WOMEN
AGING IN
PRISON

WOMEN AGING IN PRISON

A Neglected Population in the Correctional System

Ronald H. Aday
Jennifer J. Krabill

LYNNE
RIENNER
PUBLISHERS

BOULDER
LONDON

Published in the United States of America in 2011 by
Lynne Rienner Publishers, Inc.
1800 30th Street, Boulder, Colorado 80301
www.rienner.com

and in the United Kingdom by
Lynne Rienner Publishers, Inc.
3 Henrietta Street, Covent Garden, London WC2E 8LU

Library of Congress Cataloging-in-Publication Data
Aday, Ron H.
   Women aging in prison : a neglected population in the correctional system
   / Ronald H. Aday and Jennifer J. Krabill.
         p. cm.
   Includes bibliographical references and index.
   ISBN 978-1-58826-764-1 (hbk. : alk. paper)
   1. Women prisoners—United States. 2. Older women—United States.
I. Krabill, Jennifer J. II. Title.
   HV9471.A33 2011
   365'.608460973—dc22

                                                        2010043822

British Cataloguing in Publication Data
A Cataloguing in Publication record for this book
is available from the British Library.

Printed and bound in the United States of America

The paper used in this publication meets the requirements
of the American National Standard for Permanence of
Paper for Printed Library Materials Z39.48-1992.

5   4   3   2   1

Contents

Tables

1

Older Women in Prison

THE GRAYING OF AMERICA IS HAVING A TREMENDOUS INFLUENCE on almost all of our social institutions, including our nation's prison system. Elderly inmates are considered the fastest growing group of inmates in most states' prison systems, and as the general population becomes grayer so too will the prison population. It may seem unusual to think of older women as criminals; however, older incarcerated women are also a distinct reality. While the graying of prisoners in the United States mirrors the growth of an aging population, older inmates suffer from the complications of accelerated aging. Many women arrive in prison after years of unhealthy living, victimization, and drug use, and as they age in place become even more vulnerable to the rigors of incarceration. The exposure to the stressors of prison life frequently only makes them sicker and more costly to manage. As inmates remain in prison for longer periods, and in greater numbers, they are having dynamic policy implications for correctional systems already facing rising health-care costs and strapped economies.

Only recently has the involvement of older women with crime and criminal justice agencies become the subject of increased scrutiny (Caldwell, Jarvis & Rosefield, 2001; Krabill & Aday, 2005; Williams & Rikard, 2004). The special needs of female inmates have been largely overshadowed by a preoccupation with the predominantly male prison population. While the rate of increase in the overall number of women in prison has been phenomenal, male inmates continue to constitute the majority of prisoners. The fact that female inmates account for only a fragment of the total prison population has been used to excuse the system's failure to address the unique needs of female offenders (Acoca, 1998; Wahidin, 2004). In many state correctional systems, female

1

offenders have become nothing more than an afterthought in a primarily male dominated system. Anderson (2006) has recently argued that the justification for this disparity is no longer valid given the current rise of female incarceration rates. As a result, there has been a renewed call for rethinking gender, crime, and justice (Renzetti, Goodstein & Miller, 2006).

One primary reason limited attention has been granted to aging prisoners is this small, yet growing, segment of the population surfaces from controversies surrounding the most effective measure for defining oldness (Aday, 2003). In general, most experts concur that 65—the age typically used in distinguishing later adulthood for persons residing in mainstream society—would be an inappropriate benchmark to apply in institutional settings. Given that occupants arrive at the facilities with background demographic and lifestyle characteristics that predispose them to certain health complications, and consequently, notice marked declines in physical, cognitive, mental, and social functioning at younger ages than their free-world counterparts, the age at which oldness begins must be adjusted accordingly. Most experts now agree that 50-year-old inmates possess health characteristics of someone at least ten years older (Williams, 2006), and many states now use this age to characterize what constitutes an elderly inmate.

Age and Gender Pathways to Crime

Over the past several decades, older individuals have witnessed a dramatic increase in all areas of society. As arrest statistics inform us, the aging of the baby boom generation has altered the composition of the population at large and has also affected the demographics of those who will come into contact with the criminal justice system in any given year. Although younger individuals (persons in the 15–19 and 20–24 year age ranges) continue to represent the largest segment of persons who are arrested and are overrepresented among arrests in comparison to their presence within the total US population, the 50 and older category is currently experiencing a transition that exceeds the rate of growth that had once been projected. As Table 1.1 indicates, in 1998, persons age 50 and over accounted for approximately 473,162, or 4.2 percent, of all arrests. This figure rose to 895,419 in 2009 comprising 8.4 percent of arrests from all age groups. As Table 1.1 shows, the significant rise in the number of older citizen arrests actually occurred during the 5 years from 2004 to 2009. Major increases in criminal activity

Table 1.1 Gender Differences in Number and Percentage of Arrests for All Crimes, Age 50 and Over, 1998–2009

| | Number of Arrests | | | |
	1998	2004	2009	Percent Change
Males				
50–54	194,912	266,395	377,048	+93.4
55–59	98,742	127,852	190,341	+92.7
60–64	51,319	59,614	85,009	+65.6
65+	53,325	49,672	64,082	+20.1
Total	398,298	503,533	716,480	+44.4
Females				
50–54	38,805	62,340	99,500	+156.4
55–59	17,457	26,702	42,964	+146.1
60–64	8,300	11,597	18,592	+124.0
65+	10,302	10,638	17,883	+73.5
Total	74,864	92,639	178,939	+139.0
Total	473,162	533,969	895,419	+89.2

Source: US Department of Justice, Bureau of Justice Statistics, *Sourcebook of Criminal Justice Statistics,* 1998, 2004, 2009 (Washington, DC: USGPO).

were apparent for both males and females for all age categories shown, with the exception for those 65 years of age or older. As can be garnered from the available data, the most significant increase witnessed within this time frame has been among women who are between the ages of 50 and 54 years. In a little more than a decade, the numbers rose from 38,805 offenders in 1998 to 99,500 in 2009, resulting in a 156 percent increase. Additional segments of the population to experience significant gains in number included women 55–59 and 60–64 years of age, witnessing a 146 and 124 percent increase respectively. Surprisingly, women in the 65 and over age category practically doubled during the same time period.

The increase in the number of reported arrests from 1998 to 2009 is most dramatic when compared to a similar time period in the 1990s. For example, Aday (2003) reported an actual 3 percent decline in the number of arrests for older males 50 years and older between 1989 and 1998 and a modest 3 percent increase for older females. The only increases found for either males or females were in the 50–54 age category. Given the dramatic increases during this time frame, there is some evidence of what some might term a geriatric crime wave. It is apparent that as baby boomers continue to age, the criminal justice system will see an increasing number of older offenders in the coming decades. Truly, these numbers are indicative of the swell of baby boomers now reaching retirement age and finding jail and sometimes prison as their final retirement destination.

According to the Bureau of Justice Statistics (BJS), women made up more than a quarter of all people convicted of felony property offenses in 2009. Twenty-six percent of those convicted of felony property crimes were women, compared to 18 percent of those convicted of felony drug crimes, 10 percent of those convicted of violent felonies, and 4 percent of those convicted of felony weapons crimes. Women, in general, were greater than four times more likely to be convicted of a nonviolent felony (property or drug crime) than they were to be convicted of a violent felony.

Comparing the general patterns of growth in older male and female arrestees is only the first step in understanding who is entering the system in increasing numbers. As illustrated in Table 1.2, the crimes older women commit, at every period in time, have been heavily concentrated in the areas of drug- and property-related offenses, with significantly

Table 1.2   Gender Differences in Number of Arrests for Categories of Crimes, Age 50 and Over, 1998–2009

| | Number of Arrests | | | | | | | |
| | 1998 | | 2004 | | 2009 | | Percent Change | |
	M	F	M	F	M	F	M	F
Violent crimes								
Murder	477	85	498	88	614	82	+28	–03
Rape	1,135	10	1,160	7	1,306	10	+15	0
Robbery	885	102	1,490	169	2,234	299	+152	+193
Aggravated assault	16,115	2,456	17,454	3,225	24,007	5,133	+49	+109
Property crimes								
Burglary	2,800	590	4,254	883	7,286	1,432	+160	+159
Larceny-theft	23,372	13,167	30,321	16,809	43,801	27,420	+87	+108
Auto theft	1,167	163	1,627	238	1,796	316	+53	+93
Arson	345	99	409	118	505	132	+46	+33
Selected crimes								
Drugs	23,676	3,855	42,184	8,186	63,809	13,725	+169	+256
Other assaults	41,955	6,519	44,182	9,580	64,992	15,366	+54	+135

Source: US Department of Justice, Bureau of Justice Statistics, *Sourcebook of Criminal Justice Statistics,* 1998, 2004, 2009 (Washington, DC: USGPO).

fewer committing violent crimes. Property crimes for which older women have entered into contact with the criminal justice system in increasing numbers over the past decade include burglary, larceny/theft, as well as auto-vehicle theft. According to Uniform Crime Reports data that are shown in Table 1.2, women 50 years of age and older committed only 590 of the total burglaries that were reported by police in 1998, and yet, accounted for an estimated 1,432 that occurred in the year 2009. Similarly, we notice a dramatic rise in larceny theft when examining the arrest trends reported for 2009. Although the literature concerning female criminality has historically documented a strong correlation between the use of illegal substances, treatment for addictions, and arrests for engagement in criminal behaviors (Beck, 1999; McQuaide & Ehrenreich, 1998; Snell & Morton, 1994), the introduction of crack cocaine into the inner-city drug market, the war on drugs, and the more stringent enforcement of drug-related policies contributed to a significant rise in arrests for drug-related offenses during this period of time.

Violent offenses, as illustrated by Uniform Crime Reports data, represent only a small fraction of the total number of offenses women will engage in during any given year. As numerous studies conducted in recent years have documented, however, the proliferation of pro-arrest and mandatory arrest laws have contributed to a rise in the number of women who have been arrested for these offenses. Beginning in the 1980s, research conducted on the resolution of domestic violence disputes began to surface suggesting arrest may be a more effective deterrent to further engagement in criminal activities than would be police use of mediation and other conflict-resolution strategies (Sherman & Beck, 1984). In the following years, numerous states began implementing policies to restrict the use of police discretion. By 2002, twenty-two states had enacted regulations mandating arrests in cases involving assault and battery charges, whereas thirty-three had policies that required arrest under circumstances with persons who have been identified as having violated previously issued restraining orders (Hirschell & Buzawa, 2002). Although laws were undoubtedly created as a mechanism for protecting and preserving the well-being of women who would otherwise be on the receiving end of abuse by their significant others, they would additionally contribute to an increasing number of women entering the criminal justice system as offenders (Miller, 2006; Miller & Meloy, 2006). As of 2007, female offenders were reported as being responsible for approximately 23 percent of all violent offenses, which included 12 percent of the total number of homicides, 12 percent of robberies, and 28 percent of aggravated assaults.

The Graying Prison Populaton

The US prison population has experienced a continual growth over the past three decades, reaching a national prison census of over 1.6 million at year end 2009 (West & Sabol, 2010). This figure represents just a slight increase in the federal prison population and the first decline in the state prison population since 1977. Among this vast number are 115,308 incarcerated females. While women make up a small percentage of incarcerated adults in the US prison system, the number of women in prison is increasing at a much faster rate than that of men. The growth of female imprisonment is evident by the fact that in 1977 the United States imprisoned 24 male prisoners for every female inmate, and by 2007 the ratio had fallen to 13 male prisoners for every female prisoner. One of the major effects frequently identified as being associated with the rise in numbers of older adults committing criminal activities involves an increased presence of elders within state and federal prisons. In 2009, more than 198,000 incarcerated persons (or approximately 13 percent of inmates) were 50 years of age or older (American Correctional Association, 2010). Among this number are more than 7,000 incarcerated females age 50 years and older representing about 5 percent of the older adult prison population.

There are several factors contributing to the growth of the older female prison population. In the 1980s a fundamental shift toward a more retributive and punitive response to crime occurred. The establishment of longer mandatory sentences, the war on drugs, and the abolition of parole in some states are some of the factors contributing to the increasing number of long-term inmates (Anno et al., 2004). For example, some states have introduced sentencing laws such as "mandatory minimums" and "three strikes and you're out" legislation requiring significantly longer sentences for certain offenses (Mezey et al., 2002; Byock, 2002). As our nation has become tougher on criminals in general, there has also been a trend in our justice system toward putting women in prison and giving them longer sentences (Caldwell, Jarvis & Rosefield, 2001; Pollock, 2004; Young & Reviere, 2006). Another simple explanation for the increase in the older female population is that with a rapidly growing aging population there are now greater numbers of older females to commit crimes. While there is no evidence of a "geriatric crime wave," the fact is elderly persons, including women, are committing more serious crimes. With the possibility of spending a major portion of their lives in prison, the aging prison population has created an increasing number of end-of-life issues as more offenders are at greater risk for dying in prison (Granse, 2003).

Researching Women in Prison

The fact that incarcerated women represent a much-neglected population among scholars was first brought to the forefront by Kathryn Watterson's groundbreaking *Women in Prison* first published in 1973. Broadly exposing the reality of prison life for women incarcerated across the United States and the resilient coping strategies as they fought for survival, Watterson identified numerous topics crying out for much-needed research attention. Watterson's work, along with Carol Smart's classic work *Women, Crime and Criminology: A Feminist Critique* (1976), identified a new field of feminist inquiry (Britton, 2000). Scholars in subsequent years have addressed a variety of gendered issues ranging from women's experiences as victims to those found in the structural arrangement of contemporary women's prisons. Special attention has been given to imprisoned mothers and their children, abused women and incarceration, inequitable health care, gender disparity in prison programming, the use of violence in the control of women inmates, the general pains of imprisonment, and women's stories of survival to mention a few.

The significant growth in the women's prison population has resulted in a renewed interest in exploring the consequences of prisonization, not only for inmates themselves but also for their families and those responsible for managing the unique problems facing female prisoners. New issues continue to emerge as the prison demographic changes toward an older inmate population, resulting in prisons being confronted with any number of end-of-life issues—for example, special health-care needs such as long-term care (Mara, 2002); health-care cost and delivery (Braithwaite, Arriola & Newkirk, 2006); malign neglect toward aging female inmates (Williams & Rikard, 2004); inadequate programming and facilities (Caldwell, Jarvis & Rosefield, 2001); penal harm issues associated with dying in prison (Deaton, Aday & Wahidin, 2009–2010; Granse, 2003); and victimization in prison (Miller, 2006).

Social scientists have increasingly been drawn to US prisons for a number of reasons. The prison environment provides rare opportunities for a variety of methodological interests and purposes (Patenaude, 2004; Liebling, 1999; Miller, 2006). For example, prisons as a microcosm provide research opportunities for both qualitative and quantitative explorations. Whether conducting a national survey on the health-care needs of the new woman inmate (Young & Reviere, 2001) or an ethnographic field study focusing on the daily experiences of women aging in prison (Wahidin, 2004), the opportunity to engage in relevant research that may potentially influence public policy can be attractive. As prisons see an increase in older inmates, correctional systems responsible for formulating and financing current policies are confronted with any number of serious issues that must be addressed. Questions currently being raised by criminal justice officials and legislators alike include (see Aday, 2003): (1) Is there a limit on how much we want to spend on long-term incarceration? (2) How do we maintain a safe environment for older, frail inmates? (3) Do we build special needs facilities for aging women? (4) How do we assist older offenders so they make a successful transition into and out of prison? (5) What type of end-of-life care should be implemented for those inmates serving life in prison? (6) How can prisons better assist female inmates suffering from life-long victimization and related mental health issues? These and other pending challenges have created a sense of urgency among scholars searching to make a difference by engaging in pragmatic and policy-oriented prison research impacting aging female offenders (Deaton, Aday & Wahidin, 2009–2010).

Engaging in prison research can be a complicated endeavor, especially for those coming from the outside. Azrini Wahidin (2004) provides a lively discussion concerning the problems of "breaking in" or doing research in prison. Issues raised by other researchers include the procedural hoops involved in obtaining entry into a specific prison setting, gaining and maintaining trust of inmates and prison officials, and how to best capture the subjective experiences of those incarcerated (Liebling, 1999; Patenaude, 2004). In meeting this challenge, Alison Liebling (1999) has reflected on both the values and problems when using qualitative and quantitative styles of research in the prison setting. Liebling cautions against prison research that is devoid of "emotions." As Liebling (1999, p. 147) acknowledges, "research in any human environment without subjective feeling is almost impossible—particularly in a prison." While researching the experiences of females in prison lends itself to a qualitative approach (Wahidin, 2004), conducting actual field research where researchers can spend extended periods of time observing the prison culture can be problematic. The degree of intrusion into the prison environment, close contact with inmates and staff, and the potential for disruption can cause concern for any correctional institution (Aday, 2003; Patenaude, 2004). Rather, more structured qualitative research designs, such as focus groups or in-depth open-ended interviews, are more likely the method types utilized by contemporary prison researchers (Liebling, 1999; Patenaude, 2004; Wahidin, 2004).

Study Design and Format

In investigating the views and experiences of growing old in women's prisons, we used a three-pronged approach. First, every attempt was made to conduct a thorough review of the relevant literature for each topic presented. We found this to be a challenging task because much of the existing research on prisons had been carried out either on male samples or with younger female prison populations. In fact, existing studies only rarely used age differences when reporting on prison experiences. Only a handful of studies have actually focused on the pains of imprisonment for older female offenders. Consequently, in reviewing existing research, we were sensitive in acknowledging the importance of age when it was made available. Another challenge in integrating the literature into our findings was analyzing the diverse methodological approaches previously used in creating a better understanding of the lives of women behind bars. While numerous qualitative studies used in-depth case studies, other studies focused on larger aggregate samples across a variety of topics. Regardless, every attempt was made to ground our research with previous research findings using a comprehensive overview for each topic presented.

A second means for gaining information for addressing some of the major gaps in knowledge regarding the effects of imprisonment on older offenders involved conducting an empirical study from a broad sample of participants. One advantage of using a quantitative approach is the capability to produce a preliminary profile of older incarcerated females. In the past, prison research has frequently relied on small nonrepresentative samples, making generalizations literally impossible. A particular strength of this study is the fact it reaches across five states and provides an excellent database from which to provide a comprehensive picture of aging female offenders. Although the sample was not randomly drawn, we feel confident that a fair representation of this subgroup of prisoners was obtained, permitting some conclusive policy recommendations. With a robust sample of 327, this project provides the largest and most comprehensive study to date that examines older incarcerated women. This study will also provide the opportunity for direct comparisons between older women prisoners not only within the same state, but also between the participating states.

Finally, this study also utilized qualitative methods to explore and describe the unique prison experiences of older women. A series of focus groups were conducted in the majority of participating institutions. A cross-section of inmates from each prison was selected to gather in-depth information on family and prison relationships, the transition into prison life, health-care access and medical-staff attitudes, dying in prison, reentry issues, and the role these issues contributed to overall prison adjustment. Using a semistructured interview guide, respondents were encouraged to talk openly about their prison experiences. Collecting personal narratives from the inmates was important in providing insights into the daily routine of prison life for each prison. In most cases, the research team was able to record the focus group conversations. However, other sessions were not taped due to the privacy concerns of the subjects. In the latter cases, detailed notes were taken. As is the case when conducting research in a prison setting, researchers must be flexible when issues such as space availability, time constraints, and inmate privacy are concerned.

Numerous open-ended questions also captured the personal accounts of the women's prison experiences. For example, participants were asked to describe, in their own words, the true value of the friends they have made while in prison. In addition, they were encouraged to discuss any changes they would like to see for improving health-care services, describe in detail what it is like being an older woman in prison, or share what fears and concerns they may have about growing old or dying in prison. Those inmates who reportedly were abused prior to imprisonment were also asked to describe episodes of abusive behavior, discuss problems of intervention, and provide detailed examples of injuries sustained as a victim. Follow-up questionnaires were also mailed to a cross-section of participants encouraging inmates to share their prison experiences on a variety of additional topics, such as visitation barriers, the importance of work, and their general strategies for coping with life in prison. Overall, the subjective data provided by the women in this sample are a useful tool in enhancing our understanding by viewing these events through their own personal lens.

Research Approach

The self-report survey was long and detailed and covered a vast number of issues with important significance to older females. This portion of the study used existing instruments and quantitative analysis to explore the effects of various emotional, social, physical, and mental-health characteristics on inmate coping patterns and adjustment to prison life. Such variables included inmate support measures, Templer's Death Anxiety Scale (1970), and the Hopkins Symptom Checklist (1974) for anxiety, depression, somatization, and intrapersonal sensitivity. Other measures of chronic and functional health; incidence of abuse prior to incarceration; engagement in prison activities, education, and work programs; and measures of family support and barriers preventing linkages with the outside world were also important variables central to this study. The closed-ended questionnaire included general demographic data including age, race, education, prior occupation, and marital status. Information on each inmate's criminal history was also solicited, including most recent crime committed, age when first incarcerated, length of imprisonment, and length of time remaining. Participants who responded yes to the question about whether they had been abused prior to incarceration were also asked to complete several additional questions. One portion of the victimization section included an intimate-partner violence inventory (Eliason, Taylor & Arndt, 2005). This measure included a series of statements measuring incidents of physical, verbal, social, and sexual abuse, as well as controlling threats.

The Research Setting

Gaining access to potential study participants involved a lengthy process, especially when seeking approval in multiple states. According to standard procedure, we submitted a research proposal to each state's research and planning office (Arkansas, Mississippi, Kentucky, Georgia, and Tennessee). Chosen because of their contiguous proximity, we found that while similar, each state has its own unique organizational structure, application materials, and internal review process. Of particular interest to each state's Human Subjects Committee were issues of confidentiality and informed consent and the general objectives of the study, including an estimated timeline for completing the project. Once approval was received from each state, we submitted the proposal to the Middle Tennessee State University Institutional Review Board (IRB) for final review. The IRB, as part of the screening process, consulted with a faculty member familiar with prison research to ensure proper guidelines were being followed. After receiving final university approval, each state research and planning division was notified in writing. At that time, the warden at each participating women's prison was notified by the state office of the pending research project, and we were told at that time to contact each warden or a designated contact person to make final arrangements for our site visits.

This research was conducted in seven women's prisons: Arkansas (Grimes Unit for Women, Newport), Central Mississippi Correctional Facility (Women's Unit, Pearl), Tennessee Prison for Women (Nashville),

Kentucky Correctional Institution for Women (Pee Wee Valley, Kentucky); the three Georgia facilities included Metro State Prison (Atlanta), Pulaski State Prison (Pulaski), and Arrendale State Prison (Alto). Several institutional consistencies exist between the facilities. With the exception of the Central Mississippi Correctional Facility, which also serves as a reception unit for the state, the other six prisons housed only female inmates. All are maximum security prisons in which guards are both male and female and inmates are subject to being viewed at all times. The facilities all provide set limits on meal times, out-of-cell times, hours of visitation, visitors, and wardrobe. The seven institutions all require co-pays for health care and restrict inmates to in-prison medical services for most treatment. All facilities, with the exception of Arkansas, require inmates to walk from one building to another for meals, sick call, laundry, or commissary products. Since the initial interview process, Arkansas has since built a new mental health structure for a handful of inmates that is located near the main facility. With the exception of the Metro State Prison in Georgia and the Tennessee Prison for Women in Nashville, all prisons are located in rather remote rural areas.

Interview Procedures

The approach to inform inmates about the study varied from institution to institution. For example, in some instances prospective participants age 50 and over were contacted by prison staff via a personal notice that included a concise description of the project with stated research goals. Interested inmates were assigned a date and time corresponding with the researchers' visit. However, in the majority of cases, all inmates in the appropriate age category and with suitable mental health skills were brought to a general classroom or visitation area to meet with the research team. Potential participants were then informed about the research objectives of the study and were able to examine a copy of the research instrument including the consent form. All participation was voluntary, and a small number of eligible inmates chose not to participate. Other inmates were unable to participate due to work responsibilities, lockdown or death row status, or being confined to the infirmary. In most cases, the overwhelming majority of inmates at most institutions were more than willing to participate in the study. We received numerous comments from the women about how they felt "forgotten," and the majority were overjoyed that finally someone was interested in telling their story.

The first step in the research process was administering the 10-page survey questionnaire to all individuals agreeing to participate. A minimum of three research team members was always present during the actual data collection process. The research team provided assistance, as needed, particularly for those with visual, language, or literacy barriers. In those instances, researchers administered the questionnaire orally. On numerous occasions, inmates also helped others who needed any special attention completing the questionnaire. Once the survey was completed, small groups were formed as we transitioned into the focus group discussions. As mentioned earlier, not all inmates participated in this portion of the qualitative data gathering activity. On occasion, some women expressed the desire to speak to a member of the research team in private, while others felt more comfortable mailing their personal comments to us.

The Study Sample

Participants for this study included 327 women ranging in age from 50 to 77, with a mean age of 55.4 years. Table 1.3 provides a comparative view of the sample showing the majority (56.6 percent) of the sample is white, 37.3 percent are black, and the remaining 2.8 percent are Hispanic, Native American, or "other." One interesting factor when viewing the race category is the significant number of African Americans found in the Mississippi sample and the small number reported in Tennessee. About one-half of the total female population in Mississippi is reported as African American, so it appears there are a disproportionate number found among the older female population. Only 22.2 percent of participants reported being married. Among the others, 33.0 percent reported being divorced, 25.9 percent indicated that they were widowed, 8.3 percent stated that they were separated, and 10.5 percent reported never having been married. While there was consistency from state to state, Mississippi women were slightly more likely to have marked the separated or never married box. About two-thirds (65.5 percent) of the women reported having at least a high school degree, and 37.2 percent reported having some college education or a college degree. The smaller samples from Kentucky and Arkansas seemed slightly more likely to have attended college or received a college degree.

For 71 percent of the women, this was their first arrest leading to prison. The mean age of incarceration for this particular crime was 44 years with several women first imprisoned as early as 17 years of age

Table 1.3 Demographic Profile of Older Female Offenders

Characteristic	Total	Georgia (n = 145)	Tennessee (n = 60)	Kentucky (n = 28)	Mississippi (n = 71)	Arkansas (n = 23)
Mean age	55.4	54.8	56.1	54.8	55.0	57.0
Marital status (%)						
Married	22.2	20.3	23.3	21.4	24.3	26.1
Widowed	25.9	25.2	35.0	21.4	18.6	34.8
Divorced	33.0	37.8	30.0	39.3	27.1	21.7
Separated	8.3	5.6	5.0	7.1	17.1	8.7
Never married	10.5	11.2	6.7	10.7	12.9	8.7
Race (%)						
Caucasian	56.6	53.5	86.4	78.6	26.8	65.2
African American	37.3	38.9	8.5	21.4	67.6	26.1
Hispanic, Native American, or other	2.8	4.2	1.7	—	1.4	—
Education (%)						
8th grade or less	14.2	13.2	18.6	14.3	15.5	4.3
Some high school	20.3	20.8	16.9	10.7	29.6	8.7
High school graduate	28.3	27.1	37.3	17.9	23.9	39.1
Some college	24.9	23.6	22.0	46.4	21.1	26.1
College degree	12.3	15.3	5.1	10.7	9.9	21.7

while others committed their first offense in their 70s. The average length of time served for the current offense was 8.8 years, with the amount of time remaining to be served estimated at 17 years as reported by the inmates themselves. We removed those inmates serving life without parole, and for Arkansas the number of years left to serve for life is not formally established based on current sentencing policy. Of course, some inmates correlated their time left to be with their parole hearing, but some had realistic doubts that approval would be forthcoming.

Table 1.4 provides a summary of the criminal offenses for those participating in this study. Unlike women in younger age categories, older inmates were much more likely to be serving time for the violent crime of murder/manslaughter (41.3 percent) followed by drug-related offenses (25.1 percent). Since the sample from the Arkansas facility was chosen because of their life sentences, the overwhelming majority were serving time for capital murder. Tennessee and Georgia also had their fair share of women serving time for murder, while the samples from Mississippi and Kentucky were more likely to have committed drug offenses. A variety of other crimes are scattered throughout Table 1.4 with few other significant patterns.

Table 1.4 Current Primary Crime Offenses (percentage; n = 327)

Type of Offense	Total	Georgia	Kentucky	Tennessee	Mississippi	Arkansas
Murder/manslaughter	41.3	38.6	14.3	52.5	14.1	86.9
Assault/battery	5.9	9.1	7.1	5.1	4.1	4.3
Drug related	25.1	12.9	39.2	25.4	43.6	4.3
Theft	11.6	17.4	14.3	3.4	11.3	—
Fraud	8.5	—	3.6	5.1	16.9	—
Violation of parole	3.4	—	—	3.4	—	—
Conspiracy	3.2	—	3.6	1.7	4.2	—
Larceny	1.7	—	—	1.7	—	—
Sexual crimes	4.9	3.8	14.3	—	1.4	—
Vehicular violence	2.2	3.8	—	—	2.8	—
Burglary	2.8	—	—	—	2.8	—
Possession of firearms	4.3	—	—	—	—	4.3
Kidnapping	3.6	—	3.6	—	—	—
Other	7.7	13.6	—	1.7	—	—

Book Overview

This book is an attempt to begin the initial process of assembling a comprehensive perspective on a variety of issues facing older women in prison today. Although much has been written by way of books, chapters, and articles on incarcerated women, there has been only limited attention given to this unique group of older women with unforeseen special needs. The treatment needs of women are much different than for men, and certainly this is the case as we focus on women who are aging behind bars. As our society incurs such an enormous economic and social cost with so many mothers and grandmothers permanently locked away, acquiring a true picture of this tragic occurrence motivated us to write this book. Using a diverse approach with broad implications for the lives of these women, this book contains distinctive empirical information that provides an integration of aging issues with the field of corrections. While topics such as abuse within the confines of prison or the intimate relationships among inmates are not addressed, the issues chosen for this book are at the very heart of the lives of these aging women. The following paragraphs provide an overview of our effort to make a valuable and lasting contribution to the knowledge base of older incarcerated women.

Chapter 2 explores the relationships among aging, identity, and adjustment to prison life for women who come into the system marginal at best. Most inmates come to prison with few coping skills, having shown poor judgment in dealing with life's choices. With tendencies toward accelerated aging due to a history of inadequate health care and abusive behaviors, prison only magnifies the problems that bring people to prison in the first place. Discussed in this chapter is the fact that prison produces significantly different experiences for older female offenders, including features of self-esteem, identity management, and social relationships with others. For many inmates, this is their first introduction to prison life, resulting in feelings of apprehensiveness, frustration, and fear as they personally process the consequences of their actions. The transition to prison is especially difficult for those who will likely find themselves behind bars for the remainder of their lives.

The chapter also stresses that not only must these mothers and grandmothers overcome the stigma associated with incarceration at a time when their families need them most, but they must also cope with the stigma of being a devalued older person behind bars. As they begin to notice the realities of aging and accept distinct reminders of their own mortalities, the women acknowledge the negative stigma associated with these changes. Without exception, older incarcerated women report a continual struggle to negotiate some of the same challenges their free-world counterparts undergo on a regular basis. Personal narratives indicate that this stigma is particularly blatant in prison where ageist attitudes are rampant among prison staff members. While ageist actions are often subtle, the perception of women in prison implies that older people are specifically disadvantaged or treated in a less than desirable way because of their age. This chapter demonstrates the fact that despite the rigidity of total institutions, such restrictive environments are important sites of socialization and identity construction.

Chapter 3 provides an extensive overview of the mental and physical health concerns and issues currently confronting older female offenders. A major focus involves issues related to health policy, health-care utilization, and costs of providing health care to an aging prison population. Using aggregate data from the participating sample, it is evident the health status of the older female inmates is usually worse than their counterparts outside prison. Incarcerated inmates tend to develop health issues much earlier due to their previous lifestyles and related socioeconomic factors resulting in a projected physiological age 10 years older than their actual age. Based on personal narratives provided by the women in this study, it appears a significant degree of health anxiety is present. Inmates express their fears as well as realities of the lack of adequate health-care service delivery found in a prison setting. The correctional systems we explored require inmates to pay between $2 and

$5 for a sick-call visit. Inmates report these fees can be insurmountable for sick, aging inmates who are less likely to have a source of income. We also address the importance of race and age in determining a comprehensive health plan.

As mandatory sentencing laws have become more popular in the past 20 years, inmates are spending longer periods of time incarcerated. According to Joan Petersilia (2003), a total of 16 states have abolished parole altogether, supporting the "truth in sentencing" policies. As a result, Chapter 3 also examines the increasing number of end-of-life issues as more prisoners spend their final years in prison. Previous research has found that institutionalization can be a valid predictor of death anxiety, and for many older individuals, the critical issue is not so much about death, but how and where the death will occur. A number of correlates of fear of dying in prison are examined in this study. Comments from inmates indicate that the prospect of dying in a foreign place in a dependent and undignified state is a very distressing thought. This chapter exposes the reality that older inmates must not only cope with their fears of getting sick and dying in prison, but also cope with frequent losses on the outside. The themes of dying in prison (fate, fear, stigma, and escape) are identified, as are coping strategies such as denial, religious activities, and acceptance. A number of important policy issues emerge as states are now including a number of end-of-life services to accommodate those who will spend their final years in prison.

Chapter 4 adds to the overall understanding of incarcerated mothers and grandmothers by stressing the importance of remaining in contact with family members on the outside. This connection provides older women the much needed assistance in adjusting to the pains of imprisonment. Benefits for maintaining family connections are identified, including the importance of family rituals, forms of financial assistance, and general encouragement to adopt prosocial behaviors. The important role that letter writing, telephone calls, and family visits play in maintaining family ties are documented with extensive inmate narratives. This chapter also points out that institutional control strictly regulates how frequently the prisoners can personally initiate family contact. These regulations can prove to be emotionally costly, as receiving word from home reassures inmates that relatives have not forgotten them and they will have a home where they can return after release.

While Chapter 4 documents the importance of maintaining family relationships for both prisoners and their families, numerous barriers are identified that frequently interfere with this desired outcome. Inmates and their families frequently mentioned the issues of time, geographical distance, and money as problems restraining their contacts. In particular, aging inmates are often faced with unique problems such as aging family members who, due to health reasons, will have limited access to prison. Institutional barriers such as phone expenses and visitation restrictions are also important indicators in hindering connections to the outside. Despite the many barriers to maintaining family relationships, this chapter illustrates that the older women manage to find meaningful ways of parenting and grandparenting while behind bars. This chapter is filled with important implications for correctional officials who are called upon to identify policies that support the emotional attachment of older female inmates to their families.

Chapter 5 focuses on building a life in prison and the importance of various prison activities that serve to provide aging prisoners with "a home away from home." This chapter is important because it introduces another significant stage in the progression of changes that occurs in the transformation to a total institution. During this stage of "learning the ropes," the women begin to understand the social structure of prison, forming guidelines for shaping new social relationships. Frequently voiced by new prison arrivals are issues such as whom to trust and how to select friends or acquaintances. To cope with the physical isolation and severance of emotional ties with family and friends on the outside, inmates frequently turn to an inner circle of inmate friends for social support. This chapter documents the important exchanges of support that emerge between the women as they spend a significant portion of their life together. Prison friendships are important for older incarcerated females because they serve as a buffer against role losses and reduced social interaction with the outside world.

Chapter 5 also identifies how these women "do their time" by engaging in a variety of prison pastimes. How to cope with the boredom of prison life and unvarying schedules is an important feature of developing a successful strategy for coping with long-term incarceration. This chapter stresses the importance of work as a meaningful prison activity for the women who are capable. A prison job may not only provide limited monetary rewards, but also the social structure that creates a sense of normalcy in the women's lives. The importance of religious activities and other prison programs are singled out as crucial elements in transforming the lives of older incarcerated women. Providing helpful assistance to fellow inmates by sharing personal items such as food or a bar of soap or simply making conversation are all important in creating a social world with meaning. This chapter provides important policy implications, especially in responding to the everyday needs of women who will remain in prison indefinitely.

It has been well established that the majority of incarcerated women have experienced various incidences of abuse prior to their incarceration. However, we have few actual accounts of the past traumas that battered women bring to prison. Chapter 6 explores a wide range of abuse and battering experiences found among this group of older incarcerated women. The types of abuse identified in this study were categorized as verbal, physical, social, sexual, psychological, and controlling threats. The women explain that, as their abusive situations escalated, they attempted to leave abusive relationships, and many victims attempted to do so several times before they were able to leave permanently. Frequently fleeing for their lives, the women repeatedly tried to hide from their abuser, called the police and filed restraining orders, or turned to their family and friends as a means of seeking support.

This chapter documents not only the patterns of abusive behaviors, but also the frequent reluctance of family or authorities to come to their assistance. Also explored are not only the physical injuries received from battering incidents, but also the emotional consequences and mental anguish the women suffered, many from early childhood into later life. The factors contributing to specific abuse cases are helpful in understanding the destructive family backgrounds from which many of the women came. The posttraumatic stress symptoms identified in this subgroup reveal why these women have such difficulty in adjusting to prison life. The experiences relived in this chapter are important in understanding the total lives of this population. They help explain why these victims are so fragile mentally and why they frequently also become victims of the criminal justice system if neglected in prison.

As the numbers of lifers and older inmate populations have increased, there has been little attention given to the experiences of those aging inmates who are spending a major portion of their lives behind bars. The intent of Chapter 7 is to provide an intimate look into the life of one long-term inmate who is serving a 166-year conviction. Based on the extensive narrative provided by Judy Holbird, a Native American, the early portion of this chapter will trace her life beginning with early childhood, marriage as a teenager, and her criminal pathway leading to imprisonment. Her story is unique in that two of her children were also charged as accomplices to the crimes she committed. Of interest will be the sexual abuse she suffered as a child, the emotional abuse that was encountered in her marriage, and the financial struggles she faced prior to incarceration.

The latter sections will explore her transition into prison and the changes she has witnessed for more than 20 years. This lifer's adjustment to prison is typical of many inmates who struggle to accept their lengthy sentence by pushing back angrily at the criminal justice system. An emphasis is given to her efforts to remain an integral part of her family's life. In particular, the effective use of letter writing emerges as a key strategy in Judy's attempt to adjust to the consequences of incarceration. Her efforts to maintain her own health are also noteworthy, and her story leaves a measure of hope for those inmates seeking redemption.

Finally, Chapter 8 reviews some of the major concerns of older inmates as they consider reentry back into the free world. Important policy implications are provided in the discussion of the apprehension inmates feel due to a lack of preparation and training for a successful career, especially for those who are now old and have been isolated in prison for decades. Also discussed in this chapter are the challenges inmates face as they reunite with family members. Finding a suitable living arrangement is critical in a successful transition back to society and numerous inmates' narratives shed considerable light on this subject. Of course, some inmates' families have disengaged from those inmates serving life sentences, and in some cases, family members themselves are grown old, leaving few transition opportunities.

Given the fact that older female offenders often enter prison with high levels of anxiety, depression, apathy, and despair, it is imperative to identify and explore in further detail the recommendations these individuals would have for improving the state of their existing accommodations. Although the essence of this chapter will capture the voices of these older women as they suggest how their lives might be improved, it will also use a broader brush to address the important policy implications. Certainly, as the aging female prison population continues to grow at alarming rates, it will be imperative that correctional officials address the special needs of this population, including not only where they are housed and what they are fed, but also the multitude of mental and physical health concerns. This chapter will call attention to the fact that additional staff training is necessary as well as the implementation of new policies that serve to promote the health and wellness of this subgroup of inmates. An argument is made that, in the long run, these programs and policies will prove to be cost effective as more women are living out their lives behind bars.

2

Aging and Prison Adjustment

THERE HAS BEEN CONSIDERABLE INTEREST IN HOW INDIVIDUALS adjust to the conditions of prison life. The extent to which offender adaptations are influenced by preprison characteristics such as age, gender, and life histories, or even by the prison environments themselves, have emerged as the focus of substantial debate (Dhami, Ayton & Loewenstein, 2007). Over the past several decades, a number of studies that have addressed inmate adjustment patterns have borrowed extensively from the notion of prisonization (Haney, 2006; MacKenzie, 1987). In his seminal work, *The Prison Community,* Donald Clemmer defined prisonization as "the taking on in greater or lesser degree of the folkways, mores, customs, and general culture of the penitentiary" (1940, p. 299). While the concept of prisonization continues to intrigue scholars and plays a critical role in influencing the direction of contemporary research, most recently researchers have emphasized the specific behavioral, psychological, and emotional reactions inmates have to this event (Dhami, Ayton & Loewenstein, 2007).

This chapter explores the general effects of growing old in the confines of a prison setting. Addressed here are some of the transitional issues faced by older women entering prison for the first time in later life. The discourse presented here reflects a vision of older inmates' aging selves as they come to grips with the changes associated with physical aging. While this view is often filled with contradictions and self-doubts, some women do acknowledge some personal comforts associated with aging in prison. Examples of how these women take a proactive approach to their own aging are provided. This chapter also provides numerous illustrations of the ageist reactions from both staff and younger inmates, such as disparaging remarks or ignoring special needs these women experience. Conflict and friction that often surface between young and older prisoners are briefly identified.

Entry into Prison Life

A growing body of literature concerning the unique concerns experienced by female offenders in particular confirms that members of this population frequently arrive at prison noticeably unprepared for surviving the new challenges to which they will be exposed (Aday, 2003; Cranford & Williams, 1998; Greer, 2000). Many women, for example, enter the system with histories of low self-esteem, fractured external support systems, as well as underdeveloped coping skills (Genders & Player, 1990; Krabill & Aday, 2005; Lamb, 2010). As these individuals will naturally experience added burdens as they are suddenly introduced to a wide range of stressors to which they must ultimately adapt, it is certain that they must identify strategies for overcoming the demands imposed on them. Some offenders may undeniably respond remarkably well to the enormous transitions they are encountering. For a number of women who are confined to long-term imprisonment, this form of adaptation may involve learning to depend on staff members to identify, plan, and dictate to them their daily activities, familiarize them with the formal rules and regulations to which they must adhere, enforce extant policies, and apply the same standards when sanctioning every offender who breaches institutional regulations. For others, however, the acclimatization into prison often includes consulting with their more experienced peers who can assist them in becoming acquainted with the unwritten, informal codes of conduct. Numerous individuals have even suggested that these conversations with prison peers assist them in clarifying why they should withhold emotional expression while residing within this environment or in identifying strategies typically used in avoiding abuse or exploitation.

Although individuals who have no prior exposure to institutional living may notice that reliance on intrainstitutional supports is undeniably crucial to survival, some offenders report inevitably discovering the processes contribute to furthering any preexisting declines in psychological well-being. As Timothy Flanagan (1981) has explained in his research conducted with long-term offenders, one of the greatest fears any offender experiences from within the prison walls is related to a concept he refers to as "the assault on self." In general, the author contends that these individuals loathe the prospect that others may attempt to deprive them of their rights to vocalize their opinions, concerns, or feelings; minimize their worth or value as human beings; and assist them in removing any hint of self-esteem they may have formerly had. Specifically, inmates who have witnessed their peers mentally, psychologically, or emotionally decompose as a result of long-term incarceration, appear to be extraordinarily worried about personally losing all sense of passion, vigor, and purpose for their lives. Such has been identified as a major focus of concern for long-term and older offenders serving time in men's as well as women's prisons.

The literature has also identified the initial phase of institutionalization as one of the most trying moments older adults may have experienced in their lives (Hooyman & Kiyak, 2008). Studies conducted with elderly who have relocated to such institutions indicate it is customary for individuals to encounter stress as they dissociate from their former identities and become integrated into the new subculture (Gamliel & Hazan, 2006). Some new residents, for example, will feel extremely apprehensive, terrified, or distressed that their external supports may desert them. Others who are accustomed to the freedoms traditionally associated with independent living arrangements may become easily frustrated or angered when they realize staff will not permit them to claim their own territories, defend their personal spaces, or have unrestricted moments of privacy. Although the ease with which people adapt to confinement will naturally vary considerably depending on facility characteristics such as administrative programs or personal philosophy, most inmates quickly learn that prison life is a far cry from the outside world (Zaitzow, 2003). One participant shares her initial impressions of the realities associated with leaving her world behind:

> When you come to prison, life stops. . . . It's a completely separate community. I mean, you see what's on the news, and read stuff in the papers, and that helps you touch base, but that does not touch your life. . . . For example, I lived in New Orleans, so I knew from the papers that it flooded. . . . But that was so surreal to me as I was *here*, okay? I looked out my window and it's not flooding where I am at, so, . . . it's not real to me.

Individuals who enter prison later in life only to quickly recognize a sudden deterioration in their personal health statuses may be further saddened by the fact that reentrance and reintegration into the communities in which they were once active participants will be highly unlikely.

Although their initial reactions to incarceration are generally highly emotional, women who are serving long-term prison sentences often eventually establish their niches within the larger social structure. Prior research suggests that women who are presented with this fate quickly discover the importance of adopting an inmate identity and lifestyle as a way of adjusting to their newly presented circumstances (Zaitzow, 2003). For those who will be facing life behind bars, survival becomes a major focus of everyday concern. As inmates are typically restricted in their movement, personal possessions, and the scheduling or structuring of their daily activities (Stoller, 2003), women have often expressed the need and desire to seek ingenious ways of accommodating to the world that they now call home. We found this transition into the prison subculture to be appropriately illustrated by the following: "You find your niche in here that puts you through the day. I do my time, my job, and my little arts and crafts. . . . I could really care less about others and what they are going. When I first got here, 'Oh what's she here for?' Now I don't want to hear it as I don't care."

Michel Foucault (1995) has stressed the role of prison as the management of its inmates through continual surveillance, monitoring of spatial activity, and classification. When viewing prison as a "place," this illuminates the ways in which features such as architecture, prison sounds, and larger sociopolitical forces create a unique kind of total institution. It is such a place where prison staff and inmates learn the system of rules and through constant negotiations construct a social reality that over time comes to be seen as a "natural environment" (Stoller, 2003; Zaitzow, 2003).

The entry into the correctional system will be understandably even more traumatic for older inmates who are being incarcerated for the first time in later life. An estimated 70 percent of the females who comprised our study reported having no prior prison experience. On average, these women were first incarcerated at 44 years of age, with approximately one in three indicating that they were incarcerated for the first time at 50 or older and the oldest being 76 years of age when she began serving her current sentence. As one would anticipate from older individuals who had lived relatively sheltered lives prior to their incarcerations, many reported experiencing what has been termed "prison shock" as they attempted to adjust to their prison living. The following narrative from a 63-year-old woman who shot her husband serves as a helpful illustration that entering prison can prove to be a difficult adjustment process:

> I'd never been in jail before. I'd never been to court before. I'd never been locked up before. I'd never had a ticket before. I was a law-abiding citizen. They took me to criminal justice center and when I came in

I had never met a homosexual person in my life. I'd never met a drug addict or a person who had sold drugs. I'd never met people who kill people. I was foolish. I didn't know anything about the system. I came into it—I walked into all of it.

Overwhelmed by their situation, some inmates may go so far as to refuse to eat, sleep, or regularly participate in the routines of daily living without encouragement from prison staff. In fact, research conducted with a small sample of new elderly offenders identified members of this population as occasionally requiring the direct intervention of professional mental health services to prevent further decline (Aday, 1994a).

Numerous other women more than graciously shared the shocks they felt as newcomers to the facilities where they now reside. A 51-year-old-woman who has completed only five months of her sentence explores the pains from the lens of an individual who has yet to adjust to her new realities. As this offender explains what being an older woman in prison means to her, the emphasis remains on her inability to conceive of the day when she will no longer be faced with the daily turmoil. While her 7-year sentence may seem relatively brief in comparison to the time received by her contemporaries, the feelings of desperation are no less intense than those held by individuals sentenced to life. Discussing her experiences with the criminal justice system at large, and prison administration in particular, this individual notes:

I could never have a happy day in here, even if I stayed in prison until the day I die. . . . As it is here, this is a very lonely, depressing, and boring place to spend later life. . . . These people need to be reminded that we are humans, make mistakes, and have already been punished by the criminal justice system. . . . We should not have to be degraded every day we are here. . . . Until changes are made, and conditions improved, we cannot even try to make it through this nightmare.

Another elder who has served approximately 14 months for forgery-related charges confirms that the time spent incarcerated often elicits feelings of loneliness, apathy, and despair in older inmates. According to this 54-year-old inmate, the pains endured are no less intense for older women who will remain in the facility for brief durations than they are for those serving extended sentences. For this offender, growing old in prison means living, adapting, and continually readjusting to intolerable noise levels and crowded conditions, and the realization conditions are unlikely to improve in the near future. She expresses her feelings of alienation with the following words:

The noise is really bad to me, the feeling of being around so many people, and yet, being really alone. It is very hard to feel close to anyone in here. I don't know how it could be a better place. I don't think it could because nobody really cares about anyone else. My time here is short, and I am happy for that. I really feel for those who have spent so much of their lives in here. I don't really know how they manage.

For others who have been convicted of violent crimes, coming to grips with serving a life sentence can be a daunting task. Two older inmates who received life sentences shared the following emotional pain when sentenced:

I was in shock. As [a new offender] you have mental [thoughts] and emotions that have to be expressed because you're stuck in prison and you know there's nothing you can do about it. I could not get my mind to comprehend the concept. It took me 3 years to adjust to where I could reasonably function. It was like I had entered the twilight zone. I attempted suicide a couple of years ago, but now I want to see how my life goes.

I think I was in a numb state because of the circumstances surrounding my offense. . . . I could have never imagined . . . even in my wildest dreams. . . . All of a sudden, I had to go from living in a $350,000 home (that was fully paid for) among upper class people to this [followed by a description of insufficient access to preventative health care, sanitation, and privacy]. . . . At the time, I felt like I had been blown off the face of the earth.

In general, these quotes reveal that older women who are currently serving time become extraordinarily emotional when presented with opportunities to discuss their preliminary attempts at adjusting to unfamiliar environments. Although prior research suggests that elders who are serving long-term prison sentences are precluded from reflecting back on the crimes they have committed as they prefer not to dwell on thoughts of persons who have been harmed as a result of their actions (Leigey, 2010), a number of older women who shared their stories reminisced about the various other transitions that they faced without prior warning. Some, for example, identified the greatest challenge as involving changes in socioeconomic status, whereas others noted the greatest obstacle as being the realization that the evidence their lawyers had presented at trial had resulted in unsuccessful outcomes.

The inmate narratives suggest that women who have recently begun serving their sentences are not the only individuals to identify strains that were encountered while striving to become acclimated with the inmate subculture. Another group of women who were first institutionalized years ago recall that the often frightening memories of their first few days, weeks, or months in prison have since lingered with them. Owen (1998) reports that many women who have been issued long-term prison sentences will vividly recollect their first impressions of the institution—the rides to the facilities, receipt of prison attire, housing assignments, and introductions to their new peers—years after the incidents occurred. Without exception, several women in this study who have begun advancing in age since beginning their time confirm that the guilt, agony, and grief conjured by thoughts of the sentencing process itself could never be compensated for. Although older offenders generally prefer to refrain from reflecting upon, discussing, or dwelling on the crimes (Leigey, 2007), several in our study referred to the incident itself or experiences occurring early in their sentences when requested to explain what being an older woman in prison means to them: "I knew better, but just got caught in a bad way. Leaving behind my loved ones hurt a lot . . . as my grandkids and family needed me. When I entered prison seven years ago for aggravated assault, I lost so much and hurt so many people. Coming to prison just wasn't worth it. . . . It's no joke."

From the limited body of literature that is available concerning the experiences of female lifers, it appears that many also acknowledge the presence of anxiety about their imminent futures. Similar to their male counterparts, members of this population may approach the first days of their terms with the impression their legal representation will return in the near future, inform them misunderstandings have occurred, present compelling evidence communicating their innocence, and advocate in favor of new trials (Jose-Kempfer, 1990). The following quotes provide invaluable insights into the feelings harbored by women who are serving life sentences:

It was horrible. . . . You had the emotions that you had to express come out . . . because you're stuck here in prison, and you know, you're here because someone unjustly put you here . . . um . . . and there's nothing you can do about it. Now that the initial adjustment is over, the rest of my life stretches out with appalling length.

I was angry. I felt like I was in a living nightmare. I knew immediately the feelings of injustice. I wasn't joking coming into it. I came in saying I wasn't guilty. People laughed at me and said, "Yeah right, we're all innocent. I didn't do it either." After a while you don't say it anymore. You just kind of let them say their thing and you keep trying to get out.

Several women explain how, why, and for whom denial appears to be most likely in describing the stark contrast between the lifestyles to which they had formerly grown accustomed to living and the roles they envisioned themselves having to assume while serving their given terms: "For a long time, I couldn't say the word 25 to mandatory . . . 'cause I couldn't see myself doing life in that room with nothing but four walls. . . . I just couldn't see myself locked up all this time . . . not getting no pay and not having a television in my room." Naturally, not all women perceive the transition to prison as being so harsh that it causes excessive distress. Like individuals residing outside the walls of total institutions, some inmates may simply have more coping mechanisms available for their use. Other persons, however, have learned with added life experience to view the circumstances they may be presented with from a more positive approach. When we asked the women whether they expected prison to be like it is, several offenders confirmed that the stressors associated with long-term confinement have not been intolerable, and as one said: "I had preconceived notions from the television back then. It wasn't quite as bad as I thought it would be. But I learned very quickly that this prison is not as bad as some, and not as good as others. We're pretty well provided for here. And, we do have some privileges that actually surprised me, you know, like I can have a look at TV and stuff."

A number of older women who provided more positive narratives of their efforts to adapt to prison living indicated that they, too, entered with insecurities or feelings of apprehensiveness and have since learned these feelings need not remain static. Instead, many confirmed the assertion by Lorriane Reitzel and Beverly Harju (2000) that the emotions experienced at the time of one's arrival to prison are amenable to change. This subgroup's strategy for survival has become more pragmatic with time. As several lifers stated:

> Rehabilitation is a personal and relationship growth process. Each person must make that choice. Character quality is how to better yourself, to encourage others, a transformation process. For lifers, prison has become our home and we work at making it a better place, a community with trust. I feel as though if you follow the rules and respect those in charge you will be treated fairly.

> I enjoy my life and have become content here. . . . I believe it is better now than when I was younger, confused, lost and hurt. . . . I have a good life here, am grateful to just be able to wake up every day, and am thankful to have been given a second chance. I do one day at a time and do what they tell me to do.

I feel like I've grown as a person, because I have every opportunity to really sit and listen. I know now the choices I've made. It doesn't matter that I've been sexually abused, because I'm not the only one. There are a lot of other people out there [who are in similar situations]. . . . I have an opportunity to take classes, to improve myself while I am here—because, this may be my life.

It is evident from the stories these women have shared that adjusting to the demands that prison life presents involves a complex process that all must negotiate independently. Women who enter a prison environment with few life experiences that would permit them to learn, develop, refine, and make extensive use of effective coping mechanisms may undisputedly notice that sudden introductions to people who do not share their specific worldviews can create conditions that are conducive to them sinking into further states of despair. Other women who have internal loci of control, understand how their involvement in criminal activities contributed to their incarcerations, and are willing to take advantage of opportunities for participation in structured routines, however, noted a contrasting viewpoint. For these individuals, living inside the walls of an institutional setting has become a transformational experience. Decisions to actively explore the range of activities and services available to them, in essence, has given them the freedom to acknowledge that the initial symptoms of shock, alienation, and depression that many persons will experience upon their entrance into new environments may subside.

Emerging Aging Identities

Residing in a total institution designed for younger inmates with harsh prison environments presents significant challenges for older offenders who must respond to declines in functional health and cope with aging in place. In general, women's location in the social structure greatly shapes their social status and sense of self in later years of life (Silver, 2003), and their identities are shaped by their places in the world, where they live, and the roads they have traveled (McHugh, 2003). Because female offenders enter the system overwhelmed with issues of low self-esteem, the stigma and shame of incarceration, and histories of physical and sexual abuse (DeBell, 2001), and they are frequently given long sentences, these women will gradually face the reality of being caught up in the "prison time machine." As Azrini Wahidin and Shirley Tate have aptly stated, "Women's bodies become the object of the prison gaze as they spend their time compelled to watch the clock as their bodies age" (2005, p. 73). With advancing age and fraught with mental and physical frailties, older female inmates construct their identities within the constraints of a stigmatized setting where they are all but invisible. This negative view of aging has been reinforced by a society that has consistently viewed women's aging bodies as "deformed, ridiculous looking, and desexualized" (Silver, 2003, p. 385). Since our society generally has devalued older women by perpetuating stereotypes and portraying older women in negative, often degrading ways, growing old with respect in prison becomes an even greater challenge.

As women enter middle and later adulthood, they experience a wide range of new challenges, as they must begin to notice, acknowledge, and accept distinct reminders of their own mortalities. Without exception, older incarcerated women report a continual struggle to negotiate some of the same challenges their free-world counterparts undergo on a regular basis. While the elders who comprised our sample discussed what aging in prison means to them, several placed considerable emphasis on changes they had observed in their health statuses, personal appearances, or the roles they will occupy while participating in familial affairs. Linda, a 52-year-old black woman who began serving her current sentence four years earlier, describes the events older women who are residing in any environment can anticipate experiencing as they approach later adulthood: "The aging process, regardless of where you are living, hurts because we must all go through certain changes. . . . Our hair changes color, our faces wrinkle, and we no longer look the same as we did when we were young."

This particular narrative reinforces the notion that body image is an important part of our self-concept, and, as such, provides a basis for our identity. This offender's story confirms widely held assumptions that one's body acts as a standard that influences how we think of ourselves as well as how we perform certain tasks (O'Brien, 1980), with facial attributes being the most important determinant of attractiveness (Bernstein, 1990). Others validate the notion that changes in body image and general effects of aging are gradual processes that result from a push to respond to sensory and behavioral experiences, physical experiences, societal norms, and the reactions from society as these changes become more obvious (Pruzinski & Cash, 1990). A 50-year-old woman who had little exposure to the extraordinarily harsh conditions found in prison is now, five years later, feeling the negative effects of prison life. As she explains: "I used to always feel like I was 21 . . . but now I am starting to feel my age. Because of the neglect, poor nutrition, and feelings of loneliness, I am aging rather rapidly. It makes me very self-conscious about my age. It makes me feel so much older around these young girls who are having such a good time." One 51-year-old college-educated woman explores the possibility that the passage into later adulthood might be an inescapable, unavoidable transition that all individuals must negotiate regardless of the settings in which they reside. In this offender's own words, "Wherever you are, you will age. Aging is a part of life, whether we want to deal with it or not." In general, this offender may not appear to recognize institutionalization as being a single event that proves detrimental to her overall well-being. For example, she reports that she does not perceive her current health status as having deteriorated since she began her sentence four years earlier or view it as likely to change significantly in the upcoming years. Nonetheless, she identifies concerns for the needs of all older adults who will suffer from age-related conditions and require the use of prescription medications while incarcerated.

While some aging prisoners perceive themselves as encountering few previous life stressors such as poverty, manual labor, substance abuse, and involvement in street crimes that hasten the aging process while they are in this setting (Aday, 2003; Leigey, 2007), these women do not view institutionalization as preserving their outward physical appearances. If anything, most note they look, feel, and in return, act years older than they would have ever imagined. A 51-year-old woman who began her sentence less than one year earlier describes the pains endured in prison, "I'm mortified—so embarrassed. I've never been in trouble before . . . and now, look at me . . . I didn't have this gray hair before all of this." More disturbingly, another woman explores the thoughts and feelings of those who must negotiate the aging process from within the walls of a prison setting, stating, "I have grown old in prison. . . . I have got to be at least 150 years old. I cannot be this miserable at only 50! Prison ages the body and the soul." As this individual reports suffering from six chronic conditions, numerous somatic health conditions, symptoms of depression as well as anxiety, and will likely remain in the environment for a number of additional years, it is imperative to continue examining the specific aspects of institutionalization that deprive older women like herself of a respectable quality of life.

Since aging is defined primarily by its visible signs of aging, some of the incarcerated women expressed the importance of managing their aging identities in such a way to reduce the stigma associated with being labeled as old. By maintaining a more youthful appearance, individuals hope to retain a sense of competence in themselves and their abilities.

Several women in their mid-50s explained that even in prison, individuals become cognizant of, sensitive to, and responsive to the impressions others have of their appearances. As one older woman shared: "It would be a lot better for morale of older inmates if we could get cosmetology to color our hair. Plus, it would make our families feel better because when your hair becomes gray your family feels you are 'aging' in prison and it bothers you."

For other inmates, the notion of successful aging involves more than preserving their once youthful outward appearances. Numerous women explained that, to them, growing old with grace is more a function of maintaining the strength, stamina, and desire to continue engaging in productive roles throughout later life. As these inmates are projected to occupy the prime of their lives isolated behind bars, several explored how they are often expected by members of mainstream society to disengage and withdraw entirely from constructive pursuits. Roped off from society at large, these socially suspended older convicts report being encouraged to do no more than simply master their daily activities and rituals. However, the desire to participate in more meaningful activities is apparent. Several, for example, mentioned the importance of getting frequent exercise, eating a healthy diet, and generally taking care of themselves to the best of their ability within a restrictive environment as an important approach to counter physical aging. One elder who expressed a preference for remaining active and engaged in her social world illustrated this by offering the following comment:

> Being an older inmate has its pros and cons. It bothers me that my life is wasted by just obeying prison rules, having everything done for me. . . . Not having to worry about anything but time. To me it's a waste, but society chooses this punishment. So if not having to do anything anymore except waste time as an older inmate then I say making this place a better place would be letting me use my experience to help others on the outside. Let us have a voice to be heard and not let us grow old without a reason behind the razor wire. Older inmates should have less time to worry and think of themselves by staying physically busy. We need more recreational activities for those over age fifty.

Throughout her interview, this offender asserts that prison is no place for older adults. Given that she views the objective of incarceration as being to instill new, more socially acceptable values in those who have caused harm to another, it is unsurprising to observe this individual is a major advocate in favor of assisting aging prisoners in making the most of their time incarcerated. By introducing the reader to a range of stimulating pursuits older adults could actively participate in while serving their time, this inmate provides some reassurance that institutionalization need not be entirely negative. In essence, she confirms prior research suggesting that prison should afford women ample opportunities to develop senses of responsibility (Zaitzow, 2003).

Several women who commented on their positive approach to adaptation unsurprisingly attributed their motivations for responding constructively to the stressful situations with which they had been presented to core personality traits they had adopted years before having entered the system. Two individuals who were incarcerated for the first time in their late 40s explain how they have maintained an optimistic outlook on life despite the stigma associated with being an incarcerated older female:

> Sometimes I feel like I should be ashamed of myself this age and locked up, but then I think that, oh well, it's my own fault so [accept] it and go on. My age doesn't bother me as far as my confidence is concerned, I feel just as good about myself as any of the younger ladies. I often fail to realize I am 56 years old. If I want to do an activity, I do it. There really doesn't seem to be an age gap between women here. . . . I can see that I am older, but at this time, I have the energy and desire to live life to the fullest.

> I'm okay with the lady that I am even though I'm 54 and in prison. Sometimes youngsters here call you old or use your age against you. But I'm blessed not to look my age. I always carry myself in the same way. I respect myself. I now have more experience and can share my life, love and wisdom with the other women. I like to encourage them that they can make it, that they can smile one more smile and walk one more mile.

These approaches to successful aging are rare, especially for many older women who are already experiencing a premature entrance into the shadows of aging. Naturally most older individuals—regardless of their social or cultural contexts—desire to reach what they consider to be a good old age (Westerhof et al., 2001). In fact, a major theme from research on aging highlights that people who have the most enjoyable aging experiences are those who can actively control or maneuver their given environments. For example, Robert Atchley's (1989) continuity theory rests on the assumption that the well-adjusted older adult can use useful insights they learned from previous life events to resolve imminent crises. Specifically, this perspective projects that nearly all elders will encounter times of adversity and yet often thrive in the aftermath of these experiences. According to proponents of continuity theory, several crucial elements distinguish those who are successful in their quest to negotiate the stressors endured from their similar-aged counterparts. First, these individuals appear remarkably adept at finding the strength, courage, and commitment to surround themselves with people they know will confirm their existing notions of self. As they may eventually discover themselves in situations that would not permit isolating themselves from certain segments of the population at large, many report it is equally imperative to trivialize the value of contradictory opinion. By making conscious efforts to focus on the aspects of self that have remained relatively intact, many older incarcerated women will undeniably gain the invaluable opportunity to recognize their surroundings as ordered, predictable, and navigable.

Aging and Staff Reactions

One of the primary sources of pain that many of these older individuals will eventually have to learn to address and respond to while serving their respective sentences is directly related ageist attitudes, values, and behaviors extended to them by others who will also be occupying time and space within this environment. Since Robert Butler (1969) coined the term *ageism* nearly 50 years ago, the notion of this practice has become a distinct reality surfacing within every sector of mainstream society. In general, the phenomenon is typically recognized as occurring when younger adults adopt uninformed, simplistic, or often excessively rigid attitudes, beliefs, or opinions about the value or worth of senior citizens. This practice is most frequently associated with the processes of using age-based stereotypes for the purposes of systematically and unduly depriving an entire segment of the population access to a limited range of available goods and services. Differential treatment on the basis of age alone is indisputably concerning as it may have the capacity to prove damaging to the populations who are on the receiving end of the mistreatment. Several scholars, for example, have indicated that less than favorable words or deeds often cause victims of the discriminatory practices to suffer from reduced self-esteem, self-confidence, senses of mastery over their surroundings, or motivation for engagement in once pleasurable activities (Minichiello, Browne & Kendig, 2000; Vogt, 2007).

Recent studies speculate that total institutions appear to be unique, if not ideal, settings within which ageism can be regularly observed

(Gamliel & Hazan, 2006; McHugh, 2003). Debra Dobbs and colleagues (2008) explained that any living arrangement requiring individuals to have their daily routines planned for them, complete activities while in the company of many, and have their behaviors routinely and closely monitored creates conditions that are conducive to this event. Elders who must occupy later adulthood in nursing homes, assisted living facilities, or other long-term care facilities appear to be at high risk of encountering ageist exchanges with administrators, medical personnel, or other residents. Although many older adults who are confined to these environments may undoubtedly have cognitive declines or other major limitations that would prevent them from assuming active roles in planning for their care and custody, even minor practices such as neglecting to provide a range of stimulating activities that would likely interest the targeted population can have an impact on the elder's mental well-being.

As expected, ageism has also emerged as a commonplace occurrence within the various facets of the contemporary criminal justice system. Reflections from the interactions offenders frequently have with younger correctional officers, medical staff, and prison peers are invaluable for guiding and furthering our understanding of the forms of prejudice and discrimination that persist. Overall, these offenders concur that most conflicts they have encountered, negotiated, and overcome to date have been initiated by the combined efforts of multiple parties. Several express their frustrations with members of mainstream society who define what it means to be old, administrators and personnel who select and enforce policies based on existing notions of "oldness," and younger inmates who assist in perpetuating stereotypical beliefs by electing to actively exclude older offenders from their social circles.

In general, officers may convey signs of disrespect by overwhelming inmates with orders, initiating dialogues with them only when it is necessary to secure compliance, or rigorously applying punishments to all who violate prison policies with no consideration to extenuating circumstances such as age (Ben-David & Siflin, 1994). Although staff attitudes toward older adults may be heavily influenced by background variables such as their ages, levels of educational attainment, training, and number of years employed within the setting (Freeman, 2003), any decisions they make to act upon them may regrettably have negative consequences for the segments of the population whose lives will be guided and shaped by them. Since correctional officers in particular spend a substantial amount of time communicating directly with the inmates, they have frequently been identified as being the parties who are most likely to be present should these individuals encounter adjustment problems or need referrals to qualified professionals for advice, guidance, or assistance (Adams & Ferrandino, 2008; Vuolo & Kruttschnitt, 2008). Consequently, any signs of inattentiveness to inmate concerns or failures to invest time, effort, and energy to enhancing the physical, cognitive, emotional, or social well-being of all offenders may unfortunately leave some prisoners who are in need of their support in states of duress. As will become increasingly more evident throughout inmate narratives, the marginalized groups that are most likely to be adversely affected by staff-initiated conflicts include women, the elderly, and the mentally ill (Crawley, 2005; Crawley & Sparks, 2006).

Correctional officers who are employed in women's prisons are regularly presented with offenders who have heartfelt desires to establish open, intimate, close relationships with others but have previously encountered few opportunities to learn how to cultivate meaningful relationships. Some staff may experience the unique challenge of instructing them in setting appropriate boundaries or expressing emotions in a socially acceptable manner. Since personnel frequently appear unequipped with the specialized knowledge, skills, talents, or resources that may be necessary to adequately respond to this task, obligations to maintain order within the institution appear to be of greater concern than assisting their fellow humans to achieve personal growth. Personnel who may have been socialized to consider their positions as less significant, prestigious, or rewarding than labor performed in men's prisons have often been identified as treating female offenders as if they harbor similar attitudes, values, and behaviors as their male counterparts (Zupan, 1992; Cranford & Williams, 1998; Owen, 1998). For example, it is a relatively commonplace occurrence for officials to regard inmates who engage in self-disclosure as manipulative and respond to any emotionally charged interactions with the use of disciplinary infractions, revocations of coveted privileges, insults, or indifference (Cranford & Williams, 1998; Owen, 1998; Pollock, 2002; Greer, 2002).

As expected, persons who are confined to living within the parameters of this restrictive environment frequently harbor frustrations with their current circumstances. Many women who earnestly want to approach correctional officers for assistance, for example, have reported discovering that their methods for securing support appear to be ineffective. Distressingly, these female offenders often indicate that regardless of the steps they have taken to gain staff attention, the reactions received have primarily been dismissive. In the words of one 52-year-old woman who had served over 21 years of a life sentence:

> Being an older woman in prison means that you are ignored . . . staff generally have no time for the older inmates. . . . We often don't have activities that interest us . . . or access to someone who will take the time to listen. . . . Sometimes we just need someone to talk or vent to [and no one is there]. . . . Older inmates do not always know they matter. . . . Instead, we feel as if we are pushed to the side.

The sentiments frequently expressed by older women who perceive current policies or staff behaviors as needlessly restrictive or confining when they are taken out of the context for which they were adopted and liberally applied to female prison populations is illustrated by the statement given by this 63-year-old serving life: "They're instructed to treat us like they treat men, and we don't act like that. I've been here 13 years, and I've never seen anyone stabbed. They keep a tighter rein—a choke chain—on us with some of the rules they have here. . . . The men's institutions don't have that."

Additional research has shown that female offenders who recognize officers as viewing their roles as nothing more than performing the functions of a job, adhering strictly to procedures when instilling order, and writing up disciplinary reports for every infraction observed have higher levels of frustration, anger, and poor institutional adjustment than women who view the correctional officers as responding to their needs with greater leniency (Vuolo & Kruttschnitt, 2008). For reasons that will be outlined later, naturally the negative effect that correspondences with staff may have on inmate mood may be even greater for older women who must occupy later adulthood in prison.

Although previous research suggests an inverse relationship between offenders' age and the presence of abrasive or aggressive interactions with staff (MacKenzie, 1987), numerous older women observe less openly hostile forms of conflict or friction with correctional personnel. It is a relatively commonplace occurrence, for example, for members of this population to observe staff who are naturally more accustomed to supervising, monitoring, and reprimanding youthful offenders for their unruly behaviors yelling, screaming, or verbally abusing elders with whom they regularly interact (Aday, 2003). Among others, two women shared their insights into the nature of these behaviors as well as the contexts within which they were most likely to occur:

> I'm often bothered by the way the officers talk to us and curse us out. . . . It hurts my feelings. I cope by respecting the authority that they do have over me, no matter what age, by being obedient and staying near or on my bunk. Under the circumstances, I try to remain positive even

though I do think at times, "do these people talk to their mothers this way?"

The staff has a complex on the job vocabulary that includes "line up, straighten up, don't cross the line, hurry up and eat." . . . Even when we try to [adhere to their policies] and make them look good, they still fail to respect us. One day, these elderly ladies who obviously could not walk very well were coming down the hallway from the dorm to the dining room. One asked the officer if she could take the shortcut, and the officer yelled at her, "No, go the long way like everyone else."

Given the number of women who made general statements pertaining to conflicts with staff, or reported specific incidents they recall of having encountered problems with one or more officers while they had been incarcerated, it is unsurprising to note that an estimated 42 percent of older women reported being bothered by staff not listening to their grievances, whereas an additional 32 percent regularly worried about their relations with staff. For many offenders, the act of being under constant surveillance without adequate staff support caused them to become overwhelmed by intrusive thoughts associated with dealing with their losses of freedom, abiding by prison policies, as well as performing the jobs assigned to them. Several older women whose candid narratives related information concerning age-specific grievances reported staff had repeatedly driven them beyond the point of their capability by requiring, expecting, or encouraging active participation in the various exercise regimens, forms of prison employment, or other laborious chores that constitute daily life in this environment. A 56-year-old woman who had served over 15 years of a life sentence exemplifies strains that incarceration can place on the aged and infirm in voicing her attitudes toward the arduous labor personnel expect of inmates in her institution: "The most trying aspect of growing old in prison is the staff expects us to maintain a certain pace, keep up with the younger inmates, and do physical work that is just not possible. . . . Older women who have health problems or limitations do not need to be required to participate in the physical work outs." Although this elder identifies herself as finding value in the more moderately paced activities that the institution has to offer, she indicates that many of the existing options that her peers often feel obligated to pursue while they are incarcerated are incompatible with the goals or ambitions that most members of an aging prison population have brought with them into the system.

A growing body of literature suggests the greatest challenges that older offenders will encounter as they struggle to relate to the correctional officers with whom they regularly interact surfaces from the personnel's lack of knowledge, training, or sensitivity to gerontological issues (Aday, 2003; Kerbs & Jolley, 2009). As individuals who secure employment in this environment typically have minimal interest in working directly with the elderly, they may frequently fail to consider that certain physiological changes that accompany the aging process will result in slower response times or eliminate their abilities to engage in rigorous activities altogether. Thus, many may command elders to hurry when completing chores, walking to recreational activities or the dining hall, eating their meals, or even when voicing their concerns without knowing the impossibility of their demands. For older women whose deteriorating physical health necessitates an unrushed pace of living, however, staff demands are perceived as more serious than minor inconveniences, nuisances, or hassles to be addressed or overcome in the progression of their normal daily events. In fact, several offenders noted the presence of negative interactions with correctional personnel, if presented under the wrong circumstances, could result in further declines in health. Frustrations frequently held by these individuals are captured by the following comments:

> Growing old in prison, to me, appears to be the most horrifying experience one could have. The staff does not provide us easy enough details or listen to our needs. Sometimes we have a hard time getting up the ladder to the bunk beds, but they don't seem concerned or think we would benefit from an extra mattress.

> The officers are very low I.Q., very rude, prejudiced against whites. The people need to be reminded that we are people too. We made a mistake and the justice system has already degraded us and convicted us so we don't need to hear it every single day from medical and security officers. Then at least we could try and make it through this nightmare.

One of the most frequently reported complaints held by those who consider the line staff inattentive and irresponsive to their physical health–related concerns focuses on the amount of time they are expected to stand throughout any given day. As recent studies have estimated that approximately half of women who are aging in prison regularly encounter problems standing for head counts, with those feeling the greatest strain having increased risk of falling and sustaining injury afterwards (Williams et al., 2006), the following statement should cause administrators to reevaluate the effectiveness of existing procedures: "I don't care what we have done. [Older] inmates are not treated right. I can't walk everywhere and stand on my legs [as they require me to do]. Those of us who have health problems [such as arthritis or hip problems] just can't stand for any length of time. We have definite limits as to what we can physically do, but no one seems to care."

Although most inmate narratives have confirmed that the thoughtless, uncaring staff remarks or gestures older women observe on a regular basis are not intended to be personal attacks against individual inmates but instead represent "hidden injuries" that have unfortunately resulted from systemic demands intended to punish young male offenders, older female offenders do occasionally discover themselves forced to interact with the isolated cold, callous, insensitive officer who unarguably desires to inflict added punishment on the population he or she serves. One 52-year-old mother of nine, for example, observed the cruel and uncaring remark she received from one particular officer when she lost her son shortly after her arrival at the institution. Unlike the majority of prison personnel who extended to her their condolences and offered to assist her in the grieving process, this staff member could convey no other response than, "Well then, you shouldn't have been locked up when he died."

Several older women who provided their insights on exchanges they had engaged in with staff members throughout the duration of their sentences recognized the various constraints under which most officers must work. Elders who attempted to explore interpersonal relations from the perspective of the correctional officers occasionally attributed most of the concerns members of a graying prison population would encounter to the treatment the employees had received from the younger, more disrespectful generations who are currently entering the system in greater numbers than in previous years. Although women who acknowledged their supervisors as being untrained to accommodate their concerns, overworked, underpaid, and generally unappreciated regarded some conflicts they had witnessed as being outside the direct control or responsibility of individual officers to resolve, they struggled to comprehend why appropriate interventions could not be implemented to encourage a more hospitable atmosphere for all parties who occupy time and space within the institution. Respondents who share their visions of an environment within which employees are actively encouraged and rewarded for demonstrating open, warm, caring thoughts or gestures to those under their surveillance note: "What makes it so bad is that there are other inmates that will play the system. So they have gotten to the point that they are so guarded. If you need help, they will automatically assume you . . . I don't know if they are that overworked, or that they're apathetic, or. . . . Why don't they listen?? They don't listen . . . they just don't care."

Another group of women who expressed their visions concerning discrepancies between the ways in which correctional officers responded to the older offenders currently residing in the facilities where they work framed the nature of interactions within the context of the personnel's communications with younger offenders. Although many openly acknowledged and understood there would be a natural tendency for individuals to have more in common with, and a greater affinity toward, persons of their own ages, several individuals perceived the dialogues they had observed between particular officer-inmate dyads as closely resembling the correspondences one would anticipate surfacing within genuine friendships.

A number of offenders who commented on staff relations noted the problems becoming even more noticeable in recent years. According to one inmate, a 55-year-old woman who had served time for over 33 years, changes in the nature of these interactions incidentally occurred near the timing of transitions in the demographic composition of correctional personnel:

> Until the last 10 years, the officers for the female unit were mostly older women—women who had much experience as mothers, wives, daughters, church members. When I first began my sentence, it seemed as if whatever area an inmate was struggling with, there was someone who could relate and give her advice. . . . Today, this is not true—the staff are just out of high school . . . have no life experience. . . . There really is no interaction . . . and seems to be a lack of interest on either part.

It should be noted that inmate perceptions varied regarding their interactions with prison staff. At some facilities it was evident that inmates were more pleased with their treatment. In this instance, inmates felt prison staff showed respect to them by providing a stimulating environment designed to meet their special needs both mentally and physically.

Friction with Inmates

While many participants in our study voiced their satisfaction with younger inmates and their frequent opportunities to serve as mentors, the majority expressed dissatisfaction with the day-to-day interactions with the subgroup. Studies have found that older inmates report feeling unsafe and vulnerable to attack by younger inmates and expressed a preference for rooming with people their own age (Marquart, Merianos & Doucet, 2000; Walsh, 1990; Williams, 1989). Manuel Vega and Mitchell Silverman (1988) reported that abrasive relations with other inmates were the most disturbing incidents elderly prisoners had to cope with while incarcerated. These factors, among others, often result in fear and increasing stress for the older inmate (Kerbs & Jolley, 2009). Although few specific incidents of victimization were mentioned among our participants, other than harassment, teasing, or minor incidents, there appears to be an uneasiness associated with serving time with the younger women entering the criminal justice system today. This point is illustrated by an inmate serving life for murder who states, "Being an older inmate actually makes me feel out of place due to the fact our younger inmates are so disrespectful." Another said, "The young ones cuss us, try to push us around and hurt us sometimes." These general feelings of vulnerability and constant tension were expressed time and time again:

> Older women do not feel safe in prison because there are so many younger people in here who intimidate and try to abuse older people. They take advantage of older people because they know we can't fight back.

> It's very hard being incarcerated, but the most challenging aspect I have had to deal with is placement in a building with younger females. The women who are younger nowadays are very disrespectful of their fellow inmates. The younger they are, the worse they are. . . . Their actions are very toxic and cause older inmate[s] a lot of stress and emotional problems.

One of the most challenging aspects of residing with individuals one would not ordinarily consider befriending that was noted by many older women involved the introduction to homosexual lifestyles. Studies concerning inmate attitudes toward homosexuality have traditionally been limited in scope, with most research conducted in this area focusing extensively on the frequency with which offenders personally engage in homosexual behaviors. In general, the earliest attempts to document personal thoughts toward the practice itself as well as individuals who are active participants revealed that individuals serving time within the parameters of a prison setting held relatively negative opinions concerning their homosexual peers, often ridiculing or taunting them or using them as the subject of institutional humor (Richards, 1978). More recent research that explores attitudes observes unfavorable perceptions as being a function of race, gender, and sentence length. As Richard Tewksbury and Angela West (2000) note, those sentenced to long-term confinement typically harbor more negative attitudes toward their homosexual peers. Understandably, many individuals who will not receive the opportunity to return to the free world where they would have greater control over defining the nature, context, and outcome of interpersonal relationships may feel threatened by the presence of activities occurring in their immediate presences. More specifically, a number of these individuals have reported fears or feelings of apprehensiveness that persons will directly or indirectly convince or encourage them to become involved.

> Well, I came in as an older woman and . . . I just can't get used to the active relationships that constantly go on in prison. I've never seen anything like it! Homosexual relationships should not be tolerated. These relationships are very toxic and cause the other inmates a lot of stress and emotional problems. I wish they would stop housing the lovers together.

In some facilities, older women may even be encouraged, expected, or instructed to serve as mentoring figures to other women who are newer to the institution. Older individuals who do not personally desire to assume this enormous responsibility may discover themselves receiving requests from administration to actively extend practical, informational, or emotional support to their younger, more impressionable peers (Wahidin, 2004). As illustrated in other chapters, elder decisions to take on mentoring roles to others who have more limited familiarity with the inmate subculture can foster a sense of belonging, cohesiveness, and unity among inmates as well as ensure each offender's needs are accommodated in the most efficient manner humanly possible. Wahidin (2004) notes, however, additional circumstances under which roles that are imposed on members of an aging prison population can also contribute to conflicts or friction within the inmate social milieu. As we have yet to address how expectations for maintaining close proximity can dramatically and negatively affect the lives of those older women who desire additional opportunities for privacy, such must be acknowledged and recognized.

When making a suggestion for making prison a better place for older inmates, one inmate summed up her feelings this way, "To be able to do this time, without the fear of being hurt and things stolen from you." As a result, an overwhelming majority of the older women expressed the desire to be grouped together in a segregated area.

Special Housing Quarters

Given the variety and complexity of concerns that older incarcerated persons frequently pose regarding institutional living, policymakers have recently begun to explore the most practical and economical approaches for responding to them. Among the potential solutions that have been proposed to resolve grievances elders have with their current living arrangements, the notion of segregated housing units has sparked considerable scholarly interest. Within the past several years, a substantial body of research has proliferated to recognize the needs unique to persons who are over 50 years of age and have health conditions that would preclude them from functioning effectively in the mainstream prison environment. Numerous scholars, for example, have argued that grouping offenders by their medical needs substantially increases the level of specialized care these individuals would receive while simultaneously permitting administrators to avert the expense of offering services in every facility where the aged and infirm would otherwise likely reside (Kerbs & Jolley, 2009; Thivierge-Rikard & Thompson, 2007).

Over time, it has also become increasingly more evident that many older women would view segregation as serving a critical social function. Females who are placed in direct contact with their younger counterparts often feel as if they have no viable option but to remain on guard against others who may use their physical frailties as signs of potential weakness and vulnerability. Several individuals, for example, have expressed that they regularly refrain from congregating in communal areas as these places within the larger institution appear to be prime locations for younger, assertive, and aggressive persons to prey upon them. For them, prolonged exposure to intolerable noise levels, insults, or threats of physical injury can substantially diminish the anticipation that would otherwise be associated with formerly enjoyable pastimes. The following narratives serve as a common thread found in many responses regarding suggestions on how to make prison a better place for older inmates.

> I would like to see a senior citizens housing unit. This way the fear of being hurt by a younger inmate would be greatly reduced in the dorm. The older inmates share a lot in common but the younger inmates see

us as fools! Old fools! I think it would be nice to live with other senior citizens where we could enjoy recreation programs designed for us.

The younger women do not want us around them and will often tell us the administration should have another place for us. We have often been informed they do not want or need us here. We would appreciate separate housing accommodations so we won't have to continue to worry about being mentally abused.

The notion of segregated housing continues to be a topic of debate and policy consideration. While there have been numerous special needs units designed for older male prisoners, only a handful currently exist for women (Aday, 2003). Decisions to segregate older women from their younger counterparts would undisputedly provide many individuals who are entering into later adulthood access to a number of privileges that would improve their feelings of safety and comfort. Nonetheless, any use of this alternative would need to be accompanied by efforts to ensure that the offenders' removal from mainstream environments would not introduce them to additional extraneous burdens that could inhibit their opportunities for personal growth. In jurisdictions that have extended this option to male offenders, elders confined to geriatric facilities have occasionally reported suffering greatly from boredom or despair. For many, having limited options to engage in meaningful employment or structured activities results in them occupying countless hours in states of idleness. As James Marquart, Dorothy Merianos, and Geri Doucet (2000) have appropriately illustrated, residence away from their more energetic, youthful peers causes some individuals to limit their daily affairs to sedentary pursuits such as reading, writing, watching television, taking naps, and snacking.

Summary

This chapter reflects upon the special difficulties of adjusting to prison life for older female offenders. The shared experiences for those entering prison for the first time were obviously difficult. Due to the nature of the crimes committed by this group of aging prisoners, prison sentences are frequently long and, in some cases, bring the realization that prison life will more than likely be the final destination. Unique in this chapter was the role that aging plays in the adjustment process. Certainly, aging in any social context can be a trying event, but aging in an environment such as a total institution frequently results in a whole new set of challenges. Maintaining a positive feminine identity in a social setting that stresses control and punishment is a challenge that many women are incapable of overcoming. Compounded by poor mental and physical health, many women face the reality of a premature aging.

While some women expressed difficulty accepting their fate of being incarcerated in later life, others openly acknowledged a personal transformation. Assuming responsibility for past actions while making a pledge to do their very best in making prison a better place usually marked this evolution. The effect of imprisonment for an older female with an already beaten down self-esteem can be traumatic. This experience can be even more detrimental for marginal women who are now devalued more than ever. Certainly the negative reactions of prison officials and other younger peers are instrumental in how older women view themselves and consequently adjust to life behind bars. For some, prison may be the best option for access to health care and a compassionate support group of other older inmates. However, reducing the negative sanctions directed toward those who are old and in prison is a key component in developing a more positive prison experience. In particular, grouping older incarcerated women into a separate environment appears to be a first step in accommodating their special needs.

3

Health and Fears of Dying

WITH CORRECTIONS BUDGETS UNDER SIEGE IN RECENT DECADES to accommodate the dramatic increase in the overall prison population, states are finding it a challenging task to fund extensive physical and mental health-care services beyond the basic minimum. Critics maintain that addressing the gender-specific needs of female inmates equal to those afforded men is rarely a high priority for policymakers (Williams & Rikard, 2004). The aging of inmates in prison significantly affects the demand for health services, which only adds additional pressures for correctional systems. Despite the tremendous demand for health services and the simultaneous effort to control costs, there is little research concerning the health, well-being, and lifestyles of older inmates (Gallagher, 2001). Health habits and accessibility to prison health care has not been systematically addressed. In particular, the unique health-care needs of older women and their satisfaction or dissatisfaction with the services they receive deserve special attention.

Using aggregate data and personal narratives, this chapter is an effort to examine the health needs and functioning of older female inmates. Not only does this chapter document the deterioration of the women's health status and hence early aging, but also it brings new light to the frequent symptoms associated with poor mental health. Personal narratives from the women expose the malign neglect and lack of current policies available to address the health-care needs of aging female inmates. The constant suffering from physical pain, often the result of exposure to abusive relationships prior to incarceration, is addressed. This chapter also examines a variety of end-of-life issues as a greater number of older females spend their final years in prison. In the later stages of life, these women are faced with the reality that older inmates have no choice but to cope with their fears associated with inadequate health care and the distinct possibility of getting sick and perhaps dying in prison.

Assessing Older Inmates' Health

When assessing the health status of older inmates, it is important to include prior life experiences in combination with current health changes during incarceration (Marquart et al., 1997). Older inmates are usually in worse health than their counterparts outside prison because they develop health issues much earlier due to their previous lifestyle, socioeconomic factors, and the prison environment (Glamser & Cabana, 2003). Comorbidity is a common occurrence among aging prisoners, who frequently report multiple chronic diseases (Aday, 2003). Inmates may have illnesses such as asthma, emphysema, and arthritis (Glamser & Cabana, 2003). Various other viruses and infections contribute to the health threat among geriatric inmates. Airborne viruses such as influenza and respiration viruses are common in this age group (Falter, 1999). Parkinson's disease and Alzheimer's disease are also familiar in older inmates (Beckett, Taylor & Johnson, 2003). It has been frequently projected that inmates are usually physiologically ten years older than their actual age and they may have more chronic health issues than noninmates. In fact, 46 percent of inmates over the age of 50 reported having health problems at the time of their arrival into prison (Beckett, Taylor & Johnson, 2003). As a result, older inmates generally need more medical and mental health services than younger people (Cohn, 1999).

The issue of penal health care is of primary importance for aging female inmates, who as a general rule place a greater demand on prison medical and psychiatric services than males (Caldwell, Jarvis & Rosefield, 2001; Gibbons & Katzenbach, 2006; Shearer, 2003). Research has found that women seek health care at two and a half times the rate of males, but frequently prisons fail to adjust staffing ratios in female institutions (Ammar & Erez, 2000). Exposed to high rates of violence and victimization, many female inmates enter prison already highly marginalized in the wider society. With backgrounds of poverty and unemployment and a history of prior drug abuse, most have suffered from personal stress, trauma, and fear in many stages of their lives (Morash, Bynum & Koons, 1998). A frequent psychological consequence for women of being the victims of violence is posttraumatic stress disorder, characterized by intrusive thoughts, nightmares, and flashbacks of their earlier experiences (Braithwaite, Arriola & Newkirk, 2006). The socioeconomic hardships combined with extensive histories of violence and abuse negatively impact the short- and long-term health conditions of older women and place them at greater risk. Older inmates are, in particular, physically and mentally vulnerable and are most susceptible to the effects of incarceration.

As the number of incarcerated women continues to increase, correctional health officials can expect significant challenges because of their diverse needs. With poor health care prior to imprisonment, it is not uncommon for women entering prison to arrive with either untreated or undertreated health conditions (Maeve, 1999). Although not life threatening, chronic conditions can affect the quality of life of the female offender as well as prove costly to treat. When examining health profiles for the general population, research has found that when compared to older men, older women have higher incidents of certain debilitating diseases, including strokes, visual impairments, arthritis, hypertension, most digestive and urinary problems, incontinence, most types of orthopedic problems, depression, and diabetes (Hooyman & Kiyak, 2008). Women also face health problems specifically associated with their reproductive functions, such as breast, cervical, and uterine cancers—all of which have increased in recent years. Seventy-five percent of women with breast cancer are over age 50. In the past 25 years, the chances of a woman developing breast cancer have grown from 1 in 16 to 1 in 9 (Ebersole & Hess, 1998). Of those diagnosed with the disease, approximately one-third will die as a result.

Complications from hysterectomies are also common among older women. Compared to their male counterparts, older women experience more injuries and more days of restricted activity and bed disability. Osteoporosis, a degenerative bone condition affecting older women, causes them to be three to five times more likely to suffer from hip, back, and spine impairments. It has been reported that 20 percent of women age 50 and older have osteoporosis in both hips and spine (Speroff et al., 1996). The higher incidence of wrist, spinal, and hip fractures related to postmenopausal osteoporosis has been linked to the greater number of injuries and days of restricted activity among older women. An estimated 75 percent of postmenopausal women will fracture a hip, and approximately 35 percent will suffer spine shortening and often-painful vertebral fractures (Speroff et al., 1996).

Physical health concerns among older female inmates may result from aging in general or from previous lifestyles. Asthma, dementia,

Hepatitis B and C, tuberculosis, and HIV are prevalent among those who previously engaged in extensive alcohol consumption, smoking, sexual promiscuity, and intravenous drug use (Caldwell, Jarvis & Rosefield, 2001; Cranford & Williams, 1998; Nadel, 1997; Owen, 1998). Additionally, characteristics such as widowhood or divorce resulting in poverty, lack of insurance to afford preventative care, or improper diet prior to imprisonment contribute to the poor health among older female inmates (Caldwell, Jarvis & Rosefield, 2001; Morton, 1992; Reviere & Young, 2004). For those who have medical conditions related to poor lifestyle choices, not only must the health condition be treated, but also the inmate needs services to instruct her in correcting her high-risk behaviors that initially led to the illness. In addition, Gerri Lamb (2010) reported that incarcerated women who suffered from an abusive past were also more likely to have significantly more physical health problems and were more likely to be diagnosed with a variety of mental health problems.

Health Deterioration

Using this five-state sample, a comprehensive health profile enables us to better understand the challenges facing those who are obligated to provide health services to each and every prisoner. As Table 3.1 indicates, two-thirds of the respondents reported their health to be fair or poor, while about one-third described their health as good. Only 5.3 percent described their health as excellent—not surprising given that the mean number of chronic illnesses reported was 4.2. Although the overwhelming majority of women in this sample were between 50 and 55 years of age, they reported four times as many chronic illnesses as is likely in the 65 and older population in the general community (Hooyman & Kiyak, 2008). Table 3.2 displays the most common chronic illnesses to be mentioned by this group of older women. The leading chronic health problems were arthritis (61%), followed by hypertension (52%), stomach illness or ulcers (30%), emphysema/asthma (28%), and heart conditions (26%). Almost half (47%) indicated they felt their health to be worsening over the previous two years and participants frequently mentioned that their health status had gradually declined over the course of incarceration. Being conscious of this fact is illustrated by the following comments: "I am old and [have] done 22 years in here. I have gotten older and sicker every year." "When I came in, I didn't have any health issues. Now I have high blood pressure, high cholesterol, and

Table 3.1 Health Profile of a Sample Population (percentage; n = 327)

Characteristic	Total	Georgia	Tennessee	Kentucky	Mississippi	Arkansas
Self-reported health						
Excellent	5.3	9.0	3.3	—	1.4	13.0
Good	29.2	35.4	23.3	35.7	24.3	26.1
Fair	42.4	40.3	45.0	46.4	45.7	34.8
Poor	23.2	15.3	28.3	17.9	28.6	26.1
Self-reported mental health						
Excellent	25.2	35.9	21.7	21.4	25.7	21.7
Good	33.0	40.1	26.7	35.7	22.9	39.1
Fair	33.0	19.0	43.3	32.1	35.7	34.8
Poor	8.7	4.9	8.3	10.7	15.7	4.3
Health clinic or sick call						
Weekly	12.6	6.3	3.3	11.9	19.7	21.7
Once or twice a month	35.2	27.1	36.7	11.9	39.4	60.9
Once every few months	30.9	34.0	33.3	40.5	33.8	13.0
Hardly ever	21.3	32.6	26.7	35.7	7.0	4.3
Daily number of medications	4.7	4.7	5.0	5.4	4.9	3.3
Number of chronic illnesses	4.2	4.0	5.3	4.5	4.2	3.2
Health compared to two years ago						
Better	8.3	12.7	8.5	7.1	13.1	—
About the same	43.1	42.3	30.5	42.9	44.9	65.2
Worse	46.6	45.1	61.0	50.0	42.0	34.8

acid reflux." A 69-year-old woman who had served 23 years of a 40-year sentence stated:

> My health has gone down since I arrived here. I used to walk six miles a day before I came in here. My health deteriorated while I was serving 16 months in jail before and during my trial. When I got to prison, I had to learn to walk again because I had not gotten to walk more than 20 feet in one direction. Now, I've been having chest pains and I feel my health is failing.

These findings are similar to those reported by Elaine Genders and Elaim Player (1990), who reported older females to have an overwhelming fear of deterioration in their physical health as they served their life sentences. With a lack of proper exercise and healthy diet and as a result of dramatic weight gains, the women frequently see their health gradual-

Table 3.2 Self-Reported Chronic Illnesses (percentage; n = 327)

Illness	Total	Georgia	Tennessee	Kentucky	Mississippi	Arkansas
Hypertension	52	43	71	71	54	57
Arthritis	61	61	70	75	61	48
Blood disorders	9	10	16	11	4	4
Circulatory disorders	11	9	16	4	20	4
Heart condition	26	22	48	32	14	17
Cirrhosis/liver disease	3	4	5	7	0	0
Stomach/intestinal ulcers	30	32	22	25	30	27
Emphysema/asthma	28	23	55	46	31	30
Diabetes	21	21	21	29	21	17
Kidney disease	4	4	3	7	7	0
Nervous system disorders	16	10	32	11	22	4
Menopause problems	27	31	30	7	27	22
Menstrual problems	2	2	2	0	4	0
Pulmonary disease	4	3	7	7	11	0
Skin problems	9	6	21	11	10	0
Stroke	7	6	7	7	11	0
Urinary tract problems	8	5	12	18	10	4
Cancer	2	3	2	4	0	0
Respiratory system disorders	8	6	12	18	7	9

ly decline. As time passes them by, the feelings of vulnerability often intensify, especially in an environment grounded in protection and punishment (Maeve, 1999).

Mental Health Issues

In recent years, it has been estimated that approximately 15 percent of individuals who are 55 years of age or older and serving time in state prisons exhibit symptoms of one or more mental illnesses (Ditton, 1999; James & Glaze, 2006). In fact, 40 percent of state prisoners and 36 percent of federal prisoners report at least one mental health problem. Other research based on small convenience samples report that, in select institutions, the prevalence of specific mental conditions may be much higher, occasionally exceeding half of the older prison population (Barak, Perry & Elizur, 1995; Fazel et al., 2001; Taylor & Parrott, 1988). The rates are much higher for female inmates, with an estimated three-fourths entering prison with mental health issues. Mental illnesses prevalent among female inmates include depression, anxiety, and post-traumatic stress disorder (Aday, 2003; Caldwell, Jarvis & Rosefield, 2001; Cranford & Williams, 1998; Ross & Lawrence, 1998). Many older inmates also have anxieties associated with declining health.

When asked to report on their own mental health, 62 percent of respondents reported that it was "good" or "excellent." However, when using the Hopkins Symptoms Self-Report Inventory, 46 percent of the women in our sample were suffering from high or severe depression. Depression was most manifest overall by reports of "feeling lonely" (74%), "feeling blue" (70%), and "blaming myself for things" (60%). About the same number also reported coping with higher or severe indicators of anxiety. Anxiety was exhibited by symptoms of feeling "anxious about the future" (82%), "heart pounding or racing" (54%), and "nervousness or shakiness inside" (54%). There is growing evidence that being victimized by violent behaviors frequently leads to psychiatric consequences. Many female offenders require extensive mental health services during incarceration resulting from physical or sexual abuse endured prior to incarceration (Lamb, 2010; Young & Reviere, 2001). Our study supported this notion, as inmates reporting sexual and physical abuse prior to their incarceration were less well adjusted to prison and more likely to report significantly higher levels of depression, anxiety, and interpersonal sensitivity to others than for those reporting no abusive histories. The most commonly reported interpersonal sensitivity symptom was "feeling easily annoyed or irritated" (61%), "feelings being easily hurt" (59%), and "feeling that others do not understand you" (56%).

Depression is considered the most prevalent form of late-life psychopathology. While the rates of depression may vary when controlling for race and ethnicity, clinically relevant depressive symptoms are more common among older women when compared to those who are younger (Hooyman & Kiyak, 2008). In addition, depression is more likely to be found among the unmarried, those suffering from multiple chronic diseases (comorbidity), and individuals who lack an adequate social support system (Aranda, Lee & Wilson, 2001; Garrard et al., 1998; Taylor, McQuoid & Krishnan, 2004). Chronic diseases such as high blood pressure, arthritis, diabetes, stroke, and heart disease are significantly associated with depression (Bosworth et al., 2003; Lyness, 2004). Since older incarcerated women possess many of the characteristics mentioned above, it was not surprising that self-reported health and other indicators of functional health were found to be important predictors of depression. The prevalence of depression is also evident by self-reports as 60 percent of the women indicated that they sometimes or very often experience feelings of being depressed. Although the number of women taking antidepressants was not recorded, discussions with the women indicate that depression is a common experience. As one 63-year-old woman voiced about the consequences of doing time in a lifeless environment: "If the prison community doesn't follow through with the therapeutic side of it—giving some structure and activities, things to do, some recreational opportunities, well then, we're just vegetating. And when I see some women in here with this vacant look, it's like in a nursing home; they're just totally depressed."

It is not surprising that mental health was significantly correlated with prison adjustment. Several researchers have found this relationship to exist (Haney, 2006; Warren et al., 2004). Edward Zamble and Frank Porporino (1988) further state that emotional well-being is directly linked to adjustment, or "coping style." According to the researchers, emotionally adjusted prisoners have a tendency to strive to ameliorate the pressures of incarceration by attempting to maintain a sense of control over the prison environment. In turn, these behaviors affect how inmates are seen by staff and the subsequent treatment and care they receive. Other researchers have linked depression and poor prison coping (Kratcoski & Babb, 1990; Warren et al., 2004). Being able to delineate the symptoms of depression is of note because a self-awareness of depression and prison adjustment has been found to be a first step in alleviating depression in incarcerated adults. Lorriane Reitzel and Beverly Harju note that understanding the characteristics that predispose offenders to depression can help "in an attempt to alleviate depression and aid in the process of referral and attempt to alleviate depression and facilitate better adjustment to the environment" (2000, p. 641).

Functional Health Challenges

Functional impairments also create adverse experiences for geriatric female inmates as well as become important predictors of health-care costs (Williams et al., 2006). For instance, the decline of sensory-motor functioning becomes more detrimental in a prison environment where poor lighting and noise may pose significant problems. Presbyopia, or age-related vision loss, is made more problematic in prison settings where direct lighting and smooth surfaces combine to create glare. Presbycusis, or age-related hearing loss, is especially impairing in atmospheres, such as prisons, where there is a constant din of voices and sounds (Hooyman & Kiyak, 2008). Of notable impediment to functional ailment were loss of eyesight and hearing. Such losses can cause older prisoners to unwittingly break prison rules and risk punitive consequences. For example, several women mentioned the fact they had received a reprimand for failing to respond to a guard's orders only because they were unable to hear the command. To make matters even more problematic, vision and hearing problems often go undetected or are treated insufficiently in prison environments. As one inmate illustrated: "Eye care is a big problem. We shouldn't have to wait so long for eye-exams. We shouldn't have to pay for glasses. We often go as long as five years without a prescription change in our glasses, and glaucoma and cataract treatment is non-existent." Poor eyesight was reported by 88 percent of participants, and 69 percent reported wearing corrective lenses. In addition to poor eyesight, women reported hearing problems (32%) with 6 percent reporting the use of a hearing aid. (See Table 3.3.)

Table 3.3 Self-Reported Functional Health Status (percentage; n = 327)

Characteristic	Total	Georgia	Kentucky	Tennessee	Mississippi	Arkansas
Hearing problems	32.4	32.2	39.3	39.2	33.3	31.8
Vision problems	87.6	85.2	71.4	87.5	82.9	68.2
Wear hearing aid	6.2	6.0	0.0	1.7	0.0	4.5
Wear corrective eye lenses	69.0	67.1	82.1	57.1	58.6	78.3
Smoke cigarettes	47.6	46.3	32.1	46.4	50.0	0.0
Past drug or alcohol problem	43.4	42.3	50.0	28.6	52.9	30.4
Abused as a child or adult	50.3	50.1	60.7	51.7	47.8	52.2
Problems walking long distances	57.2	55.7	53.6	64.3	57.1	56.5
Difficulty standing for longer than 15 min.	59.3	57.7	57.1	66.1	62.9	40.9
Cannot walk independently	9.0	11.9	3.6	2.1	12.4	0.0
Require a flat, even terrain for walking	38.6	37.5	42.9	37.5	31.9	17.4
Cannot go up and down stairs	33.1	32.8	35.7	26.8	40.6	21.7
Require ground-level housing	49.7	48.3	42.9	57.1	61.4	27.3
Need a lower bunk	84.1	81.9	78.6	87.5	87.0	87.0
Health prevents you from doing things you'd like to	62.4	53.0	64.3	73.2	68.6	47.8

It should also be noted that over half also reported difficulty negoti-ating their prison environment when it came to walking long distances and standing for periods longer than 15 minutes. Over one-third felt they require a flat terrain for walking, and about the same number indicated they cannot go up and down stairs. Some 84 percent indicated they need a lower bunk, although this is often an unrealistic expectation in most institutions due to space and availability. The following comment serves as an illustration for the sentiment expressed concerning this issue: "For inmates in our age group, some have been issued a top bunk, and that's a real health issue. It is virtually impossible for some older women to climb up the ladder. I fell off the top bunk and now I have back trouble. They should take our age and health into consideration when assigning where we sleep."

Other physical problems also emerged for many participants who indicated that they were often required to walk uncomfortable dis-tances sometimes in bad weather, wait in long lines, and traverse stairs with considerable difficulty. The following narrative expresses this frustration:

> We have to walk to meals during cold winter rain. Picking up our daily meds, they make us stand in line until our turn to enter, sometimes 20 to 30 minutes in rain, sleet, and snow. It is very hard for the older women. We can't get around like the younger ones. I can't walk every-where and stand on my legs for long. I need to be on a lower level. I have trouble with the stairs—especially when I am carrying laundry or supplies from the commissary.

These findings are consistent with previous research (Williams et al., 2006) reporting that 69 percent of a large sample of older women (55 years and older) residing in California had difficulty with at least one "prison activity of daily living." Such activities include standing for head count, getting to the dining hall for meals, hearing orders from staff, dropping to the floor for alarms, and climbing on and off of a top bunk.

Other impediments to functional health included prior drug or alco-hol abuse (43%) and a continued dependency on tobacco, with 44 per-cent reporting to be regular smokers. This finding is consistent with that of Susan Cranford and Rose Williams (1998) who found that a high per-centage of incarcerated women are smokers, and this leads to an increase in hypertension, asthma, cardiovascular problems, and cancer. Women in this study who were nonsmokers complained that they suf-fered the ill effects of secondhand smoke: "I don't smoke, but I might as well for all of it that I have to breathe in. I know it's killing me. For those of us with cardio-pulmonary problems, we don't even have the luxury of living in a smoke-free environment." It should be pointed out that most states did have designated areas set aside for smoking, and several states had approved a smoke-free policy that is now in effect. Thus, it appears most correctional facilities are now more inclined to engage in preventive health measures, especially in this particular area.

Managing Physical Pain

Another factor that impedes functional health is "somatization," or the presence of physical symptoms of illness. Pain is an indicator frequently overlooked as an important measure of one's quality of life, including mobility and mental outlook. Considered a multidimensional phenomenon with physical, sensory, psychosocial, and emotional components (Lynch, 2001), pain also has the tendency to erode personality, sap energy, while evoking depression, creating sleep disorders, decreased socialization, and an eventual increase in health-care costs (Jeffery & Lubkin, 2002; Roberto, Perkins & Holland, 2007). Having lived longer and often confronted with degenerative conditions, older people are at high risk for experiencing pain. Chronic pain has frequently been linked with various health problems found among older women (Roberto & Reynolds, 2002). Loneliness and emotional pain from various situational losses coupled with boredom and depression decreases the ability to cope with physical pain (Touhy and Jett, 2008).

Due to the high rates of chronic health conditions reported by older women in prison, it is no wonder that they report persistent pain associated with problems such as osteoarthritis, back pain, angina, diabetes, and chronic sinusitis. These symptoms may or may not have medically identifiable origins, but they cause physical and emotional distress and/or impairment (Derogatis et al., 1974; North, 2002). Respondents reported several somatization symptoms. In fact, over three-fourths of the women reported sometimes or very often dealing with symptoms of lower back pain. Additionally, the majority of participants reported sometimes or frequently experiencing low levels of energy (78%), weakness in parts of the body (75%), muscle soreness (74%), numbness or tingling (69%), and hot or cold spells (63%). Also, over half of the older women indicated that their health prevented them from doing things they would like to do. Thus, managing their pain forced many of the women to withdraw from social activities that they valued such as working or recreational activities. Over two-thirds of the women reported they sometimes or frequently have difficulty sleeping, and pain was often sited as a major factor. As one woman stated: "The old suffer from back pains because of the lack of mattresses and all the metal and concrete. Lying there is really so uncomfortable, you never really get any real sleep. I wish we had thicker mattresses for those over age 50."

Others talked about the lack of appropriate medical response to those suffering from pain. And some participants claimed medications that they should or would be taking were unavailable. For instance, the women often voiced complaints that pain medication was improperly administered:

> They won't give anything for pain but Motrin, and lots of women experience much pain. Motrin is the drug for everything here and it doesn't work. Pain medications that I used to take to treat my condition are not prescribed. The drug formulary is so limited that we sometimes have to take several medications rather than the one that would be most effective. We need something for severe body pain.

> Medical personnel need to be more attentive to our needs. No one knows our bodies and the pains that we go through from day to day [like we do]. Often they fail to comply with the recommendations the outside providers have provided, and this causes our conditions to worsen. When we attend sick call, medical should also be more patient with us instead of getting agitated because of our complaints.

Ironically, the "pains of imprisonment" are not supposed to be physical. Yet, prisons are legally sanctioned to be uncomfortable, and the public's "threshold" of pain for the incarcerated is high (Haney, 2006; Johnson & Toch, 1982; Maeve & Vaughn, 2001; Vaughn & Smith, 1999). Moreover, it has long been assumed that many inmates are malingerers who feign illnesses in attempts to "get high" or gain medications to use as a commodity. As a result of these factors, it is likely that aging women behind bars experience physical pains that are discounted and go untreated.

Barriers to Health-Care Access

While older women may enter the prison setting with health problems, many indicate they do not receive adequate medical care. Although most state and federal prisons do screen inmates for arthritis, heart disease, and hypertension upon admission, many fail to screen for glaucoma and cataracts while others fail to provide necessary treatments and follow-up screenings (Young & Reviere, 2001). Some older incarcerated women have reported being repeatedly denied access to nutritional supplements, regular physical examinations, vision screenings, and mammograms (Caldwell, Jarvis & Rosefield, 2001; Mezey et al., 2002; Wahidin, 2004; Reviere & Young, 2004). Older incarcerated women who are not blatantly deprived from using available services may be strongly discouraged from seeking needed medical treatment by being forced to climb stairs to reach prison medical facilities, being labeled "hypochondriacs" for requesting treatment, and being shackled upon entering nonprison hospitals (Genders & Player, 1990; Wahidin, 2004). Reasons staff members frequently give for denying older women serving time adequate health care include a fear that they will abuse services and the number of incarcerated older females does not justify providing specialized medical services (Mezey et al., 2002; Wahidin, 2004).

Some inmates expressed a concern for the lack of preventive health care, which may be a reflection of the desire to maintain health-care costs. For example, many of the women expressed the desire for healthier diets including more fruits, vegetables, and salads. Almost one in five expressed concerns with abnormal weight gains and obesity. Participants also expressed feelings that prison health care is inadequate and difficult to access. One woman stated, "Most of the time they go against what the outside provider recommends for our needs which causes our condition to worsen." The notion that barriers to or denial of decent health services has become a significant issue in prison (Jacobi, 2005) is further illustrated by the following comment.

> Occasionally, we will run into a nurse who will just tell us the truth. To be honest with you, they will look at you and just say, "Honey, they're not going to do that because it costs too much money." Of course, this is a nurse that cares, so she won't last long, guaranteed. But there's something else; you feel like the prison system is dealing in dollars and cents, and that's all the hell you are is a commodity.

In an attempt to manage the soaring costs of caring for offenders, prisons have increasingly implemented health-care co-payment policies over the past decade (Gibbons & Katzenbach, 2006). The majority of state correctional systems require inmates to pay between $2 and $15 for a sick-call request, a doctor's visit, and in some states, for a prescription (National Institute of Corrections, 1997). These fees can be insurmountable for sick, aging inmates who are less likely than younger prisoners to have in-prison employment or a source of income outside the institution (Shadmi et al., 2006). The execution of these policies has been intended to prevent overutilization of medical services and to assure that these services are used "responsibly." While these fees are particularly detrimental to older adults in need of health services, research based on data from 36 states shows that co-payments reduce sick calls anywhere between 16 and 50 percent (Ammar & Erez, 2000). This policy has led inmates with legitimate medical concerns to delay or forgo seeking necessary treatment.

While some correctional systems do have chronic-care clinics where women may receive routine treatment, there is reason to believe that mandatory co-payments of as much as $3 to $5 may serve as a barrier to health-care access. Several women stated that they could not afford to co-pay for medical help or that the co-payment policy was unreasonable:

> We do not have the money to go to medical all the times that we really need to. We need medical to care and stop charging three dollars on the seventeen cents we make an hour. It takes three days to work to pay for this.

> Charging an inmate five dollars for sick call is ludicrous! I'm indigent and the few dollars my family sends me, they send to take care of me. I feel strongly against this practice, it's not fair. After you reach a certain age most of your family is gone and if you don't have children, there is no one to help you financially. Get rid of the co-pay so I can afford medical help.

> Every time we go to medical we have to pay. If you go there to get an aspirin you're going to pay $3 for that. Then, if it is determined that you need to see the doctor, you have to pay $3 again. Some just don't go to medical.

Other research involving aging inmates has also noted that co-pay prison procedures prevent access to health care. Heidi Strupp and Donna Willmott (2005) note that these payments represent a significant expense as older prisoners lack a steady income from friends and family outside the prison. Therefore, co-pay policies force many older female prisoners to choose between accessing medical care and purchasing necessary goods such as food and hygiene items. While more than 60 percent of the sample reported their health as "fair" or "poor," these women, as a whole, infrequently seek medical attention. Some two-thirds of the women reported visiting the health clinic between twice a month and once every two months. Only 10 percent reported going on a weekly basis, and one-fourth of the sample indicated that they rarely go to sick call.

However, it should be noted that while the majority of states require co-payments, all do allow certain services to be exempted. According to Todd Edwards (2000, p. 15), the most frequent listed exemptions include emergency services, when evaluation and treatment are immediately necessary for an offender's health; diagnosis, treatment, and testing for communicable diseases; mental health services; requested follow-up health-care services, initial or transfer health screenings, or other required medical procedures; in-patient care services such as hospitalization, extended care, hospice care, and skilled nursing services; and chronic-care clinics addressing such needs as hypertension, diabetes, or lung ailments.

Health Issues and Race

Due to the fact that a significant number of incarcerated women are African American, there is a need to address any special issues they may bring to the prison environment. Leslie Acoca (1998) has suggested morbidity factors such as diabetes, hypertension, and sickle-cell anemia are more likely to be present among this subgroup. In this study, only minor differences were observed when reviewing the inmates' access to health services, with older African American women being a little less likely to visit the health clinic. Although there were no significant racial differences in the number of daily medications reportedly consumed, Caucasians (mean = 4.5) did report significantly more chronic illnesses than their black (mean = 3.8) counterparts (t = 2.14; $p < .01$). While a small number, approximately twice as many African American women felt that their health had gotten better over the past two years. About one-half reported no significant changes compared to 39 percent of those in the Caucasian sample. Interestingly, more than half (53%) of whites felt that their health had worsened over the past two years compared to only 37 percent of African Americans. It should be noted that African American women were more likely to report prior drug and alcohol problems. However, when investigating any differences between various measures of mental health, the African American women were significantly less likely to suffer from depression and anxiety when compared to older Caucasians. Findings also revealed that Caucasians were also more likely than African Americans to report significantly more somatic complaints.

These findings may not be surprising when considering the fact that the prison literature generally supports the notion that African Americans are more resilient to the pains of incarceration than members of other ethnic groups (Wright, 1989). Previous research also suggests that African Americans may be more immune to the negative consequences of imprisonment and better able to stave off serious threats to their self-esteem (Carroll, 1982). Other research has also reported that African American women appear to feel significantly safer in prison and report fewer symptoms of psychological distress than Caucasians or Hispanics (Fagan and Lira, 1978). It has been hypothesized that perhaps living in hostile environments and other extreme life experiences prior to incarceration have better prepared African Americans for prison survival. According to Leo Carroll (1982), African Americans develop defense mechanisms to discrimination, debasement, and degradation and, as a result, typically maintain a more positive worldview.

Health and Death Concerns

Prior research has supported a significant association between one's health condition and fear of death (Benton, Christopher & Walter, 2007; Cicirelli, 1997; Fortner, Neimeyer, & Rybarczyk, 2000; Knight & Elfenbein, 1996; Lockhart et al., 2001). As health declines and greater physical problems emerge, higher levels of death anxiety are reported in elderly people (Fortner & Neimeyer, 1999). Larry Mullins and Mark Lopez (1982) found that individuals who reported worse health and diminished functional ability scored higher on the Death Anxiety Scale regardless of their age. Linda Viney's (1984) research similarly found that ill persons displayed higher death concern than well persons, and surgical patients were more anxious about death than were other patients. Research has also indicated that death anxiety increased among elderly individuals when they thought about being sick or dependent upon someone to take care of them for an extended period of time (Lockhart et al., 2001). Additional research has also suggested that other medical and somatic conditions should be examined more closely as possible determinants of death anxiety (Fortner & Neimeyer, 1999).

Coping with chronic illness and losses associated with aging can further induce stressful reactions sometimes referred to as "health anxiety" (Furer, Walker & Stein, 2007). Fears about one's personal health can be influenced by the fact that women's prisons are frequently located in predominantly rural areas and removed from easy access to health-care services (Reviere & Young, 2004). Also, the medical facilities in many state and federal prisons are simply unequipped to effectively provide the appropriate care necessary to treat older inmates (Lundstrom, 1994). Another factor contributing to health anxiety is the often unsympathetic environment of prisons, where many question whether sick inmates should receive expensive medical procedures at the same level as law-abiding citizens in the community. Although older female inmates need medical services more than any other inmate group (Caldwell, Jarvis & Rosefield, 2001), these impediments to health-care access coupled with an overwhelming fear of deterioration in their physical health are a constant reminder of the vulnerabilities facing older inmates in poor health (Genders & Player, 1990; Smyer & Gragert, 2006; Ross & Lawrence, 1998).

The harshness of prison environments can accelerate declines in inmate health, which may trigger additional devastating anxieties (Haney, 2006; Maeve & Vaughn, 2001; Tonry, 1995). Contributing to inmate health fears has been the "penal harm movement," which has gained considerable traction in prison settings during the past decade (Granse, 2003; Vaughn & Collins, 2004; Vaughn & Smith, 1999). Due to staff indifference or efforts to curb health-care costs, the quality of services provided frequently departs from the ordinary standard of care. It has been suggested that this philosophy often results in the denial or delay of medical treatment to inmates (Watson, Stimpson & Hostick 2004; Vaughn 1999). In some cases, medical staff have even been found to humiliate inmates and to deny giving care such as withholding or delaying essential medications resulting in physical and/or emotional damage to inmates (Vaughn & Smith, 1999; Vaughn & Collins, 2004). In prison, every aspect of an inmate's life, including end-of-life issues, is generally controlled by others. As a result, inmates frequently have little control over their own health care or dying experience. The prospect of dying in a foreign place in a dependent and undignified state is likely to be a very distressing thought for older adults (Aday, 2005–2006).

For the older women in this sample, there appears to be a significant link between the preoccupation with death thoughts and death anxiety. About two-thirds (67%) of the women in this sample indicated that the thought of death frequently entered their mind, and about one-half (46%) said that those thoughts bothered them. As one inmate revealed, "I am 70 years old and growing older, possibly getting real sick and dying in prison bothers me all the time." Another inmate reported, "I sometimes have flashbacks about some who have died with the same disease that I have that is incurable." As reported earlier, almost one-half (47%) of women reported that their health had progressively worsened over the previous two years, and it is no surprise that the majority of participants (77%) who were more likely to worry about getting sick in prison also exhibited a greater degree of death anxiety. Certainly a prison culture provides the ideal conditions for persistent stress and imposes "continual wear and tear on individuals and contribute[s] to the aging process and ill health" (Smyer, Gragert & LaMere, 1997). As individuals age, there is a decreased ability to adapt, leading to an increased mortality and morbidity in this population (Smyer & Gragert, 2006).

Specifically, two-thirds of the women surveyed feared having a heart attack or getting cancer while incarcerated. These fears are illustrated by one older female who responded, "If I get sick I know I will die in here." Another mentioned, "I worry about medical needs being met if I had a heart attack or was diagnosed with cancer because of past inmates who have died in here." Yet another older inmate also expressed her anxieties concerning perceived health-care needs while residing in a confined environment: "To be so sick and so locked up, and you don't have any way of getting help, and you look out there and you don't see a guard anywhere for maybe 20 or 30 minutes, and you think what if I have a heart attack and I can't get out. What if the power goes down? That really scares me." It is apparent that coping with chronic illness and losses associated with aging can induce fearful reactions, and the lack of adequate health care can have severe repercussions on an older female inmate's state of mental well-being.

For many aging prisoners, it was a very common occurrence to fear or mistrust the medical care provided in what they perceived to be a highly defective system. The prisoners were fearful that the "incompetent medical attention, more than the illness itself, would lead to death" (Watterson, 1996, p. 255). David Sudnow (1967) suggested there is a strong relationship between the perceived moral character of individuals and the amount of effort that is made to attempt revival when death appears imminent. This view is supported here as numerous women commented about the deaths of other inmates due to the perceived indifference or lack of proper response from the medical staff. For instance, participants noted:

> The death anxiety is very high, due to the lack of medical care that we get. The majority of the time, [inmates die] because they did not have the medicine that they needed, but more often, because they were left in a critical condition and couldn't get anyone to respond.

Without decent care, I will just get worse. I can tell, [and there is] nothing I can do about it. I've spent months trying to see a specialist on the outside and every day I'm getting sicker, frustrated, and one day closer to death, and when I wake up, there's no one here that gives a damn.

Additionally, inmates frequently observed their friends and acquaintances suffering from the pain and humiliation that the medical personnel have caused them due to denial or delaying of medical treatment. One older inmate stated, "I have seen a woman have a stroke and left to lie on the ground while medical personnel walked to the person and smoked and joked as they walked." Another inmate also voiced this hopeless view that so many inmates expressed when attempting to get their health-care needs addressed: "It's like they see your mouth move, but they're not hearing a word."

These perceptions are similar to those reported by Diane Young (2000) who found inmate fears are often fueled by a lack of faith in prison health-care systems as well as the view that prison care not only is nonempathetic, but also lacks the necessary resources to provide adequate care. Also, custodial priorities, poor health-care management, and incompetence are obstacles to satisfactory penal health care. As one inmate voiced, "I feel that sometimes it [death] could be prevented or wouldn't have happened as soon if they wouldn't be taken off their meds." And another suggested, "It's upsetting if it's a case of not being diagnosed properly or receiving medical care." One woman gave an eye-opening description of what several inmates in her pod witnessed as another inmate died due to perceived staff indifference and incompetency:

I was in my cell when I heard . . . "Get a guard! Get a guard! She's foaming at the mouth!" The guard went running in there, looked in the door and said, "I want you to roll over and shut up! I am tired of hearing you beat on this door." She said, "I'm telling you, she's dying. Her eyes are rolled back in her head, She's dying." So she finally, after twenty minutes, got on the radio and got another guard up there. They went in the room and tried to resuscitate her. They put the tube down, and instead of running it into her airway, they run it down into her stomach and blew her up with the air that they was expecting to be putting in her lung.

It has been acknowledged that medical facilities in many state and federal prisons are simply unequipped to effectively provide the appropriate care necessary to treat advanced chronic diseases commonly found among older inmates (Gibbons & Katzenbach, 2006; Lundstrom, 1994). This fact is illustrated by the following comment: "They die in here all the time. Even young people die in here 27 years old from diseases and heart attacks. Here, they are not very well equipped to handle a heart attack. They have to go call somebody in to get you. They got an EKG machine, but still, that ain't nothing if you are having a heart attack. You know, they need a medical hospital here." These experiences of observing others die in prison became telling reminders of the fact that they too may very well become victims of an inadequate or substandard health-care response. Several comments made by inmates, such as "The system has neglected them. . . . It makes me feel like I'm next" or "They go to medical, get Mylanta and die," illustrate the fears and concerns expressed by this vulnerable prison population. It is apparent that as these women age they have to deal with many issues relating to incarceration and the possibility of dying in prison. They may have no other choice but to accept the idea of dying in a harsh prison environment, the constant deterioration of their health, and the lack of health care within the prison, all of which increases the risk of dying in prison.

Coping with Death Fears

Older female offenders by the very nature of their fragile mental and physical health condition have difficulty coping with a harsh prison environment that engenders considerable stress and anxiety (Aday, 2003; Reviere & Young, 2004). As we have learned from earlier comments, it is the experience of neglect, denigration, humiliation, and lack of care and treatment that gives aging and dying in prison a new significance. The lack of control over one's health and one's body has been suggested as a major cause for many to fear death in prison. While views of death in prison have been found to contain negative connotations, other models have included positive views of death acceptance that symbolized death as passage to a better afterlife or death as a relief or escape from pain (Gesser, Wong & Reker, 1987; Klug & Sinha, 1987; Martin & Salovey, 1996).

To address specific ways older incarcerated women managed their feelings toward dying in prison, older women in this study were asked, "What does dying in prison mean to you?" and "How do you cope with the thought of dying in prison?" This question prompted a wide range of responses, including notions from a small group of the women that the thought was so overwhelming they just couldn't comprehend the prospect of spending their final days behind bars. Other women expressed fear or grief reactions such as sadness or responded with bouts of crying and depression. For this vulnerable prison population, experiencing a gradual deterioration of their health, common themes emerged such as denial and avoidance and the importance of religious activities and beliefs as valid coping strategies.

Thoughts of Dying in Prison

Previous research has reported that dying in prison carries tremendous negative stigma. Inmates frequently associate dying in prison with an experience devoid of "dignity and peace" (Aday, 2005–2006; Bolger, 2004). Numerous inmates who had witnessed or were aware of inmates in their facility dying expressed a variety of emotions when considering the possibility. Responses about dying in prison were varied, ranging from feelings of hopelessness, sadness, fear, and anger to "the worst-case scenario." Respondents frequently mentioned the negative stigma associated with dying in prison, especially the emotional pain and suffering that such an event might have on the inmate's family. One inmate succinctly describes her feelings about what it means to die in prison, "It also means I'm a sister, grandmother, mother, and I feel like after 10 years it's going to be a waste to die here." Another woman felt, "It's more of an embarrassment for my family, not me since I would be dead," and another shared a similar sentiment, "I have thought about dying in here, how terrible it would be for my children and family." These thoughts are similar to those suggested by Frank Glamser and Donald Cabana (2003), who compared dying in prison to a wasted life, and Maggie Bolger (2004), who reported that dying in prison was a huge letdown for the family.

Other inmates expressed similar views about dying in prison. As one inmate commented, "My life would be a waste," and another stated, "It means that I have failed God." A 61-year-old female commented further about the stigma of aging and dying in prison: "It is a bad feeling to have to sit here day after day, year after year getting older every year just to set around here every day wondering if I will ever get to go back to my family before I leave this earth. I wouldn't want to have to leave here in a body bag. That would hurt my family so much." Ira Byock (2002) has stated that dying prisoners are considered a highly marginal group and devalued by society as well as by prison staff. Inmates may feel the added shame from dying in prison and frequently regret the lack of opportunity to atone for their behavior. A successful return to the community would be a sign of forgiveness and redemption (Blanchette & Brown, 2006). For example, for one older woman, dying in prison would mean: "I would not have the opportunity to physically bless my family. I want to renew my relationship with my family and live as a law-abiding, productive citizen."

The majority (83%) of respondents indicated they have no fear of death; the process of actually dying is the most troubling. As one woman expressed, "My concern is not with what happens after death, but with the process of dying . . . the pain, the dignity." The stigma of dying in prison is often associated with dying alone. In particular, being disconnected from loved ones at life's end can have a compelling impact. These fears are supported by Richard Kalish (1985), who maintained the view that when people consider the prospect of death, they need, more than ever, the assurance that their close friends and family will not abandon them to die alone. As one inmate expressed, "I want to be with my family when I die. I want to tell them that everything is okay." Another responded, "Dying in here would be the most terrible thing to happen, not being able to see my family . . . being alone to die by yourself."

Denial and Avoidance

Denial has been reported as one of the most useful ways of coping with the fear of dying in prison (Maull, 1991). About one-third of aging male prisoners were found to use avoidance or denial as a coping strategy when death thoughts surfaced (Aday, 2005–2006). The older women in our study clearly used similar techniques to cope with their thoughts about dying in prison. For example, numerous offenders made similar comments: "I never give it a second or first thought." "It's hard to deal with the thought of dying in prison. I can't deal with the thought." "I don't think about dying in prison." Still others strived to identify leisurely pursuits to preoccupy their minds and found that thumbing through the pages of a good book or listening to music leaves them with few opportunities to worry about death.

Talking with others about their concerns and fears or engaging in recreational activities were also used to avoid unwanted death thoughts. For those who rely on pleasant conversations to lessen their fears, relatives outside the institution provide them with an opportunity for laughter that makes fears of dying behind bars less painful. One inmate reported that when someone she knew died in prison she coped by thinking more about her family. As she indicated, "I have even called home after a death. It makes you want to reach out after someone dies." Another woman recalled that she usually called home and joked with family members to take her mind off of prison deaths when she had difficulty coping. Some women reported reaching out to other inmates to allay their concerns about their vulnerable situations. Two-thirds of the participants mentioned they frequently talked with other inmates about their health status, and one-third also reported sharing their fears and concerns about getting sick and dying in prison.

Death Acceptance

Confirming the assertion that many inmates neither anticipate nor fear dying behind bars (Granse, 2003), some women insisted that they refuse to dwell on this very real possibility. Christina Rocke and Katie Cherry (2002) suggest that accepting one's own death is a final task in late life. Moreover, Fleet Maull states that it is very difficult to accept one's own death, but many people are able to accept the "realization of the inevitable" (1991, p. 139). Research has also suggested that most older adults have been given ample time to consider their own mortality, and this process apparently allows them to have less fear and become more accepting of death (Rocke & Cherry, 2002). Among those who do not brood over death-related fears, one woman explained, "Yes I think about dying in here nearly every day, but if it's my time to go, so be it." It appears that many women have accepted the fact that death happens to everyone, and as one inmate stated, "Whether in prison or not, dying is part of life regardless of where you are." Other examples of acceptance include such comments as "I try very hard not to let death cross my mind, but when it does I feel it was meant to be" and "I can't live forever whether I'm in prison or out."

Another symbolic measure of acceptance of death includes the view that death can serve as an opportunity to escape an intolerable situation (Martin & Salovey, 1996). Thus, for many of the older women inmates, dying in prison was viewed as an escape or a relief from a life filled with pain and frustration. This supports previous prison research of male inmates, who also found death in prison to be an escape from isolation, illness, and the pains of imprisonment (Aday, 2005–2006; Heflick, 2005). As one older woman offender said: "Knowing one day that I will not suffer any longer in this house, I focus on positive thoughts about release and freedom." Therefore, in some situations disenfranchised inmates embraced death as an end to their suffering. For them, prison life provides nothing to look forward to but more frustrations and humiliating situations.

Although religious beliefs were not comprehensively addressed in this study, there was some support for the notion that inmates who reported participating in religious activities were less likely to have heightened death anxiety (Fortner, Neimeyer & Rybarczyk, 2000). When asked how the older women offenders coped with their fears of dying behind bars, the majority of the respondents turned to prayer or other spiritual activities. Among those who found prayer, trust in "God's will," or other religious practices to be sources of hope, one woman explained that "if a person's heart is right with God, they have no fear of death or eternity." Several other women commented: "I talk to God about it" and "I pray all day and read my Bible and do as God have me to do and be nice as I can to everyone" or "I give it to God and he gives me peace." The religious theme supports the commonly held view that religious beliefs provide an important buffer against the fear of death (Wink & Scott, 2005).

Viewing death as a passage to a better afterlife is purported to be helpful in coming to terms with one's mortality (Martin & Salovey, 1996). To soften the thought of dying in prison, a significant number of women viewed death as a passage into a new world or an afterlife. Several women declared, "I will be in a better place; my family and friends will know that," "I know if it happens it happens, I will be in a much better place," and "When the Lord gets ready for me, I got to go, it will be a better place." Even though there is conflicting literature about the correlation between the belief in an afterlife and death anxiety, it is viewed as an important coping mechanism for many people (Rose & O'Sullivan, 2002). The women inmates in this study did use the belief in an afterlife as a positive coping mechanism toward the thought of dying in prison, and it is apparent this view provided the courage to be more accepting of their mortality.

Summary

Older female offenders were found to possess a significant number of health problems as well as a high degree of anxiety and depression. This study explored the role that prison health-care practices played in contributing to older female offenders' concerns about the adequacy of their health care in this vulnerable condition. Katherine Maeve (1999) has suggested that for some inmates prison was their opportunity to get healthy, especially for those with little access to health care prior to imprisonment. Some inmates tend to view medical care in prison as a buffer against the hostile nature of prisons (Mahan, 1984). This view is quickly discarded by the realities of what is really possible within correctional health-care systems where resources are quite scarce. Prior research has also found that inmates typically hold negative views of prison health care (Aday, 2003; Young, 2000). Similar to the findings discussed in this chapter, other research has expressed the notion that health-care treatment has been characterized as having a total disregard for prisoners by responding in either an abrupt or unresponsive manner, is often delayed, or is frequently misdirected (Fearn and Parker, 2005).

This chapter also looked specifically at how the inmates' declining health and the lack of medical care influenced their fears of death. Older inmates with multiple health conditions and who are mentally fragile frequently find themselves engaging in thoughts about dying in prison. However, the preoccupation with death for community dwellers was not that significant in a study by Richard Kalish and David Reynolds (1974). They discovered that only one out of six respondents reported thinking about death daily, and one-fourth said that they never thought of their own death at all. Earlier findings have found that individuals are more likely to think about death due to their personal situations such as advancing age, illness, and the death of others (Lowenthal, Thurnher & Chiriboga, 1975; Riley, 1970). This seems to clearly be the case for older incarcerated females who are living in such a vulnerable state of existence. Living in a harsh prison environment with little control over their own health care only serves to heighten fears about dying in prison.

By their very nature, total institutions strip away a person's identity and their sense of self through a process of isolation and homogenization (Kamerman, 1988). Inadequate facilities and poor health care both serve as constant reminders of their status as prisoners. If prison steals away the dignity and true identity of those who are in a vulnerable state of existence, the journey into the unknown becomes more ominous. As many women indicated, the notion of dying in a total institution reflects immeasurably on one's personal identity. According to Jack Kamerman, "this 'prisoner' is the final version of the self . . . each person's dying day is Judgment Day" (p. 46). Thus, when thoughts arise about dying in a total institution, questions may arise concerning the inmates' self-worth. In some cases, family members may have already deserted them. The thought of spending one's final days behind bars creates a variety of emotions, including anxiety, anger, and frustration mixed with the slightest glimpse of hope. Certainly understanding this population's unique health characteristics and consequential personal vulnerabilities is essential to understanding and managing this special subgroup of inmates.

4

Connections to
the Free World

THIS CHAPTER UNDERSCORES THE IMPORTANCE OF VIEWING INCAR-
cerated women as part of their family context. Major benefits of
staying in touch with family members include maintaining an important
link with the outside in addition to the emotional and financial support
that frequently is provided. However, prison policies often restrict the
ability of inmates to maintain connections with family members,
whether corresponding by letter, phone, or face-to-face visits. This
chapter will expand our understanding of the challenges of these older
women when faced with prolonged separation, traumatic family histories, and the institutional and personal obstacles for maintaining important family roles and relationships. In particular, parenting and grandparenting from prison can be challenging for individuals with extended
prison sentences. Using personal narratives, this chapter exposes the lit-
eral pain and emotional turmoil as well as the joy and excitement that
older females experience when confronted with the challenges of staying connected. It is apparent from the experiences shared in this chapter
that the inmates and their families tend to partner to do the prison time
together. Families are often pulled into an unforgiving system where
they are also susceptible to the pains of imprisonment.

Families are viewed as the cornerstone of our lives. It is the social
context whereby our identity is affirmed, where we learn to respect and
to trust. Families provide us with important rituals and traditions and
give special meaning to our lives. Inmates indicate that a relationship
with their family is their most significant concern while incarcerated
(Sellen et al., 2006). Although prisoners are frequently seen in terms of
their criminal activities, we must remember they are not isolated individuals without important connections to families and other community

members. Each inmate has a family history and the majority of them continue to share their lives with family members. Research has demonstrated that inmates who are able to maintain contact with family members experience more positive outcomes with the transition to prison life. Moreover, scholars have been able to identify the services family members are most likely to perform for incarcerated women (Lindquist, 2000; Casey-Acevedo & Bakken, 2002). Most suggest families provide offenders the presence of support when crises arise; provision of financial assistance, childcare, or similar practical forms of assistance; encouragement to adopt prosocial behaviors; as well as the assurance the individuals will have homes where they can return upon release. Such support not only makes the transition into the institutional setting easier to accept for older women, but it also facilitates a smoother transition back into mainstream society after their sentences end.

The act of imprisonment itself has an immediate and dramatic effect on an individual's social life. Relational developmental theory maintains that a woman's identity and well-being are grounded in her ability to maintain relationships with significant others, especially family members (Miller, 1993). For female offenders, incarceration can have a devastating impact on the lives of family members, especially if they leave children or aging parents behind who must now rely on others for support (Krabill & Aday, 2005; Poehlmann, 2005; Pollock, 2004). The fact that families left behind are faced with financial hardships as well as emotional issues can weigh heavily on the minds of incarcerated mothers. Knowing family members are suffering from stigma associated with incarceration, depression, anxiety, sadness, loneliness, uncertainty, and feelings of abandonment may lead to certain depressive symptoms on the part of inmates (Christian, 2005; Hoffmann, Dickinson & Dunn, 2007; Poehlmann, 2005). Relationship disconnections may also lead inmates to face similar emotional trauma by experiencing shame, separation anxiety, guilt, failure, and abandonment to mention a few (Luke, 2002; Aday, 1994a).

Family Relations

Table 4.1 provides a glimpse into the family life of older incarcerated females. The overwhelming majority have a variety of immediate family members (parents, siblings, children, and grandchildren) who at least provide a pool from which support may be available. As indicated, various connection methods such as writing, visits, or phone calls

Table 4.1 Indicators of Family Support (n = 327)

Support Measures	Percentage
Do you have living ____?	
Parents	57.2
Brothers/sisters	86.5
Children	90.2
Grandchildren	77.8
Remain in contact with them?	88.2
How often do you receive visits from family members?	
Never	33.0
Occasionally (1–2 times a year)	26.5
Fairly often (monthly)	23.8
Very often (weekly)	16.7
How often do you receive letters from family members?	
Never	11.1
Occasionally (1–2 times a year)	15.1
Fairly often (monthly)	38.2
Very often (weekly)	35.4
How often do you talk on the phone to family members?	
Never	20.6
Occasionally (1–2 times a year)	12.0
Fairly often (monthly)	19.6
Very often (weekly)	47.9
Feel a strong emotional closeness with family/friends on the outside?	83.7
Feel you could turn to family/friends for advice and guidance?	86.5
Have family/friends on the outside you can depend on?	89.8
Overall, how satisfied are you with family relationships?	
Very satisfied	54.0
Fairly satisfied	25.9
Not very satisfied	19.1

are used to remain in contact with family members. The majority report that they still feel a strong emotional closeness with their family and feel comfortable turning to them for advice and guidance. As a result, the women tend to feel either very or fairly satisfied with their family relationships. Of course, this does not mean that families do not struggle to remain in touch or are not abusive and dysfunctional, but certainly the perception indicates relatively strong family foundations for the majority.

The literature has identified numerous institutional and personal benefits associated with inmates maintaining contact with the outside world and this is the case for most all of the women in our study. Personal benefits range from emotional support to financial support for the commissary. Researchers have also suggested that if family members through regular contact are able to preserve the inmate's status as a spouse, parent, or son or daughter, both the inmate and family may have a more positive mental outlook (Lindquist, 2000; Schafer, 1994). Remaining connected enables inmates the opportunity to retain an instrumental role in family rituals as well as staying involved in the day-to-day decisions. When families make special efforts to remain in contact, this symbolically helps reassure convicted siblings, parents, and grandparents that family members still care and support them as a person (Casey-Acevedo & Bakken, 2002). Maintaining ties to the community can also be an important factor for inmate adjustment. Making possible inmates' contact with family members while incarcerated through telephone, letter writing, or prison visitation has been positively linked with improved behavior while imprisoned (Casey-Acevedo & Bakken, 2002; Hensley, Koscheski & Tewksbury, 2002). Some prison officials tend to view family visitation as an important managerial tool to maintain inmate conduct (Rosen, 2001). For example, George Kiser (1991) notes a positive relationship between communication with family and participation in structured prison programming.

Heidi Strupp and Donna Willmott (2005) emphasize the important role that outside emotional support often plays in the lives of older incarcerated women as they maintain the hope of reunification for years on end. By continually engaging in positive communication, inmates can draw on the social support of family and friends and better adjust to the stresses and strains of prison life. Being able to actively participate in the parenting role can be an important motivator for improving self-esteem and purpose in life. Formal letter writing, video visitation, book programs, and structured prison visits have been significant activities leading to improved behavior. In particular, family social support has been found to reduce prisoner anxiety and improve their life view. This is a factor frequently overlooked by policymakers who create barriers that hinder families from maintaining close ties with their loved ones in prison. The following comments serve as illustrations of the utmost importance of family interaction and support:

> My children and I communicate well with each other. We are an open family and can talk and share our emotions about a wide range of issues. We have dealt with the pain and feelings about the past and my years away from home. As a result, my family continues to support me emotionally, spiritually, etc.

> I have a very warm and supportive family. They may not be perfect, but they are usually understanding. All know about the reasons I am incarcerated and support my decisions. Members of my family write,

send packages, pictures, and their love. Their support has provided me with a great lift.

Research concerning adjustment to long-term imprisonment suggests the increased time spent in prison encourages individuals to value their supports as individuals of worth. Inmates are able to reflect on the repertoire of knowledge, skills, and resources already available to themselves before making unwarranted requests from family on the outside. They are able to convey empathy, straightforwardness, and willingness to reciprocate when asking for help, as well as understand and accept each exchange is key to maintaining positive relationships (Rasch, 1981; Johnson & Chernoff, 2002; Johnson & Dobrzanska, 2005). Consequently, older women who appeared reticent to rely extensively on family for support unsurprisingly identified the present as a time when former self-serving, materialistic attitudes were quickly being replaced by consideration for the needs of others. Numerous offenders indicated that they made conscious decisions to refrain from placing added burdens on relatives who have limited time, talents, or motivations to assist them. Rather, they used the experience of imprisonment as teachable moments to instill in themselves the levels of self-sufficiency they would ultimately need for survival postrelease:

> I had grown up dependent on family a lot. We had some issues financially. I had always used [resources provided by] my family, kids, all of that over there to make me okay. . . . To be in here now is sad, heartbreaking really . . . but it is better for me and is making me grow up. . . . It is forcing me to realize I must depend on my own power.

One 50-year-old offender who is currently serving a 14-year sentence for embezzlement charges explains the imperativeness of identifying, securing, and developing a willingness to contact family for financial assistance after informing the researchers of her current health concerns. As she has battled cancers, strokes, and other chronic conditions, received no thorough medical examination while incarcerated, and had gained 21 pounds since being institutionalized the previous year, this older woman has become a major advocate for taking proactive measures toward preventative health care. While this individual regularly walks and attempts to self-regulate her mood, stress, and salt intake levels, the presence of a balanced diet remains a major concern for her. According to her, the fact that earnings from full-time prison employment total no more than 65 cents per day requires continual requests from external supports to achieve the noted goals: "It's expensive in here . . . a real battle to eat healthfully. I'm mortified—so embarrassed . . . to . . . cost my family . . . to cause them to suffer . . . but I had to ask [my husband] for the money—for my health. With his help, I can eat a more healthy diet by buying special foods at the canteen." Older offenders who must rely on children, grandchildren, and others for whom one should be providing care will understandably feel extraordinarily guilty about the prospects of having to make such requests for assistance (Leigey, 2007). For one inmate, her entrance into prison was near the time when her husband was making plans to retire, creating a significant financial hardship. Other women expressed that they experienced feelings such as guilt, humiliation, or embarrassment due to the fact that they had let their families down by committing crimes leading to their incarceration.

The prospect of being separated from family members, missing friends and outside social activities, or coping with family members who have forgotten them are constant worries that frequently burdened a number of older women as well. Many elders expressed how excruciatingly painful separation appears to be for them in comparing this deprivation to others, such as material losses, they will invariably encounter over the course of their sentences. Margaret Leigey (2007) reported that older inmates appeared very distressed by this adversity as it was one facet of prison life that most offenders fail to psychologically prepare themselves for addressing. As law-abiding citizens, nearly every participant had experienced times when they had been forced to relinquish cherished possessions. Few, however, had endured social losses nearing the magnitude of those with which institutionalization would present them. For elders who may be unaccustomed to others planning their social engagements, adjustment to prison would be nearly impossible to achieve. Two older offenders currently serving life examine the personal loss associated with losing critical connections with their children:

> The hardest aspect of doing time in here is the mental and emotional strain of being unable to be with my daughter. . . . I can't be a mother. . . . It's not the stress of them [the officers] yelling and screaming at me "You've got to do this" as that's to be expected with institutionalization. . . . Rather, it's what I've lost.

> I lost hope. I've kept my head down. . . . I will not be allowed to see my grandbaby because her father doesn't agree with having me there because I'm a lifer. I have no contact with him. When I lose my daughter I lose my grandchild. I've lost all future generations of my family.

One important factor that may impact family relations centers around the history of involvement with the criminal justice system. At the very least, inmates will have been through the court process, having spent some time in jail for the current offense. Any prior involvement with the criminal justice system could affect the inmate's social relationships in several ways. Each arrest and conviction carries with it a certain social stigma that may influence a family's negative reaction toward the offender. Drug-related crimes and murder/manslaughter are both common crimes for older female offenders. In numerous cases, older women have struck back in relationships, taking the lives of abusive husbands. Such crimes may lead to serious stigma and initial ostracism on the part of surviving children (Aday, 1994a). Other families may become frustrated with offenders who repeatedly commit crimes and withdraw their support. As one 59-year-old inmate proclaimed, "After my arrest, I had a falling out with my family. I have no contact with any of my five children, no phone calls, no letters, nothing." Other repeat offenders provided examples of how family members had finally lost their patience with their behavior.

> I've been in and out of here a lot. My relationship with my family is not like it used to be as far as contact this time. This time it's different. I don't see them as much. I don't talk to them as much. I got out and went back into my old ways and ended up back in here. I caused them too much pain. It's really rough.

> When I came for the first time, they were all there for me. Like my mom always said, "Everybody makes mistakes." They supported me financially, came to visit and everything. When I returned for the second and third times, however, they never came to visit, and I received very little money from them. By then, they had discovered I was no longer just smoking crack but was selling it as well. They wanted to show me they did not condone this behavior.

Although a number of older offenders who are serving long-term prison sentences have reported the presence of continued interaction with family and friends, many indicate the passage of time diminishes the frequency of correspondences (Strupp & Willmott, 2005). The following passage suggests the common feeling that time decreases the emotional connection these incarcerated women could realistically anticipate receiving from their loved ones:

> I am not really sure how my children would react to an emergency. There is a void, and they are not being told what is happening to us.

They're just so used to being away from us. Like my mom . . . it's like she doesn't know anything about me because we have been separated so long. . . . If something happened, I don't think it would affect her the same as if I were at home and something happened. I've been in here 15 years and [my children] are treating me like, well you're just mom, that's it.

Research in the area of long-term confinement suggests many individuals, upon entering prison, will adapt to their surroundings by noting family and friends have lives, joys, and frustrations of their own to attend to and have limited leisure time to use developing an appreciation of the stressors commonly encountered in the prison environment (Flanagan, 1980). As offenders know that outsiders receive no specific details concerning their unique plights, and thus have no awareness about what, how much, or how often support should be extended, many quickly learn to accept they would be better served adopting a "do your own time" frame of reference toward institutionalization (Richards, 1978; Flanagan, 1981). Through their reluctance to contact loved ones at the onset of every grievance encountered in their routine lives, long-term offenders are spared the pain that could ensue if external supports ever elected to abandon them. For many inmates, the sense of independence necessary for survival in contemporary correctional institutions may even be most easily gained by severing all connections to the free world (Aday, 2003). This fact is evident by the following inmate who discusses her family estrangement: "I worry about being forgotten by everyone. It often seems as if I am a ghost to my family, and it's hard for me to understand why. I thought we had such a strong relationship, but now, I no longer receive support from any of them. It's like I'm no longer on the face of the earth."

While most elders prefer to avoid enmeshed relations, many realize if they do not maintain some degree of contact during their sentences, they may not have sufficient time upon release to reestablish critical ties (Wilson & Vito, 1986; Santos, 1995). Thus, knowing there is some semblance of an intact support system composed of individuals who are willing to maintain reasonable levels of involvement in the inmate's life can serve as a protective function against adverse effects of duress. Even when connections to one or more siblings, children, or other loved ones are severed, receiving information concerning the lives of these individuals from other connections may contribute to heightened morale (Leigey, 2007). For example, the older women in our study indicated an important link between talking on the phone, receiving family visits or letters, and feelings of loneliness and hopelessness about the future. As expected, the more frequent the family contacts, the more likelihood the respondents felt emotionally close to and dependent upon their respective families. As a result, those who infrequently or never received visits, made phone contact, or communicated through letters were more likely to be dissatisfied with their family relationships.

Family Visits

The Bureau of Justice Statistics reports that in 1999 only 43 percent of inmates housed in state prison facilities had received a personal visit from at least one child since incarceration (Mumola, 2000). A relatively sizable body of literature documents that older inmates, even long-termers, do maintain fairly intact social support systems while incarcerated (Aday, 1994b; Gallagher, 1990; Hoffmann, Dickinson & Dunn, 2007). Face-to-face visits can be the most appealing and positive activity for maintaining and improving family solidarity. Although one-third of the women indicated they never receive visitors, four out of five remain in contact in some way (visit, letters, or phone). Certainly, family visits are an important indicator of inmate well-being as over one-half of those individuals who report never receiving family visits also feel unloved and dissatisfied with their family relationships. While an overwhelming majority felt they could rely on their family/friends network on the outside, 68 percent of the women who indicated they couldn't rely on family reported never receiving family visits (see Table 4.1).

Previous research has suggested marital status to be an important factor in whether visits to inmates occur. Administering questionnaires to 442 older male and female inmates, Peter Kratcoski and Susan Babb (1990) found that having no spouse decreases the potential for visitation and increases the likelihood of isolation among older female inmates. Marital status also appears to be an important indicator for family visits among our sample. For example, slightly over one-third of older married offenders report they receive visitors on a weekly basis compared to 10 percent for women divorced and 16 percent for those widowed. Only 6 percent of those in the never-married and separated categories report weekly visits. Well over one-half of the never-married inmates report never receiving family visits compared to one out of three for inmates who were separated, widowed, or divorced. One married inmate serving time reported that compared to other inmates, she feels most fortunate: "My husband comes every Saturday and Sunday, even though it isn't always convenient. I really appreciate the support he continues to provide me here. My son and grandchildren [ages three and five] also come regularly. If I were to miss their visits, I couldn't cope. I live from visit to visit."

Among those who illustrate the critical role engaging in face-to-face interactions with family members plays in their adaptation to their new and often unfamiliar surroundings, several explain how spending quality time with siblings, children, and grandchildren enhances their feelings of closeness toward members of the outside world while reassuring them they would indeed have individuals to whom they could turn for advice and guidance as needed: "Family visits are always warm and I always look forward to them. They are times to catch up on legal matters, family matters, and personal concerns. I encourage visits as we need to stay connected. After all, I was the center of the family and I want to continue be a part of that."

A final group reported the uneasiness is greatest following their visits with loved ones. Concerns, for these individuals, may focus on the information left unstated during the brief time together or the amount of time they must wait before receiving additional opportunities to correspond with the relative. Specific to aging prisoners, moments following the exchange can involve anxieties associated with the realization the prior visit may have been a final correspondence. Several explained that although all visits are valued, there occasionally remains the uncertainty they will ultimately receive unexpected news of parents or siblings passing before they have shared their farewells. One 56-year-old offender—who has received extensive support from her family members who have taken the initiative to visit occasionally, provide advice or guidance as needed, and assist in maintaining emotionally close connections—describes her postvisitation grieving processes: "I receive visits from my daddy about twice per year. We're very close and enjoy the visits. However, he's 92 years old and we both know each visit could be his last, so visits can get very emotional. I encourage visits not necessarily for me, but for him as well. We try to make the best of what little time we have left together." Other elders who have close attachments to external supports observe how the abovementioned uncertainties cause considerable discomforts that intensify during the final moments of the exchange and can, for some, last weeks in duration:

> I always encourage visits, but the pain is deep after they leave. I always feel as if I am the body at the funeral, with them going by one last time to view the remains. As the visiting hours end, we all try not to cry, but it is hard not to.

Visits are typically very emotional and intense. . . . While I love having visits and wish they could come and see me more often . . . after they leave, I feel very sad, empty, and alone. . . . I normally get over these feelings after about a week.

The presence of visitors near special occasions can impose on the older female offenders additional, often unanticipated, strains (Krabill & Aday, 2005). Leigey (2007) explores why the attitudes, behaviors, and information revealed during holidays appears extraordinarily important to older offenders in her research conducted with long-term male offenders. For these individuals, the passage of time often results in a transition from the receipt of frequent face-to-face exchanges to interacting only near seasonal festivities. Major milestones or special occasions that would likely encourage relatives to visit them, for example, may include Christmas, Thanksgiving, birthdays, times of family crises, or dates of anticipated parole hearings. Relatives also frequent the institution when loved ones appear in need of financial support. It has been noted that some family members presume institutions accommodate all of the offenders' basic needs. Therefore, when some individuals think inmates have funds available in their personal savings accounts, they consider it an opportunity to borrow from the offender. When these conditions exist, visits to the institution may become increasingly more commonplace (Leigey, 2007).

Older women who willingly share their reservations associated with receiving visits that may occur at predictable, yet often inconvenient, times note:

This time of year [December] is very hard for me. . . . I don't like holidays. . . . I don't even like to have visits during the season . . . because they serve as a reminder that my daughter has had two children while I have been incarcerated. Even though they're all teenagers now—the oldest being 20—they all ask "Grandma, when are they ever going to let you come home?"

Another woman revealed that she becomes extremely depressed around Thanksgiving, with the feeling not subsiding until after the first of the year. Another notes, "Christmas lights are depressing because they remind me of things that aren't here." As other inmates are also likely to have their loved ones present for regularly observed national or religious holidays, which makes the noisy and crowded visitation areas more uncomfortable than they ordinarily appear during regularly scheduled contact hours (Leigey, 2007), one can easily understand how and why some older women would prefer to refrain from addressing or even acknowledging the presence of serious issues at such times. As these women age in prison, holidays serve as painful reminders of the events happening in the free world, events that many of them in all probability will never experience again.

Johanna Christian (2005) expresses concern for inmates and relatives who, prior to their parole hearings, research verdicts from similar cases, become excited about the prospects of successful outcomes, and begin preparing prematurely for impending releases. As the trials begin, victims present their recollections of the crimes committed, and the offenders return to the facility where they have been housed; it becomes excruciatingly painful for all parties involved, with relatives striving to conceal the feelings of sorrow until the return home. Unsurprisingly, the notification of any future hearings may cause family to appear less than responsive to subsequent invitations. One 53-year-old woman who is currently serving a long sentence explores the shift from enthusiasm to grief to indifference that may ensue in the process as she notes: "I already had a date to return home and was going to have my own place. . . . My daughter had the two bedroom apartment in her basement all set up. . . . When I got to the board, however, we had to listen to the victim's family, 'yap, yap, yap' and the commissioner pulled my date. So I understand why my daughter won't go to my next parole hearing."

Others who willingly shared factors that contributed to less than favorable exchanges between the parties indicate that major milestones appear most problematic when they are provided limited forewarning to prepare for the visit. For older female offenders, continued communications near funerals or other major family events may be highly valued experiences as they permit individuals to seek and establish closure on critical roles they formerly assumed (Krabill & Aday, 2005). As administration typically restricts their freedom to attend out-of-state funerals and requires those who are permitted to leave the facility to have heightened security present with them at all times, family visits to the institution following tragedies naturally serve as alternative forums through which inmates and loved ones may share in the grieving process. Several note it is not the presence of relatives during trying times that causes emotional reactions, but rather, their lack of awareness about the atmosphere within which information would be conveyed. One 60-year-old woman whose spouse, siblings, children, and grandchildren visit her on a monthly basis confirms the hardships unplanned visits cause:

My nephew occasionally travels from Hot Springs, Arkansas, to Georgia for court appearances and to inform me of deaths in the family. . . . These visits are often unannounced and unexpected and leave me sad, depressed, grieving, and without hope. We have not been afforded private environments where we could share our personal grievances. . . . Instead, we have often been distracted by other families and children. This, in return, has made it impossible for us to focus on the conversations being exchanged.

Visits following important family affairs may not be necessary, desired, or valued as women who must welcome relatives into their new living environments often shed so many tears following the exchange they need consolation from staff members before returning to their cells. Even the presence of loved ones after joyous occasions such as births, graduations, or weddings may contribute to unwanted feelings of exclusion (Kiser, 1991). Older women who document the pains they have personally experienced after such occasions note: "I do not think constantly about my children or whether they will visit. To do my time, I cannot let it upset me either way. . . . If they come to visit me, fine, if they don't, that's fine as well. At first it was hard accepting what I have no control over, but now, I have come to the realization that I cannot live out there and in here too." Given the variety of emotions visits may instill in inmates and prospective visitors, some older offenders feel uncomfortable with engaging in this form of correspondence. Leigey (2007) has indicated older male offenders view visits as times when all involved parties engage in relatively superficial disclosures without providing the others insights into the matters that are occurring in their absences.

Time, Distance, and Money Issues

Great distances typically separate those who are incarcerated from their families, and these geographical constraints can be an important issue in determining whether an inmate will in fact receive family visits. Women typically are placed in prisons an average of 160 miles from their children (Travis, McBride & Solomon, 2005). Prior research has found that inmates are less likely to receive visits when families live greater distances from the prison (Arditti & Few, 2006; Christian, 2005; Pollock, 2004). In particular, women inmates whose relatives desire to maintain face-to-face contact have to overcome the fact that many women's prisons are frequently located in remote geographical locations (Aday, 2003), which translates into extensive travel time. Also, as with other contemporary families, prison families can be quite mobile, which creates visiting constraints. As one inmate states, "All my family live in Kentucky. The trip is over 1,300 miles both ways." And another voiced, "All my family lives four and one-half hours from here and that makes nine hours of driving. Some live out of state which is even further."

Families must also make considerable preparation on the part of siblings, children, and grandchildren well in advance of the trip (Arditti & Few, 2006). Richard Tewksbury and Matthew DeMichele (2005), for example, projected individuals begin making arrangements more than one week prior to the departure date. In general, the time spent planning may involve requesting vacation time from employers, consulting the schedules of children's academic and extracurricular activities, and identifying prison policies concerning the attire, personal possessions, or conduct permitted on the premises (Comfort, 2003; Christian, 2005). Although older women appear to have limited direct involvement in the planning processes in our study, the following narratives confirm they are keenly aware of the sacrifices their loved ones must make to ensure even the briefest visits: "When my children were young, my parents made the long journey twice per month. As they became more involved with friends and school activities, developing lives of their own, I began to discourage my parents from visiting. I still wanted to see them, but I knew this was probably best for everyone."

For those traveling long distances, this also includes reserving finances to purchase bus passes, hotel accommodations, snacks, and when permitted by the institution, care packages for offenders who infrequently receive clothing and other essentials (Christian, 2005). Tewksbury and DeMichele (2005) estimate relatives spend $25 per month on visitation alone, with the figure nearing $250 when other forms of correspondence are included. Naturally, the size of the group with which potential visitors would be traveling as well as the degree to which inmates perceive the administrators as effectively accommodating their unique needs can enormously impact the expense of any anticipated visits. While institutions and nonprofit organizations have noted the critical roles that maintaining contact plays in institutional adjustment and have responded through the development of programming to minimize the burdens associated with visiting imprisoned women, most focus exclusively on assisting children who may otherwise be unable to correspond with their mothers. Given the large number of impoverished individuals serving time in women's prisons, however, the expense of communication could encourage some relatives to forgo corresponding altogether. One woman who willingly shared her experience with loved ones who could not personally afford to remain in touch as frequently as desired explains: "Family visits are sometimes planned, but because of problems with transportation or finances, they usually do not come. This is always a disappointment for me, but I try to understand their circumstances. In fact, my mother has only been here to see me once in my 10 years of incarceration."

The challenges associated with visiting may be intensified if prospective guests have young children who must accompany them on the journey. Joyce Arditti and April Few (2006), in fact, have identified the greatest hurdle most ever encounter as negotiating a balance between performing their child-rearing duties and preparing for, initiating, and sustaining interactions with the inmate. Although the act of frequenting women's prisons involves overcoming fewer obstacles than institutions for men, as the visitors are less likely to be subjected to heightened security from staff or heated conflicts initiated by the other inmates, the processes of traveling long distances via public transportation, waiting in long lines at the prison, encountering the confiscation of strollers, toys, or other necessities, and encouraging children to sit still and be quiet during the visit are exchanged for only a few moments of conversation with the offender (Comfort, 2003), and many undoubtedly perceive the burdens experienced as greater than the benefits gained from visits. While older women acknowledge the treatment received by their visitors is dependent on the shifts and staff present at the time of the interaction, several observed incidents when their young loved ones were subjected to the unnecessarily inhumane treatment, stringent orders, and foul language one would anticipate to be directed toward inmate populations.

Entering the visitation room may present relatives with a number of additional stressors that, for individuals who do not frequent correctional institutions on a regular basis, may strongly discourage repeat visits. Many contemporary institutions may require visitors to remain behind a partition while corresponding with their relatives and to have staff present to monitor exchanges. Relatives for whom the lack of privacy or opportunities to express affection pose no burdens discover the furniture to be extraordinarily uncomfortable. For individuals who have their own age-related health limitations and have recently traveled long distances via bus or other mass transportation vehicles, the decision to visit prison evolves into a form of punishment issued to law-abiding citizens. When coupled with a large number of visitors crowded into small visiting areas, it is understandable that many older adults express indifference or disdain toward receiving frequent visits (Leigey, 2007).

Women who would undeniably prefer to share time with their relatives understand the identified barriers make travel trying, if not impractical, to achieve. One elder explores how her relatives who have no other reliable adults who could travel with them to assist in child supervision have no option but to postpone visits until life circumstances appear more favorable:

> I have a grandson who is 8 months old and has been here once. . . . Since the weather is bad now, and my son is working night shifts, my daughter-in-law does not want to come with him by herself, and I can't really blame her. I wouldn't want to bring a young child under these conditions, either, but they'll be back in March, and I'll eventually be back home to watch him grow up.

While this individual appears assured the temporary separation from loved ones will not impair the quality of family relationships, for others, the prospect of maintaining ties seems less likely.

Institutional Barriers

While approximately two-thirds of the respondents receive visits at least once or twice per year, with a number engaging in face-to-face correspondences on a monthly or weekly basis, most women acknowledge the challenges both inmates and their families experience during the process of visitation. Recent research has found that prison communication policies have become more restrictive on visitation (Hoffmann, Dickinson & Dunn, 2007). Prison officials are more concerned with security measures than inmates staying in touch with family members. Elaine Genders and Elaine Player (1990) have poignantly expressed the unique concerns older female lifers experience when confronted with current prison policies. According to them, inmates may appear extraordinarily anxious about the encounter days before external supports arrive at the institution, with many failing to notice the feelings subside after the time spent together has concluded. Apprehensions and frustrations endured while preparing for visits stem from the recognition staff may be discourteous to their guests, provoke conflict with visitors, and place inmates in awkward positions of defending their loved ones' honors. Leigey (2007) notes many elders identify administrators as viewing visitors no differently than inmates, perceiving them as deserving of punishment, and therefore, creating unsafe visitation areas and conditions with the intent of strongly discouraging the prospects of future visits. Numerous offenders confirm such problems, including the psychological barriers inmates have to overcome in order to receive family visits. For many inmates the process is filled with tension as family members are carefully screened coming into the visitation area. In some cases, the process becomes too stressful: "I discourage family visits because of the way the officers humiliate family members. If my relatives visited, I do not think I would be able to refrain from saying or doing something I would regret later on. I would rather sacrifice not seeing them than have them go through such an ordeal."

Women who explored the interaction process attributed their anxieties to reservations about the types of sensitive information they could freely exchange with visitors, the prospects of others gaining access to personal confidences, and the levels of support they could reasonably provide relatives in need of comforting. While few institutions have policies that strictly prohibit inmates and visitors from embracing, most have regulations requiring correctional officers to be present throughout the duration of the visit (Hoffmann, Dickinson & Dunn, 2007). As visits may revolve around the discussion of personal problems such as what children may be encountering at home, school, or social events, the coping mechanisms each has found most effective in dealing with the loss of a family member, or plans being made in preparation for the offender's ultimate release (Arditti & Few, 2006), it is evident such restrictions for privacy may have a negative impact on the actual therapeutic intimacy families are seeking.

Elders who may recognize contemporary practices were designed to protect the well-being of all involved parties, but continue to struggle to understand why barriers must inadvertently preclude individuals from expressing affection toward loved ones, explain experiences with family visits:

> Families are put through a real battle before they ever walk through the door. Even for just a brief visit, . . . they're going to get pat searched, . . . and you never know when her skirt may be a little too short, or he ain't got this or that. . . . They are forced to do this time with us! . . . A little differently, of course, but they are experiencing many of the same painful emotions. You have to have a guard sit with you during visits. You cannot hold family members. . . . Sometimes you may want to wipe a tear, but you cannot do that.

Others explore how, within the context of institutional settings, specific behaviors, feelings, and statements must be withheld to protect recipients from experiencing heightened emotions. Many examined, for example, that when in the presence of children or grandchildren, maintaining close relations involves establishing boundaries that cannot be crossed. As visits that are not carefully planned have the potential to instill in younger populations impressions their loved ones' lives are in imminent danger (Casey-Acevedo & Bakken, 2002), elders realize decisions to express their true sentiments could result in their listeners requesting further clarification of the issues discussed, joining them in tears, or vacating the premises before the dialogue is completed.

Telephone and Letter Connections

Written correspondence and telephone calls are also important methods for maintaining connections with the outside world. For some inmates these methods are used in conjunction with face-to-face visits, but for inmates whose family members for whatever reason are unable to make personal visits, phone calls or letters become their only link with the outside world. Although the regularity with which older women report using the telephone for correspondences with external supports is limited in scope, available evidence suggests members of this population are very receptive to drawing upon the degrees of accessibility this medium affords them. Among our sample, letter writing and utilizing the telephone are the more popular ways older women use to remain in touch with immediate families. As Table 4.1 shows, members of this population rely on using these two mediums for the purpose of maintaining ties with family members, although 20 percent report never talking on the phone. Elaine Gallagher (1990) reported in an earlier study that older inmates engaged in more frequent telephone conversations and letters per month when compared to younger inmates. Others have confirmed that telephone calls are regular occurrences for older offenders by suggesting that over half of those sentenced to life without parole (53 percent) place or receive weekly telephone calls (Leigey, 2007). One older woman shared the critical role engagement in this activity had in maintaining her connections to external supports in noting, "I call home once or twice a week and can talk for 25 minutes. I can get more done in this conversation than I could in a visit. My kids are usually all there, and I can usually talk to all of them at once. So it really doesn't matter to me if they come frequently or not."

Since these individuals are restricted in the number of visitors they are permitted to receive per session, or in the information they could reasonably communicate in letters, the opportunity to correspond by phone serves an invaluable purpose. However, stringent guidelines appeared directly responsible for the pains experienced by the estimated one-third of respondents who reported only occasionally, rarely, or never talking on the phone with loved ones. Specific hurdles elders were required to endure before calls could be initiated or retrieved involved the presence of a limited number of telephones on the premises, the relatively narrow timeframes within which any outgoing calls could be placed, the confined social areas where existing phone services are located, as well as the irregularities with which existing lines appeared to be in working order. Azrini Wahidin's (2004) research conducted with older female offenders indicated that when there are few accessible phone lines available for inmates to use and high demand for contacting external supports, older, passive populations may feel compelled to forgo placing calls to avoid conflict with younger, more aggressive peers. The women frequently complained of the crowdedness present in the commons areas where the phones were located, as well as the frictions that can ensue when making calls. As one woman complained: "We have 96 women in the dorm and four phones. Nowhere in prison is there 'privacy' for an inmate [to place a call]. . . . The public at large does not [care to assist in minimizing] the long lines or wait times [that must be negotiated to] use the phone in [what we consider to be] our own homes." Other issues such as having the opportunity to make calls when family members would more likely be available, the fact the phones frequently do not work properly, or simply being cut off during conversation were also mentioned as important obstacles.

Another prison policy that restricts inmate-family phone call occurrence is the unusually high financial charges associated with collect long-distance calls. State prison facilities have contracted with phone companies resulting in a multi-million dollar windfall. Some correctional facilities even receive a commission from the phone companies (Warren, 2002). While for some the price of this phone call may appear relatively insignificant, relatives who have children with needs of their own would be unlikely to have the financial resources that are necessary to place long-distance calls to the institution on an ongoing basis. Older women who identify requests for continued calls as unwelcome burdens explain why they perceive it as much easier to live without hearing their families' voices:

> Out of state phone calls are very expensive for our families. My four daughters have all received good educations, have established themselves in professional roles, and have the financial security necessary

to call me. Since their children are now in college, and this can be quite expensive, however, I do not demand this type of support from them.

A 15 minute phone call costs approximately $20, and that is quite expensive for many of us. Any out of state calls to be placed from here must be pre-paid by credit card to the company [administrators have selected]. Since my father, who is 92 years old, does not have a credit card, other family would have to be involved to pay for me to call him.

I have to limit my calls to twice a month.

Some inmates may even identify the cost of a relatively brief telephone conversation as exceeding the price of gasoline or other travel expenses, making visitations the preferred method of communication (Leigey, 2007).

Letter writing is also an important forum whereby inmates are able to communicate with family members. Several studies have focused specifically on letter writing as a possible medium for older offenders to use in corresponding with members of the free world. One compared the number of letters this population sends or receives in a given month to those exchanged by their younger counterparts and estimated members of both groups typically average approximately six letters each (Gallagher, 1990). Presenting a slightly less optimistic portrait of how frequently letter exchanges occur in this environment, another study suggested only approximately 38 percent of older offenders can anticipate "often" or "very often" using this form of correspondence with members of the free world (Aday, 2003). As several have projected letters to be among the various methods long-term offenders rely heavily upon to remain in touch with family when visits become too tiresome to attempt on regular bases (Vega & Silverman, 1988), with mail being a particularly useful medium for communicating with one's children (Leigey, 2007), it is important to recognize that the low levels of educational attainment or poor written communication skills that older offenders frequently have when entering prison do not prevent them from using postal services.

For an estimated three-quarters of older female offenders (see Table 4.1), the act of writing letters serves a critical function in facilitating communication with external supports. After reading, writing letters was listed as the second most frequent activity these older women participate in on a weekly basis. Women who described the meaning placed on this valued activity suggest written correspondences permit them to construct written records of the activities to which they are currently being exposed, and to preserve the memories. In a sense, writing letters for this population can serve as an important therapeutic activity as well as a means for staying connected with the outside world. Similar to family visits, the receipt of letters can also serve as a sign of caring and love. One 60-year-old female incarcerated for more than 20 years stresses why "mail call and the exchange of letters is one of the most looked to events in prison":

> We get our share of junk mail mostly from Christian Ministries, but a card or a letter and money deposited in one's account are specific examples that people care. They are thinking about you. It says you're important to someone and missed! I've gone months and years even without a simple mailing from some of my family and that really hurts.

Regardless of the materials they send or receive via mail, however, several older women express gratitude for the opportunities to regularly attend mail call as this occasion provides them needed structure to their otherwise mundane routines. One explores the meaning assigned to the event, stating: "If they don't do mail call, we're like 'Where's the mail? Where's the mail?'"

While letter writing may appear an ideal resource for helping older women document their journeys through the criminal justice system, many will inevitably discover written correspondences are often inadequate forums for transmitting personal information. Offenders who would not want others accessing their personal confidences express their dissatisfactions with correctional personnel randomly spot-checking letters for contraband items (Hoffmann, Dickinson & Dunn, 2007). Older adults who have low reading and writing levels, high stress levels, depression, and apathy toward engagement in thought-provoking activity may be unable to write or enjoy expressing their thoughts on paper (Leigey, 2007).

Although written correspondence is considered the cheapest way to maintain connection with family members, indigent prisoners may not have necessary funds to mail letters on a frequent basis. As one study discovered, the majority (57 percent) of all state prison facilities require inmates alone to pay for all postage for the letters they send (Hoffmann, Dickinson & Dunn, 2007). In the past, it was more common for inmates and institutions to share in the postage expense. Some inmates in our study did express that cost was a factor in not corresponding as frequently or with as many people as they would like. For example, one woman who had an immediate goal to downsize her personal property (mostly legal and spiritual papers) stated, "I can't afford the postage to have it mailed out." Several women did mention their continuous challenge of having the discretionary funds to mail letters.

Parenting from Prison

Being separated from family members can prove to be difficult for many older female inmates. Not being able to fulfill the role of parent or grandparent every day can be frustrating. Some older female inmates serving life sentences have been unable to interact with their grandchildren in the "free world." This can be a tremendous stigma for both the grandmother, who knows she cannot provide her grandchild the emotional support she formerly did, and for the grandchild who continually inquires as to when grandma will be returning home. For some older inmates serving long sentences, visitation from family or friends on the outside can cause a continuous grief reaction with each visit. For these inmates, it becomes easier to do the time by requesting their families and members of the free world not visit. This technique of compartmentalization is one way some older females tend to cope with long-term incarceration and family separation (Aday, 2003).

The Bureau of Justice estimates approximately 65 percent of females serving time in state institutions have children under 18 years of age, with mothers having, on average, 2.38 children each (Greenfield & Snell, 1999). Many of these women were living with the children at the time of the offense, serving as primary caregivers, and performing the duties with no support from others (Cranford & Williams, 1998). The number of mothers in prison has increased some 122 percent from approximately 29,500 in 1991 to 65,600 in 2007 (West & Sabol, 2008). We found that 90 percent of older female offenders participating in this project were serving prison sentences while trying to also fulfill parental obligations. A sizable body of literature has surfaced to document the imperativeness of mother-child relationships for women who must establish, nurture, and preserve them from within prison (Loper et al., 2009; Mumola, 2000). Regardless of age, the parenting role continues to be an important factor in the lives of mothers attempting to maintain contact with their children.

According to Barbara Owen (1998), many identify their children as the most important people in their lives. For a number of incarcerated women who support children and value and covet the motherhood role, the anticipation that they may ultimately receive opportunities for release and return home to their sons and daughters governs their every behavior. Women who had to place their children in the care of others may now attempt to prove themselves as "good mothers" to inmates, staff, and others with whom they regularly interact. Some may demonstrate their commitment to parenting by strategically placing reminders of their children throughout their cells, conversing with others about child-rearing duties, and most importantly, distancing themselves from peers who have initiated, aided in, or otherwise supported the commission of crimes against children. Others who have focused on the experiences of older women project their fitness to mother is highlighted throughout the mentoring they provide to the younger women with whom they must now reside (Krabill & Aday, 2005). When mothers notice their peers engaging in behaviors that may be incongruent with their own value systems, for example, many may express their disapproval by reacting as they would if they witnessed their children speaking or acting in a similar manner.

As parenthood appears to be a coveted status for women who are currently serving time in prison, particularly for those who entered the setting when their children were young in age, many older offenders express sincere gratitude for the assistance family provided them with childcare. Although the mean age of incarceration (44.38 years) was well above the average age of incarceration (Greenfield & Snell, 1999), many had entered the setting as young mothers and had relied extensively on the generosity of relatives to rear their sons and daughters. In general, relinquishing one's child-rearing responsibilities involves placing enormous burdens on single, undereducated women of color who, while they volunteer to help, may also be living on fixed incomes, caring for multiple dependents, coping with chronic health conditions, and receiving no encouragement to assume this responsibility or plan strategies that would assist them in tending to their personal needs while caring for the child (Ruiz, 2002). Children's entrances into their home environments frequently require forgoing paid employment, helping the younger individuals cope with the separation, concealing negative emotions one may have about the offense, accepting rejection from former supports, managing any adverse physical or mental health reactions to the accumulated stressors, and if the strains become too overwhelming, preparing alternative living arrangements for children whose lives have been repeatedly disrupted (Hayslip & Kaminski, 2005). Occasionally, such may also involve increased contact with professionals in legal, medical, and mental health arenas as needed (Dressel & Barnhill, 1994). While adding children to the home environment increases stress levels, grandmothers are often content to assist in this capacity as they realize children will receive better care from them than they did while living with the biological mothers (Owen, 1998).

Recent research conducted on parenthood as experienced in prison presents a promising picture of the level of communication older offenders have with their children. Leigey (2007), for example, reported 37 percent of elders who were serving non–life without parole sentences had at least some contact with their children—in the form of letters or telephone conversations—in the month prior to the interviews. This percentage appeared to be significantly higher (47 percent) for those who were sentenced to life without parole. The author further confirmed the importance inmates place on contact with children in noting the presence of children increases one's overall level of communication with the outside world. According to Leigey (2007), older inmates with children were, in general, more likely than their nonparent peers to have received visits in the previous month or engaged in telephone conversations in the previous week.

Surprisingly, research that focuses on childcare as a critical element incarcerated women receive from maintaining family relationships may not always address the value mothers place on resting assured their sons' and daughters' needs are sufficiently accommodated. Instead, much of the information provided about this task as it is viewed from the perspective of incarcerated mothers emphasizes the feelings of guilt women may endure for placing themselves in positions where they can no longer perform their various parenting obligations (Moe & Ferraro, 2007) or, when focusing explicitly on current living arrangements, discusses only how frequently women receive permission from the new guardians to communicate with their children (Enos, 2001; Poehlmann, 2005). Given their attitudes toward child-rearing must encompass more than notions of this as a temporary holding pattern until the mother and child can be reunified, additional research is needed to document how women, specifically long-term offenders, regard their own parents as substitute guardians. Several elders who recognize the sacrifices their parents made on their behalf express their gratitude in stating: "My parents raised my three children. Mom always kept me informed of the events that were occurring in the lives of the children, and asked my opinion on various issues. In response, I deferred to her decisions because she was doing my job. They were excellent parents to my brothers and me, so I trusted they would be with my children as well." As it is well documented that children of incarcerated women are at increased risks of encountering problems that are associated with stigmatization by peers, rapidly depleting coping mechanisms, declines in school performance, development of negative attitudes toward female authority figures, or delinquency (Laughlin et al., 2008), the recognition that external supports would willingly reserve time for caring for their young proves comforting to many.

While most contemporary studies that focus on motherhood have presented the concern from the perspective of women in their 30s, as this is the age of most incarcerated mothers (Greenfield & Snell, 1999; Laughlin et al., 2008), some are beginning to explore the experiences of being a mother who is aging in this environment (Wahidin, 2004). Studies that have addressed the pains associated with infrequent contact indicate the removal from the free world causes continuous grief about being absent or unavailable when children are born, encountering major life events, or needing discipline or support (Hairston, 1991; Leigey, 2007; Young & Smith, 2000). While these studies provide invaluable insights into the often painful experiences of elders who are striving to negotiate their parenting responsibilities from inside the walls of a setting where control over interactions is undeniably restricted, they fail to account for the frustrations older women feel as they perceive themselves unable to fulfill their obligations as mothers. The following narratives provided by female offenders serving in various institutions illustrate these frustrations:

> My mind . . . my head is still out there. . . . It becomes a major stress and strain on you. When you call home, for example, you have no control over what will be said. . . . [When your children speak] you can't acknowledge them. . . . You become immune, numb. Because there is nothing you can do, you must separate life out there from life in here.

> You have to learn to let go, but I haven't been able to. . . . My daughter is my daughter, and I can't separate it. . . . It hurts. . . . When our children are suffering out there, you know, it makes the mothers suffer because they can't do anything for their children.

> I haven't seen my daughter since Thanksgiving of last year. She is HIV positive and is basically on a medical battle. She is currently in the hospital in another area of the United States, and there is no approved list for the hospital. . . . I can't call her, and if she is dying, they won't make a call to the chapel.

The loss of contact with family and friends outside prison is a major concern for any prisoner, but for long-term inmates the fear that these relationships will be irrevocably lost creates a unique set of concerns. Over the course of time, families change as new family members arrive through birth and marriage while some will exit through death. These events may occur without the prisoner's participation and, in some cases, knowledge (Santos, 1995). As a result, some women serving long sentences and without family contact have a "frozen" picture of life on the outside as they left it. As one such lifer noted: "When I came in, my little girl was 7 or 8 years old. And since I haven't gotten to see her, I've been thinking . . . okay, I've still got that age in my mind. . . . Then when I go off, hey, she's grown up now and has two kids."

Although administrators must understandably expand extant parenting programming and services to accommodate the growing demands of women with young children, scholars are now beginning to identify the unique concerns older female offenders have for the physical, mental, and emotional well-being of adult offspring. Owen (1998) provides justification for this focus of research in noting approximately one-quarter of incarcerated women have children over 18 years of age, with members of this population failing to view their parental obligations as arbitrarily ceasing the moments their sons and daughters enter adulthood. Two older women who confirm the imperativeness of providing older women assistance in preserving critical connections explore their desires to compensate for the time apart by helping children in negotiating any current challenges they may be experiencing in noting:

> My children were 11, 7, and 5 at the time of the offense, and now they are 43, 38, and 36 . . . with children of their own . . . so I've missed out on the best years of their lives. I just haven't been able to be there for them, to assist them in growing up or to be present for any important events in their lives. I really wish this had not been the case.

> Sometimes I've prayed I wouldn't have to keep going through this. Every day its just heartbreaking knowing that my children are out there, with their only parent locked up . . . and that I can't help them . . . can't be there for them. . . . I feel guilty for that and hope they can forgive me for not being there. This is one of the hardest things to deal with for many mothers in here.

Similar to their younger peers, and older male counterparts, these individuals desire to receive regular information about the events their children must experience in their absence, permission to exchange physical affection with one another, and opportunities to maximize the advantages of the extended visitation hours (Wahidin, 2004). The older women in our study viewed the institutions' communication, and specifically visitation, policies as excessively harsh, unevenly applied by offenders' age ranges, trivializing the importance of concerns posed to staff, and consequently, systematically depriving them of rights to preserve their most cherished relationships. Sentiments expressed in response to frustrations encountered while parenting in this setting are illustrated in the following statements from older offenders whose children visit once or twice per year, who provide advice or guidance if needed, and who maintain a relationship perceived as emotionally close:

> We can hug and kiss our children at the beginning and end of each visit, but however, cannot touch them during the time spent together unless they are under 10 years of age. My children are in their late thirties and I would enjoy holding their hands or rubbing their shoulders . . . but physical contact is not permitted. I usually verbally support the decisions of my children when talking with my grandchildren. I also try to commend my children on their values and encourage them to focus on building a positive character, and be there for them as a sounding board when they need me. Sometimes they just want me to listen, and I do.

> My kids would be angry if anything happened to me while I am here. They would be going off. That's why I have found somebody I have become close to and can trust talking to them. The other day, I gave my roommate my daughter's telephone number and told her if anything happens to me, call her at home. That's the only way my kids would ever know anything. My kids have had to get to know me. . . . After a friend of mine got out, she went and visited my kids. They were tickled to death to meet her as she was someone who knew me and could tell them something about me.

As most older women reported having children, further explorations into this critical issue will undoubtedly become increasingly more important in the coming years, especially for those serving long sentences and how those relationships are maintained after years of physical separation.

The Grandparenting Role

Although research concerning the role of parenting from within the walls of prison is undoubtedly gaining heightened attention, the act of grandparenting remains an understudied phenomenon. Similar to what has been done with other forms of correspondence, several have attempted to explain the meaning of this interaction by identifying the number of offenders who have grandchildren, the frequency of contact, the feelings offenders have toward current interaction patterns, and the meanings they assign to the general role of grandparenting. In one of the first studies to explore grandparenting within the context of prison settings, Monika Reed and Francis Glamser (1979) indicated that approximately one-half (9 of 18) of respondents had grandchildren, but only five had ever seen them. For these offenders, the absence of direct contact did not appear to affect their perceptions of themselves as grandparents. Rather, they believed that the opportunity to pass on a legacy to future generations was considerably more important than having close, intimate connections.

This role appears to be even more likely to be assumed by older female offenders than their male counterparts. Ronald Aday (2003), for example, projected that while approximately half (53 percent) of the older male prison population could anticipate having grandchildren, the estimate was near 65 percent for older female offenders. According to him, most grandmothers attempt to remain in contact with later generations of family members, but regard themselves as being somewhat restricted in the types of support they can extend to them. Institutional regulations, parental concerns, and older children's fears of stigmatization by peers are among the many barriers these individuals must overcome in order to correspond. As older adults who reside in mainstream society depend on the presence of continued contacts and degrees of closeness with their children and in-laws to gain access to the lives of grandchildren (Fingerman, 2004), such is even more critical for those occupying later adulthood in correctional institutions. In fact, one woman who is serving a life sentence explores the frustrations encountered when becoming aware that distant connections could prevent her from cultivating, nurturing, or maintaining relationships with her daughter, grandchildren, and any subsequent generations:

> I've lost all hope and have kept my head down. Not only have I lost my life, but my daughter has also lost hers by my sentence. I will not be allowed to have my grandbaby because her father doesn't agree with having me there because I'm a lifer. I have no contact with him. When I lose my daughter, I lose my grandchild. I have lost all future generations of my family.

Most recently, Leigey (2007) has identified how valuable having regular communications with other supports can be in gaining access to the lives of one's grandchildren in her research with older male prisoners serving time in two Mid-Atlantic facilities. Findings from this study project that individuals who experience reduced contact with external supports with the passage of time may view the sadness expressed as surfacing from their realizations that they will never receive the opportunities to cultivate meaningful relationships with their grandchildren. For these, the hopes of having the desired relationships must be quickly replaced by acceptance or contentment with the occasional visit or photograph. One woman examined the transition from the feelings of regret, sorrow, and depression nearly every elder must acknowledge to a willingness to use the resources available to them in adapting to the challenges they are presented: "Since my incarceration, I have been unable to fully participate in the lives of my grandchildren. Through the institution's 'Story Book' program, however, I can occasionally send them taped messages or read portions of books to them. I wish we had a program that permitted our grandchildren to spend more quality time with us." Under extreme circumstances, Leigey (2007) reports limited contact with members of the larger family unit may cause inmates to receive no information concerning new additions and to thus have no projected estimate of how many grandchildren they may even have. If nothing else, it is a tremendous challenge for the women to maintain a viable connection with their grandchildren who they feel are so precious.

Summary

This chapter clearly illustrates the important role the family plays in the lives of this group of older female offenders. While less than half of the women in this study reported receiving visits on a weekly or monthly basis, other means of communication were used in maintaining connections to the outside. The fact that one-third of the women indicated they never received visits from family members is cause for concern. Being separated from significant others on the outside can prove to be difficult for many older female inmates and their families alike. Not being able to fulfill the role of parent or grandparent can be frustrating, and the loss of this unique feminine role can be devastating to one's self-concept. Some older inmates serving long sentences have never had the opportunity to interact with their grandchildren in the free world and some have not even laid eyes on their grandchildren. This can be a tremendous stigma for a grandmother to know that her grandchildren have always had to live with the fact that "grandma is in prison." Of course, some family members have pulled away from the inmates and others have died, leaving many feeling helpless and all alone.

The research evidence suggests, however, that intergenerational bonds remain remarkably strong for the majority of women. A significant number remain satisfied with their family relationships and are involved in kinship roles despite serving long sentences. There is evidence that when prisoners do maintain regular contact with family members the adjustment to prison is more positive and inmates appear to have more to live for. However, from the narratives presented here, numerous institutional barriers remain as obstacles for families to stay in touch. Whether it be time, distance, money, or existing institutional rules and regulations that discourage regular family contact, a policy that keeps families together would be beneficial for all concerned parties.

5

Making a Life in Prison

OR THE MAJORITY OF INMATES, LIVING IN PRISON MEANS GIVING up many things that were once important on the outside. While the surroundings of prison may fail to simulate a home environment, finding meaningful activities behind bars can be an important ingredient for a successful adjustment to prison. Over a half-century ago, Gresham Sykes (1958) introduced the "deprivation" model as a framework from which to capture the experience of incarceration. With longer sentences, overcrowded conditions, and not much empathy for rehabilitative programs, little has occurred inside contemporary prisons to alter this view. Extreme deprivations leading to a "mortification and curtailment of self" (Goffman, 1961) and "institutional neurosis" (Ham, 1980) tend to provoke a wide range of sociopsychological reactions. Harsh confinement frequently leads to feelings of frustration, anger, powerlessness, fear, sadness, and resentment (Haney, 2006). For individuals hoping to survive or even thrive in a total institution, prisoner adaptation, survival skills, and specific methods of coping may vary widely. For example, Kevin Wright (1991) indicated that it is not simply the prison structure itself that matters most, but rather the subtle ways each prisoner socially constructs a meaningful life in prison that is important in understanding the assimilation process.

Regardless of their respective pathways to prison adjustment, Hans Toch (2006) has noted that it is clear that the management of time, the "doing" of "time," is the dominant challenge for inmates. Some evidence suggests that the number of social activities available such as work, adult education, religious activities, and other interpersonal interactions is important to facilitating the process. Nonetheless, it is up to the individual inmate to regulate the quality, structure, and function of those activities (Bill, 1998; Bond, Thompson & Malloy, 2005; Sappington, 1996). This chapter will assess the importance of the various activities and pastimes utilized by inmates as a means of social support. In particular, the important role that friendships play in the lives of older females appears to be a critical element in the adjustment process.

The Meaning of Friendships

Friendship is a rather problematic concept due to the fact there is no simple definition of the relationship. People usually define friends by subjective indicators such as someone they can trust or confide in (Adams, 1989). On the other hand, researchers have examined more objective factors such as patterns of reciprocity. Regardless, the concept of "friend" has been used to refer to a broad spectrum of relationships ranging from short-term, superficial ones to long-standing, committed bonds (Johnson & Troll, 1994). Research has found that friendship characteristics may vary by the social and physical circumstances of the aging process (Rawlings, 1992). For example, a decline in physical function can hinder mobility and a capacity to socialize. It has also been hypothesized that reciprocity is likely to influence friendship definitions because equivalent exchanges are normally expected (Liang, Krause & Bennett, 2001). Regardless, friendship relationships are considered voluntary and determined by personal choices or availability of a suitable pool of candidates.

Recent prison research has documented the value of interpersonal relationships in helping women cope with the pains of incarceration (Severance, 2005; Greer, 2000; Jiang & Winfree, 2006). Likewise, we found that the majority of women tended to portray friends that they had made in prison as extremely significant persons in their lives. Most women were able to single out another inmate as someone whom they relied on for support. When asked to describe the "true value of their prison friends," common responses representing a supportive theme included:

> The true value of my friends is having someone who loves you unconditionally, and one who accepts you for the person you are. The friends I have found are true and genuine.

> They are faithful and dependable. I love them. We have been there for one another, whether it be eating together, talking, going to church or

just sitting down and really talking and mostly listening. The friends I have made here are very special, valuable people.

Another woman talked about the value of friendships later in life, "As I get older, I'm realizing the value of relationships and friends. For years, I resented having to have inmates as friends." It has been stated, "friends are the family we choose for ourselves" (Maggio, 1996, p. 270). This may be especially the case for people who have been separated for long periods of time from extended family. Being truncated from family places friends into roles previously performed by family members and often described as "fictive" or "affiliated" kin. This appears to be the case for females who are serving long sentences and turn almost exclusively to their peers in prison for support and comfort. As one older woman stated:

> A close friend here is like having extended family. They are supportive, enjoy some of the same things I do, most of all we give comfort to each other. It allows you to have someone to confide in and share with. Without these friends, prison would be unbearable. I have many lifer friends who are like family. They are there when I need them and they pray for me. They are someone to depend on at all times.

Thus, for numerous inmates, the closest friends they have made in prison now function as typical family members. As one lifer indicated, "I have many lifer friends who are like family. I feel like they are a part of my soul, especially my Christian sisters." Others talk about friends as "someone who listens," "someone who is there no matter what the reason," "someone to talk with." The narratives provided here support previous findings that found "the friendships inmates established with each other were a critical component of the way they did their time" (Kruttschnitt, Gartner & Miller, 2000).

Relationship Motivations

Social factors play an important role in determining female prison adjustment, including the degree of social support from other inmates. The importance of informal supports in the lives of older people has been extensively documented (Johnson & Troll, 1994; Liang, Krause & Bennett, 2001). Social relationships function to not only provide a supportive network, but also as the sustainment of one's social identity (Stevens & Van Tilburg, 2000). Informal reciprocal relationships, especially those that provide support to others, are a crucial component of an older person's physical and mental well-being, feelings of personal control, and overall morale (Hooyman & Kiyak, 2008). Research has also found that even the perception that a support network is available has been linked to improved mental health (Cohen, Gottlieb & Underwood, 2001; Liang, Krause & Bennett, 2001). In providing a supportive environment, friends can also combat the effects of negative life experiences that are problematical or stressful in nature (Stevens & Van Tilburg, 2000).

Shanhe Jiang and Thomas Winfree (2006) have suggested through anecdotal evidence and other qualitative studies that female offenders have a significant need for social support while incarcerated. Certainly, dealing with the stressors of imprisonment would qualify as a life situation where social supports would prove invaluable as older female inmates find themselves struggling for survival on a daily basis. Susan Cranford and Rose Williams state, "Most female inmates have an essential need for companionship, primarily due to loneliness and isolation from loved ones—children, spouses, parents, siblings, and significant others" (1998, p. 132). To cope with the physical isolation and severance of emotional ties with family and friends on the outside, inmates frequently turn to an inner circle of inmate friends for social support. Many inmates will identify with the prison subculture, which provides a new reference group, social relationships, and rationalizations that help neutralize feelings of isolation and rejection (Silverman & Vega, 1996). Dorothy Henderson, Janet Schaeffer, and Linda Brown (1998) note that the incarcerated women's lives are shaped by their need to be connected to one another. Considering this need for connection and the findings that women receive fewer and less frequent visits than men from family and friends (Aday, 2003; Kratcoski & Babb, 1990), the importance of within-prison social supports is obvious.

Establishing Social Supports

As important as friends may be for an older person's well-being, it may be rather difficult to find suitable companionship or receive timely support and affirmation in a prison setting. Although it would seem that when entering prison, an individual would be instantly exposed to endless opportunities to meet new friends, the opposite is quite often the case. Establishing a connection with a total stranger can be a challenging process and the ease with which women form new relationships varies greatly (Severance, 2005). The process by which older incarcerated women elect to invite peers to join their existing friendship circles is most effectively illustrated through an examination of the central tenets of homophily theory. Proponents of homophily theory (Thoits, 1986; Suitor, Pillemer & Keeton, 1995; McPherson, Smith-Lovin & Cook, 2001) contend individuals generally use similarities such as age; race and ethnicity; housing arrangements; personality traits; educational, vocational, or recreational programming; and major life transitions to guide them in this selection process.

Age and Proximity

Relationships in prison are controlled, to a significant degree, by living arrangements. When women enter into the system, they typically do not receive the opportunity to exercise their own voices in placement decisions and, thus, cannot negotiate a residence preference among persons of their own age. Instead, their housing placements are largely determined for them. Overall, assignments are motivated and made on the basis of institutional rather than personal preferences. Some institutions may assign inmates to specific cells while others provide inmates with an open dormitory lifestyle. In general, these are the individuals with whom they are most likely to engage in frequent face-to-face correspondences, receive opportunities to reveal their attitudes concerning pressing concerns, or extend advice, guidance, or support without appearing unnecessarily inquisitive, judgmental, or intrusive. As one lifer who is serving life without parole noted, "My greatest need when I arrived was to be able to talk to someone without fear of disinterest, judgment or repeating confidential things." Two inmates discuss the importance of finding compatible roommates based on random assignments:

> The people you live with directly, regardless of age, are the ones to help. You form a bond, especially if you live in a certain unit. If something happens, like a death in the family or if you become sick, most of the women in the unit will be there for you. I haven't seen many people here who wouldn't ask someone to help them.

> I receive support on a daily basis from my roommate. I don't think there is anything that I don't feel I could discuss with her. . . . I also try to be as supportive of her as I can. . . . I consider myself very lucky to have the good roommate I have. We have lived together over 8 years and have never had an argument . . . which makes this kind of living easier than it would be for most.

Unfortunately, assignments to specific units are typically based on factors beyond one's immediate control and involve frequent interactions with peers one would not otherwise consider ideal candidates for friendship. Instead, offenders are generally placed in double bunk arrangements with complete strangers according to factors including the nature of their current offenses, custody levels, medical statuses, prior prison histories, levels of institutional adjustment, and space availabilities. As one older woman noted: "I have just been assigned a new roommate. We tend to just keep to ourselves and rarely talk to each other. Although we share our small space together about the only thing we have in common is the crime we committed. I do have other friends living nearby that I talk to and I've made friends in the library where I work." In fact, rarely does staff regard inmate compatibility as necessities for placement. As the needs of prison administration undoubtedly outweigh individual inmate personalities or preferences when assignments are made, with offenders often receiving no guarantee they will remain with specific inmates throughout the duration of their sentences, many perceive themselves as limited in the degree to which they may freely, openly, and comfortably express themselves within this environment (Johnson & Chernoff, 2002). This view is illustrated with the following: "All the privacy you have from the time you wake up one morning until . . . the next is the amount of time you are in the shower, going to mealtime, or using the telephone. . . . The rest of the time, you are in the room with that roommate . . . another female you know absolutely nothing about together all day and night." It is obvious that for some, coping with life in a total institution means withdrawing from their social environment. It is plausible that when women are unable to live up to the expectation that they should be cooperative and supportive of others, they can experience distress and frustration.

Although certain environmental barriers are evident, one of the most common similarities older women use in selecting prospective friends is age. In fact, about two-thirds of the offenders in our sample identify their closest friends as someone similar in age. Using an age cohort perspective, it can be argued that a particular living generation brings its own attitudes, beliefs, and values to bear on social situations held in common (Cockerham, 1991). In other words, there tends to be a certain comfort level for those who associate with others sharing similar experiences along the life course. As one 62-year-old woman stated:

> I can't see myself confiding in a young person when I have a 21-year-old daughter and a 34-year-old daughter myself. So I cannot confide in

someone who is under them. That's basically it. I just don't have that much in common with the younger ones. They are into their own music and stuff. Sometimes it is necessary to interact, but I would never share anything personal.

While age appears a significant variable that influences the decisions made by community-dwelling elders, it is even more critical for women who are occupying later adulthood within prison settings. According to continuity theory (Atchley, 1989), older adults often preserve existing social structures by applying familiar strategies. Developing and maintaining a relationship with others who share a similar history can provide a sense of continuation and familiarity. Understandably, most women will seek companionship with peers who share the desires for safety, privacy, quietness, and appropriate activities to deter them from ruminating over the crimes committed (Krabill & Aday, 2005). This point is illustrated by the following 55-year-old: "I live in an open dorm and there's four of us to a quarter. One roommate I talk to is 52 and similar to my age. We sleep right across from each other. And then the other two across from us on the other side, they're young and I don't interact much with them." Older individuals who are serving life sentences and elect to avoid interactions with members of this population, for example, attribute their decisions to observations that younger peers rarely share their interests, concerns, and life experiences; extend to them the respect they recall inmates providing elders when they first entered prison; or appear sincere when expressing an interest in or inquiring about their well-being (Leigey, 2007). Instead, those who select friends on the basis of age indicate the youth with whom they regularly intermingle are frequently loud, apathetic toward any opportunities for self-improvement institutions may afford them, and instead, continually engage in behaviors that violate extant prison policies. As several inmates commented:

> My first impression of them [young inmates] was that they were at day camp. Some are back for the third time. They don't seem to care. I tend to choose my associates with care. You run with trouble, you are trouble. I do my very best to keep my distance and try to hang around with my older friends.

> When I look at the young women, see the open sexuality, and hear the foul language . . . words I have never heard of. When they talk about the things they're gonna do to each other. It's like another world, but what are we going to do? We are stuck here with these people and just have to make the best of it.

> It is difficult being older and being housed with younger women. Their attitudes are different as well as their goals for each day. I view this as an unfortunate diversion in the later part of my life and an indicator that I'm losing valuable time. Younger people see it as a "stepping stone" or a "time out" and will jump back into life with little or no problem.

In general, scholars who have attempted to address inmate rationalizations for this practice concur that the presence of intolerable noise levels (Walsh, 1990; Aday, 2003), aggressive behaviors (Kratcoski & Babb, 1990), or discrepancies in lifestyles, orientations to the future, goals for incarceration, or attitudes toward active involvement in available structured programming (Wahidin, 2004) occasionally preclude them from establishing genuine friendships with others who are situated in this environment.

Self-Disclosure Constraints

Some respondents indicated that they were very selective about the individuals with whom they chose to develop friendships as well as the type of information they were willing to share. Research has suggested that many older women appear constrained from entrusting even the peers with whom they share the closest bonds with personal confidences (Greer, 2000). Studies that focus on the structure of relationships in prisons report women who establish intimate connections are more likely to notice a "dark side" to relationships and as a result limit self-disclosure to superficial topics. While trust is considered an important foundation for social and emotional support, it is a rather difficult trait to find in most prison relationships. Only 14 percent of the women were willing to discuss all personal matters with their fellow inmates. Although 45 percent of the women were willing to discuss some personal matters with their fellow inmates, one-fourth reported they felt comfortable discussing only superficial topics. Thus, the perceived shortcomings of other inmates frequently contribute to the fact that many women choose to closely monitor their interactions with others. The following comments illustrate this fact as these women expressed concern over sharing intimate details of their lives with other inmates:

> You pick and choose a lot what you are going to talk about. Like, if somebody wants to talk to you, you're careful how you respond, because you don't want to get too close. You don't want to feed into

their problems, because you have enough of your own. You're cordial but distant.

If you find one person you can get close to in all the time you're here, you're lucky. There's a fifty/fifty chance that that person could be your bud for ten years and all of a sudden one day they turn on you. And you don't know why, and you don't understand it. So be careful.

Yet another inmate provides a similar view of the tendency to engage in shallow communication, especially in situations where there is little trust, by stating, "I don't talk about my thoughts, I just talk about what I do."

Table 5.1 provides a descriptive overview of the self-disclosure patterns of those participating in this study. Older females were more likely to make conversations about the prison environment including issues such as prison food or staff as well as sharing positive things in their lives. Inmates were less likely to exchange "personal" information concerning their medical conditions, finances, or family relationships. For example, about 70 percent rarely or never discussed their financial situation with others, and an even greater number (80 percent) refused to talk about things from their past that might make them feel ashamed. About one-half indicated that they never or rarely discussed topics that angered, depressed, or saddened them. Several rationalized their decisions to maintain degrees of distance in the discussion of family relationships with other inmates by explaining how their inability to perform familial

Table 5.1 Inmate Conversations and Self-Disclosure (percentage; n = 327)

Conversation Topic	Never	Rarely	Sometimes	Often
Food or other conditions here	00.0	08.3	50.0	41.1
Things you are happy about	00.0	20.8	33.3	45.8
People who work here	20.8	16.7	41.4	20.8
Things you are annoyed about	08.3	29.2	37.5	16.7
Your feelings about being here	12.5	33.3	33.3	20.8
Your past life prior to prison	20.8	29.2	33.3	16.7
Activities that brought you here	16.7	20.2	37.5	16.7
Your relationship with family	04.2	44.8	20.8	20.2
Your health or illnesses	08.3	58.3	16.7	16.7
Your financial situation	33.3	37.5	20.8	08.3
Things you are ashamed of	29.2	50.0	20.8	00.0
Things you are angry about	08.7	43.5	30.4	17.4
Things you are depressed about	25.0	33.3	29.2	12.5
Things you are sad about	16.7	37.5	25.0	20.8

responsibilities invoked negative emotions—feelings of abandonment, resentfulness, anger, and bitterness—in the family as well as the involved inmate. After conversations with family members, as these older women return to their social circles with lingering feelings of shame or sadness, they note the obligation to refrain from expressing such issues with peers.

Using discretion in determining the topics of conversation, however, serves an invaluable purpose in coping with life in this environment. For example, discussing only general issues such as sources of personal happiness, food, and personnel with their peers enables them to maintain a certain degree of anonymity. However, this closed approach may limit the emotional support that intimacy affords. This may be especially true for those who enter the facility with no prior exposure to confinement and no external supports who can relate to the prison stressors they are now encountering. Sharing personal information provides opportunities to acquaint themselves with peers who are undergoing comparable challenges, understand apprehensions, and orient them to the new roles (Gutheil, 1991). Two long-term inmates who have been incarcerated more than 25 years illustrate the lack of intimacy frequently in their lives:

> From time to time, I try to talk to my peers about the emotional changes I've begun to go through as I'm aging. What I've found is that they had rather not discuss it. They seem to get agitated, uncomfortable. So, I've sort of let go of discussing it. Sometimes, I allow myself to get into gripe sessions. It doesn't help, only intensifies the anger.

> Everyone in here holds back. Maybe it's just the way we protect ourselves. You have to be careful who you associate with, and avoid the pedophiles and baby killers. . . . The more willing you are to stay away from some people, the better you will cope. You can't take on all of their problems, or you'll be overwhelmed. And *never* bare your soul to anyone. I have seen what happens to people who have.

Although maintaining a degree of distance is necessary to survival of incarceration, Azrini Wahidin (2004) emphasizes the need for sharing other topics as complete withdrawal may be perceived by others with disdain and severely restrict one's access to needed assistance. Theresa Severance (2005) reported that many women in her sample were not comfortable sharing intimate information for fear of idle chatter. However, some women did report being able to share intimate personal information.

> My friends listen when I talk and keep my heart issue private. I've been blessed to have found three people I can communicate with on

any level. We can have conversations that aren't drug related. We don't tell war stories. We have goals and we frequently talk about them and continue to encourage each other as we do our time together.

Me and my best friend always talk to each other, because it helps. You have to have somebody real close to you or it makes the time a lot harder. You don't trust everybody, but the main people, it makes you feel good to have someone you can trust.

Other inmates were hesitant to form close relationships due to the tenuous nature of prison friendships. Similar to previous research among community elders (Johnson & Troll, 1994) voluntary relationships may dissolve or at least weaken when friendship patterns are perceived as temporary. Rather than enjoying the benefits of attachment to their fellow peers, some inmates choose to remain distant: "I have found several friends that are close in age to me, but I won't allow myself to become too emotionally attached. I keep an emotional barrier between myself and my friends so that I won't be devastated when they leave." However, most inmates are probably able to overcome this fear. For example, another inmate proclaimed that she relies mainly on three other women in the prison—her so-called prison sisters. Although this 52-year-old inmate has heard repeatedly "Don't make friends cause they leave," she continues to rely on her three prison sisters for emotional support and advice. She states, "I know I'll miss them should they leave prison."

Helping Patterns and Support

Research has shown that most people have a need to be needed and to feel that they are contributing. Additionally, many older women grew up with a tradition of service, and they want to continue to be useful and to help others regardless of their current circumstance (Deichman & Kociecki, 1989). However, information concerning the helping patterns adopted by individuals who occupy later life in prison has, until recently, appeared limited in scope. Anecdotal evidence from the narratives of inmates who have undergone extensive screenings and training to serve as volunteers, however, indicates older adults can benefit substantially from performing such tasks as sitting with the terminally ill or writing letters, cleaning pods, pushing wheelchairs, and serving as "seeing eye" peers for others who have physical or mental health limitations that would otherwise preclude them from fully functioning in this environment (Anno, 2004; Byock, 2002; Hunsberger, 2000). As Table 5.2 demonstrates, the women in our study frequently provided each other with assistance. Severance (2005) has suggested that social and emotional support is essential for the health and well-being of women in prison. It is evident from the responses shown in Table 5.2 that establishing relationships proves to be quite beneficial for the majority of women. Although many women receive constant support from their family circle on the outside, inside connections are also apparently very important. Most women reported they have a supportive network—people they can confide in and rely on for emotional support and understanding. Almost 80 percent indicated that the friends they had made in prison were very important to them as well as sharing common interests. In fact, Severance makes the claim from similar research that supportive connections appear significantly more beneficial for some inmates who are willing to acknowledge that this is the case.

Although willingness to engage in reciprocal exchanges is undeniably imperative to the well-being of older offenders, most elders will acknowledge the reward is greatest when friends have established boundaries concerning the degree of support that is acceptable to give or receive. As Margaret Leigey (2007) highlighted in her research conduct-

Table 5.2 Measures of Inmate Support (n = 327)

Support Indicators	Percentage
Perceived support network	
I frequently provide some type of assistance to a fellow inmate.	83.8
I feel personally responsible for the well-being of my fellow inmates.	43.1
There are fellow inmates here who share my interests and concerns.	82.0
I have fellow inmates here I can depend on whenever I need them.	78.9
There is always someone I can talk to about my day-to-day problems.	71.4
I have fellow inmates I can confide in about my personal problems.	64.8
I can call on my friends whenever I need them.	64.6
There are plenty of people I can rely on in case of trouble.	51.0
The friends I have made here are very important to me.	77.6
My relationships with fellow inmates provide me a sense of well-being.	69.5
Assistance received from prison friends	
I have received gifts from some of my prison friends.	51.6
Other inmates have been there to console me when I'm upset.	74.2
My friends here frequently listen to my problems.	71.0
I have received emotional support from my friends.	63.4
My friends here provide me with companionship.	45.2
Other inmates have cared for me when ill or assisted with my daily needs.	56.6
I frequently receive advice or help in making personal decisions.	52.7

ed with older men who are serving sentences of life without parole, the provision of too much assistance may discourage recipients from seeking or receiving guidance from trained professionals, or foster a sense of dependency on individuals who may not have the time, patience, skills, or desire to provide continued support. This, in return, not only affects the quality of life experienced by the offender who is extending one's services, but also interferes with the recipient achieving the personal growth that is desired. Consequently, less than one-half feel personal responsibility for the well-being of their prison friends. As two inmates expressed:

> I resent this is a costly prison and that the institutional policy against borrowing, loaning or lending personal items does not benefit women who are less fortunate than myself. . . . The hardest thing about incarceration is having been raised to help, coming here, and being punished for living in accordance with my values.

> I believe prison forces inmates to break every rule in the Bible. If you see someone who is hungry, you feed them. Although it is against the rule, I offer sneaky help. I see a little lady so hungry—it breaks my heart! I also don't comply with the regulations that prohibit hugging. I've only been written up three times in 23 years so I am confident that the staff knows I'm not a problem.

Although the presence of intergenerational friendships may rarely appear to be the norm, older offenders who have befriended one or more younger peers while incarcerated report these connections frequently serve an invaluable purpose in their adjustment to institutionalization. As older women have often served the longest sentences and have accumulated the greatest body of knowledge about the institution, its culture, policies, and procedures for handling any grievances that may arise, staff may naturally anticipate and assume that they will nurture, guide, and advise their younger peers (Wahidin, 2004). In general, long-term offenders appear extremely interested in working closely with correctional personnel to ensure the presence of a safe environment for all individuals who reside within the walls of the facility (Flanagan, 1982, 1995). During their sentences, a number may have undergone major transitions that resulted in them developing an appreciation and sense of empathy, consideration, and respect for the well-being of their fellow peers. Naturally, one method these elders may elect to demonstrate their interest in complying with the responsibilities they have been assigned involves mentoring or serving as a parental figure to the younger adults with whom they must now regularly interact. Older individuals who are serving life sentences, for example, occasionally strive to identify others who resemble their earlier selves, provide them insights into behaviors they may desire to refrain from engaging in, casually monitor their actions, and periodically extend to them reminders in attempts to prevent them from making the mistakes, receiving the punishments, and suffering the consequences they experienced earlier in their terms (Johnson & Dobrzanska, 2005). Two inmates in their 60s who are serving life without parole illustrate this point:

> I live in the intake unit and I spend most of my day talking with new people giving advice. Being in here with all these new people, I try and talk with some of the young girls. Their life is ruined worse than mine. I've found that my life isn't as bad as theirs. First time for them being here and what they are here for . . . it's just pitiful. I have more wisdom and I share my life, love, and wisdom with other younger inmates to encourage them.

> My two young dorm mates come to me for advice. When I see them doing something they shouldn't be doing or headed in the wrong direction, I correct them. I tell them "everybody's" got an opinion, but this is what I think you ought to do, and it's up to you whether you want to do it or not. They usually change their ways; the way they talk and treat people.

By sharing their life, love, and wisdom with others, these elders create for themselves niches within which they can continue to enjoy active lifestyles, avoid pejorative stereotypes about the aging process, and eliminate any fears they may have formerly had about the negative effects of physiological or psychological deterioration (Aday, 2003). As the expectation for older offenders to mentor their younger, more inexperienced peers is considerably greater in women's prisons than it is in institutions housing men (Wahidin, 2004), the advantages associated with mixed age interactions may be greater than once expected.

In return, older offenders who once entered the institution after years of involvement in work, recreational pursuits, or other activities that promote the establishment of intergenerational relationships report that any opportunities they may receive to socialize with younger offenders assists them in maintaining their independence as long as humanly possible. Specifically, these inmates often acknowledge they receive much gratification from noticing their younger friends appear willing to defend their honors when conflicts with aggressive peers arise, assist them in completing chores and other strenuous tasks they would be unable to complete independently, or share with them news concerning current events they would unlikely hear from family, friends, or acquaintances who reside outside the walls of the institutional setting (Leigey, 2007). Others report benefiting substantially from encouragement to remain busy, alert, and engaged in the larger inmate subculture (Marquart, Merianos & Doucet, 2000).

Prison Pastimes

Prison life means giving up, not only friends and family, but also favorite leisure activities such as going shopping or to the movies. The routine of life behind bars can lead to boredom and monotony. With prison life a reality for years to come, inmates often struggle in finding a useful purpose. Although many critics oppose the presence of leisurely pursuits behind bars, social and recreational activities play an important role in the lives of inmates. The benefits of therapeutic programming are particularly relevant for older people because it is commonly recognized that the processes of aging slow down significantly when people remain active and involved. For example, previous research has found that engaging in social activities was linked with improved physical function and also predicted a reduced decline in functional status over time (Everard et al., 2000; Menec, 2003; Unger, Anderson Johnson & Marks, 1997). Research in a variety of social environments has also highlighted the positive influence that social attachments can have on the psychological well-being of those choosing to socially engage with others (House, Landis & Umberson, 1988; Rowe & Kahn, 1998; Wilson & Spink, 2006). Additional research has repeatedly reported a positive association between network resources and various measures of life satisfaction and/or emotional well-being.

Prisoners who are strongly encouraged to develop prosocial outlets within which they could channel their energies, for example, may benefit substantially from momentarily escaping the stressful nature of incarceration, releasing mounting tensions, and improving their trades, problem-solving skills, social skills, and senses of self-esteem (Vega & Silverman, 1988). Innovative programming for elderly inmates has been found to give inmates a reason to get up in the morning because there are things to anticipate (Harrison, 2006). Toch (2006) suggests some individuals approach doing time by pursuing passive distractions while other inmates feel continuous activity is critical to their survival. Table 5.3 provides a summary of the various types of formal and informal activities older women utilize to pass the time. As noted in this table, reading and writing have been identified as two of the most popular passive activities older women may pursue while incarcerated. Both serve the invaluable purpose of permitting participants to momentarily escape the stressors associated with institutional living while maintaining or reestablishing bonds with any external supports whose lives may have also been disrupted, altered, or impaired by the nature of their criminal activities. As older, long-term prisoners begin to notice that visits are becoming increasingly more infrequent, the exchange of letters may gradually replace face-to-face conversations as the primary medium through which information is transmitted to one another. These elders may be keenly aware they may continue to encounter circumstances that will require them to approach family, friends, and other external supports for needed assistance.

Although older offenders may treasure the acts of reading and writing as such forms of recreation permit them to correspond with members of the free world, other elders identify the pursuits as serving a range of purposes independent of this function. In addition to reading letters from home, for example, several value the information contained within the books, magazines, and other print materials available through the institutions' libraries or educational programs. Leigey (2007) indicated the respondents she interviewed identified themselves as most likely to acquire resources that could provide them learning experiences to which they would otherwise receive limited exposure. The narrative provided

Table 5.3 Prison Activities (percentage; n = 327)

Activity	Total	Georgia	Kentucky	Tennessee	Mississippi	Arkansas
Playing cards	50.1	51.0	67.8	41.6	46.5	43.4
Crafting	31.5	16.5	35.7	53.3	8.4	43.4
Exercising	39.0	42.7	53.6	30.0	25.3	43.4
Listening to music	52.5	62.7	57.1	48.3	46.5	47.8
Reading	76.0	83.4	78.5	66.6	73.2	78.2
Writing letters	70.1	75.1	85.7	66.6	49.3	73.9
Religious/spiritual activities	65.5	69.5	57.1	53.3	64.8	82.6
Watching TV	44.1	41.2	46.7	45.4	39.1	51.7
Talking/conversations	48.6	49.0	57.1	53.3	64.8	52.1
Helping others	61.0	63.4	57.1	60.0	50.7	73.9
Being alone	43.3	37.2	46.4	45.0	35.2	47.8
Educational programs	31.8	33.8	39.3	30.0	25.3	30.4
Working	49.6	43.4	57.1	50.0	32.4	65.2

below stresses the importance of reading as an activity that permits inmates to expand their knowledge:

> I have always been an avid reader. . . . I usually lay down about 9:00 P.M. and read for a few hours. I read a wide range, but prefer classics. . . . We don't have a lot to choose from in our library as it contains mostly romance and true crime. . . . Whenever I get the chance, however, I will select classic books. For me, reading late at night is something I always look forward to. It's my private time and I love letting my mind get lost in a good book.

Watching television is another activity that is a popular pastime for incarcerated women. This activity provides a useful, and to some the only, link to the outside world. In some institutions where inmates are serving their time in more private cells, they may have the opportunity of having a television in their own room. This is a definite advantage for those who enjoy watching specific programming. For example, one inmate reacts to her personal situation:

> I had my own TV until a power surge destroyed it. This was a significant loss for me because I'm a channel surfer and I only like a few channels like Animal Planet that the others in the dayroom won't watch. The dayroom is always crowded and it is hard to enjoy watching TV with so many people. You never know what program will be running. I'm now trying to save money to buy another TV.

Numerous others mentioned the conflicts that tend to emerge between inmates who have difficulty agreeing on specific television programming. Some complained of the noise and foul language associated with watching programs in a group setting, especially with younger women.

While passive activities such as reading, writing, or engaging in religious activities were mentioned more frequently, other inmates engage in more formal prison programs as a way to fill their time. Activity not only compensates for external stimulus deprivation, but it also contributes to a more immediate feeling of contentment. As Toch stresses, "Activity stabilizes the economy of the body and the mind by discharging tension, modulating moods, and providing point and focus to restlessness" (2006, p. 31). As one inmate serving life responded when asked, "How do you deal with time?": "You have to keep yourself busy. You have to do something with your time. I go to school five days a week. And, I've got groups during the day, and at night, two hours at a time. We have crochet groups. They bring in stuff for us to make hats and sweaters and blankets for the homeless, the needy, or hurricane victims."

For some, engaging in prison activities may come with a more specific purpose other than just to combat tension or boredom. At this level, some inmates may select activities in terms of their ego-enhancing or self-actualizing capacity. Engaging in certain activities that provide personal growth can serve as an important source of accomplishment. As one lifer serving time for capital murder stated:

> I have been in Anger Management and Shelter for the Storm, a program that teaches us how to cope with dysfunctional families and the long-term effects of childhood sexual abuse. . . . I've got my certificate in culinary arts and I've already got my GED while here. I've signed up for every available program . . . so I've made good use of my time. These programs have permitted me to make peace with my past and gain a sense of serenity. I feel so much better about myself now.

With the exception of women incarcerated in Georgia and Mississippi, crafting is a popular and available activity for those who have the time and inclination. However, according to one inmate, some take crafting activities to the extreme:

> It's easy (very easy) to get institutionalized in here. A number of women I live with have used arts and crafts to cope with imprisonment. Some may use these to supplement their income or to provide gifts for family and friends. For a few, however, cross-stitching, crocheting, plastic canvas, and painting have become similar to an addiction. They have little time for anything else.

The provisions for prison programming may vary from one prison community to another. While it has been suggested that a room for crafts be set aside for the geriatric population, this is not always the case (Neeley, Addison & Craig-Moreland, 1997). In the absence of structured activities and space, informal initiatives by the inmates themselves can fill this void:

> During our lobby time we can socialize, get our ice, and just basically hang out. I use this time to help the girls with any problems they might be having with crafts, legal work, or whatever. . . . I also have had a class for ladies interested in learning to crochet, and all of the things that are made to charity. . . . I enjoy teaching the women something that will keep their mind occupied and hands busy, such as cross-stitching. I find that it is the best stress reliever in the world.

Education Programs

Prison educational programming has been identified as accommodating the needs of the most ill-prepared offenders while paying relatively limited attention to those inmates who have successfully mastered the most fundamental academic skills. The Bureau of Justice reports that in 2000, nearly every state institution offered inmates opportunities to participate in some form of educational programming. Among these, most included basic adult education or secondary education options, whereas few offered collegiate instruction (Harlow, 2003). Any available programs are generally created with the intent of providing inmates free-of-cost instruction in subjects that prepare them to successfully complete the General Education Development (GED) examination. While the guidelines for progression through the curriculum vary by state, most involve year-round, self-paced, or whenever needed, independent instruction.

As older offenders have historically been identified as entering prison with significant educational deficiencies (Aday, 2003; Leigey, 2007), participation in formal course work may prove to be an invaluable experience for those who elect to utilize the various resources that are available to them. With one-third of the older women in this five-state sample lacking a high school diploma, pursuing the GED was a common occurrence. As one inmate pointed out, this seems to be the rule, especially for the women in their age group: "The older women are the ones who are going to school to get their GED. The younger ones come in here on drugs. They're young and they don't care. If you are 25 or younger, you can take college classes for free. They rarely take advantage of this opportunity." A few occasionally even receive the opportunities, through correspondence course work, to pursue baccalaureate or graduate degrees. Long-term offenders who have enrolled in prison education programs express their gratification for occasions to engage in lifelong learning, occupy their minds in constructive pursuits, gain the skills necessary to complete tasks peers take for granted, improve personal conduct, and serve as role models to younger offenders who also lack formal academic training (Leigey, 2007). The following illustrates how numerous older women are engaged in their educational pursuits: "I'm taking classes through my work—Business Electrical Maintenance Training—and I also graduated from the horticulture program. I am now taking classes offered by Jefferson Technical College through a Canteen Scholarship. I'm not certain how I qualified, but maybe because of my GPA. I only have to pay $20 of the $276 tuition."

Although participating in advanced educational programming is a popular consideration for those who are highly motivated, certain barriers do exist for some inmates who wish to continue their education behind bars. One common barrier is the lack of available funding for those individuals that may not have a scholarship or a family capable of financial support. An inmate makes this point with the following narrative: "I would love to take college courses to fill the void in my life, but they are costly. Taking them would place a burden on my family to cover the expense. As there are no courses offered designed with the older woman in mind—for example, nothing about menopause—I do not think asking them for the money would be worth it." At another institution, a number of inmates complained of the closure of the educational program that was once available. At one time indigent inmates could apply for a Pell Grant, which would pay for their college tuition, but that program no longer exists. As one inmate stated, "I went to college before they took the program away. I got a degree and I would love to continue my education, but now that is impossible without financial support." Another who recalls a time when the institution did encourage participation in higher education explains the benefits accrued from the experience and expresses her continued interest in the prospects of lifelong learning: "Take advantage of all of the opportunities they offer here. By participating in available programming, you will receive a chance to start your life over again, to grow, and to live. Then when you get out, you can live a better, more productive, life."

A substantial body of literature, however, suggests such opportunities fail to effectively accommodate the diverse needs of older or female offenders. Lori Girshick's (1999) research illuminates the very real concerns experienced by long-term offenders who, upon entering prison, identify a desire for rehabilitation. Many who elect to wisely use their time in prison by becoming actively involved in programs that would permit them to overcome their preincarceration lifestyles may pursue educational options, only to notice after achieving their goals, the feelings of accomplishment or personal growth may be replaced by those of boredom, apathy, or despair. Leigey's (2007) research documents frustrations long-term offenders observe as it identifies a positive correlation between the length of time served and the likelihood of having participated in course work while in prison. As the author explains, those offenders who have occupied the most years in this environment frequently describe themselves as having been "programmed out," and as a result, express disinterest in furthering their studies.

Older women frequently harbor more deeply entrenched feelings of indifference toward the educational opportunities afforded. Similar to their male counterparts, female offenders often perceive the selection of available topics as unnecessarily restrictive. Women who have entered the system under the impression that prison administration would place considerable value on the presence of lifelong learning frequently discover the breadth of existing programming fails to adequately reflect the variety of which they had been informed (Wahidin, 2004). Instead of receiving invaluable information they could later use to ensure successful transitions back into mainstream society, many will inevitably notice themselves participating in courses that were designed to serve the needs of younger students. Any options that are offered exclusively for this population typically appear to be slightly modified alternatives to the sections attended by their peers. Moreover, opportunities for advanced instruction that may be conducive to the needs of women who have mastered the most rudimentary mathematics and literacy skills frequently have few available slots, long wait lists, and fees for instruction. Naturally, these characteristics make any learning that may occur in this environment incidental in nature. As formal grievances to appropriate authorities require years to resolve, immediate, short-term solutions are generally considered to be the responsibility of individual inmates to identify and implement. Although some may initially have the drive to fulfill this critical objective, the passage of time may substantially reduce their levels of motivation for independent learning (Wahidin, 2004).

In recent years, prisons that house a large number of older offenders have acknowledged the imperativeness of creatively identifying, proposing, and adopting a variety of new courses for use with older adult populations. More specifically, several have expanded their curriculums to include workshops on securing Medicare or Social Security, coping with grief and bereavement issues, living with chronic illnesses, properly taking their medications, enhancing memories, reducing stress, becoming more assertive in interactions with staff and peers, and fulfilling their roles as grandparents (Anno et al., 2004). Few institutions, however, have taken the initiative to promote active involvement in these options. Similar to other research (Leigey, 2007), relatively few of the older female offenders in our sample indicated they had the opportunity to attend such informative programs.

While the advantages associated with participation in prison programming are well-documented, institutions housing female offenders have proven the slowest in responding to extant concerns. A long history of research concerning the nature of women's imprisonment portrays programming as failing to address the needs of individuals who enter after extended histories of poverty, abuse, poor educational and vocational training, inadequate preventative health care, addictions, and low self-esteem (Curry, 2001; Flanagan, 1995; Koons et al., 1995; Nadel, 1997; Phillips & Harm, 1998). Most institutions overlook women's needs for safe environments within which they receive permission to freely explore factors that contributed to their poor lifestyle decisions, prepare them for career advancement, and provide them skills they may ultimately need to successfully reintegrate into mainstream society, with any activities they offer that achieve these critical objectives being entirely accidental in nature (Wahidin, 2004). Instead, opportunities have traditionally emphasized, honored, and rewarded continued pursuit of trivial, monotonous, domestic tasks that encourage continued dependency on the system and external supports to accommodate basic needs.

Work Opportunities

Another frequently identified activity older offenders involve themselves in to occupy the time in prison are various forms of prison employment. According to the Bureau of Justice, an estimated 60 percent of the total inmate population spend at least a portion of their sentences working. Specific to older offenders, those who are most likely to work include offenders that have prior work and prison experiences, have served more time in prison, are serving non–life without parole sentences, and are in good physical health (Leigey, 2007; Sabath & Cowles, 1988). Individuals who have recently entered the facility and have prior exposure to paid employment may discover their expertise assists them in obtaining coveted positions, linking them with other offenders who have similar interests in the chosen arena, and preparing for any leadership roles they may later encounter while serving time (Leigey, 2007). Moreover, those who have already established niches within the system may notice sentence length serves as a predictor of employment as offenders who have occupied more time in this environment have turned to structured institutional pursuits to fill the void associated with reduced contact with the outside world. In fact, older offenders often creatively establish for themselves "careers" out of their participation in this arena, and in the process, identify an activity that serves an invaluable purpose in contributing to heightened morale and institutional adjustment. An inmate serving life provides the following primary example:

> They have an inmate work program here. It's called PIE [Prison Industry Enhancement]. They pay us minimum wage. The company is

Actronix and they built a factory here on the grounds. We get 20 percent of our check to spend, 40 percent goes to the prison, and 5 percent goes to the victim's fund. Some goes to child support if mandated by courts. The rest is put in saving for when the inmate is released. I've worked free for 28 years, so I'm glad to be in the program. Getting a paycheck has lifted my self-esteem. I feel better paying taxes, doing my part as a citizen.

This illustrates the important function of work, and in this particular case, work that contributes to the financial independence of the inmate. However, the majority of older incarcerated women will not have such an opportunity, as in-prison industries are not readily available in most communities.

In general, most inmates who currently hold prison jobs are employed in the areas of facility support service completing exhausting tasks such as laundry, food preparation, janitorial work, or similar activities that must be accomplished in order for administration to successfully sustain institutional operations. Inmates who are not directly involved in these pursuits may receive value from manufacturing goods or services such as prints, furniture, or caskets that will eventually be distributed to area businesses. When available, such assignments may initially be made upon close consideration of the inmates' criminal histories, security classifications, prior work assignments, and medical conditions. As one inmate who had a significant health issue mentioned:

I have a health issue that, if my supervisor learned about it, I would lose my job. I know I have some problems, okay? To keep my job, even though I don't do anything more than click on this mouse, I am required to be able to lift X number of pounds. If they found out, I would be unemployed. And I need that job. . . . So, yes, I am concerned about this.

Although age has traditionally not been used as a deciding factor in the making of placement decisions, as of 2003, fifteen states had begun to identify geriatric status as a major determinant when older offenders were involved in work assignments (Aday, 2003).

For older offenders who have received placement exclusively on the basis of age, the advantages that are associated with the receipt of geriatric status are plentiful. Individuals who reside in states that house a large number of older offenders may notice themselves placed in positions that involve reduced working hours; require minimal speed, agility, stamina, or overall use of physical exertion; and have opportunities for early release. As one inmate who works full-time in the prison library recalls, "Half of my pay goes to a program that reduces my serve out by one day for every 40 hours I work." Specific tasks that have recently been creatively designed and adopted to accommodate the diverse needs of an aging prison population include sedentary activities such as legal research or pod cleaning. As more individuals are now anticipating the prospects of spending later adulthood in prison, many scholars are strongly advocating in favor of compensating inmates who do not possess the strength or stamina necessary to perform rigorous tasks for engagement in these as well as other activities that were once considered to be performed only on a voluntary basis (Aday, 2003; Stojkovic, 2007; Williams & Rikard, 2004).

Older offenders who are eligible for prison employment receive numerous physical, mental, and social benefits as a result of their labor. Commonly noted advantages include the satisfaction of receiving small, monetary wages for their time and talents, paying restitution to their victims, creating some semblance of professional identities, and establishing contacts with staff who could later assist them in preparing for release. For those elders who no longer have any contact with their external supports, prison employment may be the only resource they have available for securing the finances necessary to purchase items at the commissary (Leigey, 2007). Other inmates also stressed the value of work:

> My work keeps me mentally alert and provides me a sense of accomplishment. When I close out at the end of the day, I have an inner peace. . . . I could not imagine spending time without ever seeing the fruits of my labor. After arriving, I was informed that I would never work a day. However, I had always worked and begged for a job. . . . And I haven't missed a day since receiving it.

> Give me a little place to grow a few veggies and a place to sit in the shade and see more of life's beauty, which is free for all of us. Let the older prisoners have something to do that can benefit the outside. We can knit and work with our hands. Let us have an input to the future generations so they won't have to experience incarceration.

Clearly, work assignments are a critical phase of a female's incarceration experience and play an important role in helping inmates to maintain their maximum productivity and highest sense of self-worth.

Although additional policies are being constructed to accommodate this growing demand, the number of elders who would require special consideration exceeds the number of positions that are currently available. Leigey's (2007) research based on qualitative interviews conducted with 25 older offenders who are serving life without parole explores the frustrations elders experience when the demand for age-appropriate tasks exceeds the slots institutions have open to extend to them. In her research, the author discovered a small percentage identified administrators as distributing work assignments on the basis of age alone. As undemanding tasks such as laundry folding were rare, even the oldest man incarcerated was expected to fulfill the same requirements as his younger colleagues if he desired to maintain his employment status. Other studies based on the experiences of "lifer" populations have confirmed Leigey's findings by also stating that it is relatively common for the oldest offenders to be observed working positions that are considered to be physically exhausting, requiring continued exposure to inclement weather, and involving close supervision by prison guards (Abramsky, 2004).

Summary

In sum, our respondents explained, older incarcerated women identify, borrow, and make extensive use of numerous strategies to cope with the stressors that institutionalization imposes on them. Unarguably, one of the most effective strategies for counteracting prison stress involves the establishment of close interpersonal relationships with one's fellow offenders. As the older women's narratives clearly suggest, prison friendships fill a critical void in their social lives when contacts to external supports cannot be established. Given that members of one's peer network are typically bonded together by shared experiences (such as locations of residence, enjoyed activities and pastimes, or even core attitudes, beliefs, values, and assumptions about the world at large), they may possess a wealth of information that can be easily handed down in times of crises or need. The older women who comprised our sample, for example, speak rather candidly about relying on individuals of similar ages, housing arrangements, and work assignments.

As they complete their narratives that focus on life in prison, our participants discuss in vivid detail some of the activities they engage in while serving their respective sentences. In the process, many openly share the personal impacts that any opportunities received to become actively involved in structured pursuits such as working or religious/spiritual activities have had on their morale and mental well-being. Although their involvement in more informal, passive activities (reading, letter writing, and so on) continues to occupy the central role in their daily routines, women who are advancing in age in prison facilities are beginning to recognize the importance of taking proactive measures to protect or shield themselves against the deleterious effects of institutionalization. Even participation in activities (such as educational programs) that are widely known for attracting few elder inmate audiences can serve an indispensable function in enhancing the self-esteem and life satisfaction of older incarcerated women who desire and elect to participate in them. Women who share their experiences concerning their involvement in this critical area, for example, express much gratification for receiving the chance to return to school and complete basic (or in some cases, even more advanced) academic training. Although few talked in elaborate detail about activities or programs that had been specifically initiated within their given institutions with the older adult population directly in mind, it is clear from the stories shared that such will unarguably gain increasingly more recognition in the coming years.

Although most older women eventually identify activities that permit them to occupy their time during incarceration, their experiences are not reflective of every inmate. A number of women, for example, report being bored and missing friends or outside social events. Others were better adjusted and thrived on spending quiet time alone reading, writing letters, or meditating. Older women who have some interest in pursuing structured programs that were designed to transform the lives of new, younger offenders, detest the bureaucratic obstacles that must be overcome before participation is possible. They often resent supervising staff who may reject their program request on the grounds that first priority must be given to those inmates who are anticipating returning back to the free world. A number of inmates at the various institutions expressed disappointment at not having the opportunity to participate in these progressive programs. In particular, those inmates who are going up for parole in the immediate future feel such participation would prove to be an advantage in making their case for successful reentry. Instead, the decision to remain in one's cell, fantasizing about events occurring outside the walls of the prison setting, becomes a common occurrence (Wahidin, 2004) as inmates live inside the walls passing the time away.

6

The Pervasive Context of Intimate Partner Abuse

DOMESTIC VIOLENCE AGAINST WOMEN IS AN EXTRAORDINARILY pervasive problem in our culture and is considered a serious problem for women across the life cycle. Abuse by an intimate partner occurs among women of all races, ethnic backgrounds, educational levels, and socioeconomic status. To our knowledge, little attention has been given to older women in prison who have literally experienced years of physical and mental abuse prior to their incarceration. Understanding how older women make sense of these life experiences may be helpful as we consider how to assist women coming into the criminal justice system. While it is common knowledge that incarcerated women have been frequent victims of abuse, little is actually known about their abuse histories, especially those that focus on intimate partner violence. The trauma suffered at the hands of their abusers has been known to have significant negative consequences, frequently leading to maladaptive behaviors resulting in incarceration. It should also be recognized that women who have been victims of abuse often have more difficulty finding a comfort level in a prison environment, where shades of abuse may continue. For battered women, adjustment to prison life can be a daunting task.

One-half of the women who participated in this comprehensive project reported they had been victims of physical or sexual abuse prior to incarceration. Countless others had also experienced various forms of emotional and verbal abuse. In fact, many of these women indicated they had been in the abusive relationship for many years. The typical victim was 28 years of age (range 17–38) when the abuse started, and the mean number of years these incarcerated women reported being in an abusive adult relationship prior to incarceration was 11 years.

129

Information addressed in this chapter includes the types of abuse endured, types of actions and strategies taken to stop the violence, and the informal and formal sources the women turned to for help. Compelling narratives are also shared about the types of injuries the women sustained, traumatic events that occurred after the women tried to seek help, episodes of abuse that the women felt were the most devastating, and their general feelings about the abuse and their abusers. It should be mentioned that although the majority of the abused sample answered the closed-ended questions on patterns of abuse, some women chose not to respond. Some mentioned the process was simply too painful emotionally to go back in time to relive their abusive past. After reading and hearing some of the personal accounts, this decision was an easy one to understand.

Explanations for Abuse

For many years, researchers have attempted to identify both individual and social factors that might explain why a person is more likely to be abusive. Numerous sociological, biological, and psychological perspectives have been introduced as possible explanations for abusive interrelationships. For example, any number of biochemical theories, including glandular and hormonal imbalances and neurological flaws, have been suggested as possible causes of violent behavior (Gosselin, 2005). On the other hand, social theories link domestic violence to the social structures and cultural norms that legitimize abusive behavior. The culture of violence posits that the implied approval for violence in our society is acknowledged by the use of physical violence to settle family disagreements. Other views include the notion that violence is learned by being handed down from generation to generation or the feminist view that wife battering can be traced to the patriarchal system, which has been used to suppress and control women for centuries (Zosky, 1999).

Other theorists concede that a sizable number of domestic perpetrators exhibit behaviors associated with personality disorders (Dutton, 2007). Such individual-level explanations focus primarily on mental illness, self-esteem problems, or undue stressful situations (Miller & Wellford, 1997). Those supporting this view argue that violence is more likely to occur when individuals have difficulty maintaining self-control or have the need to control others. Of course, when coupled with the presence of alcohol and drugs, this frequently leads to a highly volatile situation, putting women at risk of abuse. It has been suggested that approximately 2 percent of the population could possibly qualify as habitual female batterers (Dutton & Golant, 1995). Sometimes batterers themselves will suggest that they were provoked by their partner's verbal abuse, and they may perceive their physical abuse as an equivalent response (Miller & Wellford, 1997).

Since these clusters of theories, among others, have struggled, on an individual basis, to provide an adequate explanation for domestic violence, some have suggested that taking a more integrated approach would be more fruitful. Such an approach identifies the interrelationships of multiple variables from the individual to society (Miller & Wellford, 1997). There are, however, certain factors that increase the likelihood that a woman will be battered. The first of these is a history of childhood physical and/or sexual abuse (Logan et al., 2006). It has been theorized that this is because victims of abuse in early life develop a sense of "learned helplessness" and do not develop the appropriate skills to escape further battering. Lenore Walker asserts that learned helplessness can be acquired early in childhood from "experiences of non-contingency between response and outcome" (2000, p. 10). Another theory postulates that victims of childhood abuse develop low self-esteem, and in later life, they are more likely to become inured to violent relationships. Or victims of childhood domestic abuse may be desperate to leave their abusive situations and take up with partners they do not know all that well; they may be unaware of this partner's violent tendencies. In addition, a history of childhood abuse has been linked with substance abuse, which has, in turn, been linked with an increased risk of partner abuse among adult women (Jarvis, Copeland & Walton, 1998; Plichta, 2004; Woods, 2005).

While domestic abuse occurs among women at all levels of socioeconomic status, poverty has been found to be an additional risk for battering. Poverty is associated with broken families, limited resources, and exposure to climates of violence, crime, and substance abuse. Additionally, it has been noted that poverty is linked with physical and mental health problems, which increase a woman's chances of being victimized in general (Logan et al., 2006). Another risk factor that is related to violence and abuse is unemployment. Joblessness increases a female's chances of being victimized, and it has been cited as a stressor and impetus for violence among batterers. Moreover, the unemployment of a batterer may be predictive of an increase in the frequency and severity of partner abuse (Walker, 2000).

Women as Victims

It is well documented that a vast number of incarcerated women have suffered various incidents of sexual and physical violence in childhood, with similar experiences of abuse continuing into adulthood and beyond (Beaulaurier et al., 2005; Bradley & Davino, 2002; Zink et al., 2006; Zink et al., 2003). Female prisoners report a much higher incidence of abuse than women in the general population, with estimates ranging from 40 to 80 percent (Browne, Miller & Maguin, 1999; Kubiak 2005; Seijeoung, 2003). This lifelong experience of violence and abuse leads to maladaptive behaviors such as substance abuse and violent behavior and can serve as a contributing factor of incarceration (Heney & Kristiansen, 1998; Maeve, 1999, 2000; Zust, 2009).

Female offenders frequently enter the criminal justice system after years of battering in their intimate adult relationships (Eliason, Taylor & Arndt, 2005). Exposed to high rates of violence and victimization, many female inmates enter prison with backgrounds of poverty and unemployment and a history of prior drug abuse. As a consequence, women enter prison as socially marginal at best, having suffered from personal stress, trauma, and fear in many stages of their lives (Morash, Bynum & Koons, 1998). It is not surprising that high rates of mental illness have been found among incarcerated women (Bradley & Davino, 2002). A frequent psychological consequence of violence against women is posttraumatic stress disorder (PTSD), characterized by intrusive thoughts, nightmares, and flashbacks (Braithwaite, Arriola & Newkirk, 2006). The socioeconomic hardships, combined with extensive histories of violence and abuse, negatively impact the lives of this subgroup of prisoners.

Abused women also suffer from multiple physical health problems as a result of their abusive relationships. Headaches, stomach ulcers, and gastrointestinal problems are only a few physical health-related problems that victimized women experience (Coker, Smith, Bethea et al., 2000). High blood pressure, epilepsy, migraine, arthritis, and diabetes are other types of health problems that can be aggravated by victimization (Campbell, 2002; Stein & Barrett-Connor, 2000). In addition, battered women may experience other health problems from severe abuse such as undiagnosed hearing and vision problems, dizziness, cognitive difficulties, and concentration issues (Valera & Bernbaum, 2003). Abused women have also been known to have higher rates of stress-related problems such as abdominal pain and appetite loss compared to women without abusive histories. A sample taken from a health maintenance organization found that women with abusive histories reported anywhere from a 50 to 70 percent increase in stress-related health problems (Campbell, 2002).

Reasons for incarceration among battered women may be directly or indirectly related to abuse. The most direct link occurs when a woman is incarcerated for killing her abusive partner. It has been estimated that 72 to 80 percent of women charged with killing their abusive partners accept a plea or are convicted and often receive lengthy prison sentences (Leonard, 2002). A contributing factor to this is that the majority of battered women who kill cannot afford the services of a private attorney at the time of their arrest, and they are frequently assigned public criminal defense representatives who are overworked and underskilled (LaBelle, 2002). Additionally, attorneys who represent battered women who kill may have little understanding of the dynamics of abuse and its psychological responses. Or, these lawyers may be reticent in admitting abuse records into evidence for fear that the prosecution will turn them into a motive for a crime of revenge (Leonard, 2002). The fact that women most often use weapons to kill is another factor in harsh sentencing (Walker, 2000).

Regardless of the crime for which they are sentenced, battered women who are imprisoned may suffer mentally and emotionally as a result of abuse, and prison experiences often exacerbate these illnesses. Women who suffer from PTSD are in an especially precarious environment. Because the deleterious manifestations of this illness are often precipitated by cues that remind victims of their trauma, female inmates with this condition can suffer extreme anxiety, rage, and depression due to mandatory strip searches, male authority figures, and the fear of sexual assault from prison guards (Eliason, Taylor & Arndt, 2005; Kubiak, 2005). Additionally, symptoms of PTSD are sometimes interpreted by prison security as attempts to manipulate or inveigle. Thus, it is not surprising that women who suffer from PTSD have been found to have unique problems with prison adjustment (Eliason, Taylor & Arndt, 2005). In addition to creating problems with prison adjustment, a history of intimate partner abuse also causes difficulties for incarcerated women in transitioning back into the community after release. Because of this, it has been suggested that battered women would benefit from trauma and intimate partner violence interventions while incarcerated (Eliason, Taylor & Arndt, 2005; Leonard, 2002).

Older incarcerated women with a history of abuse may face additional problems. First, women who are now over 50 years of age were raised in an era when child abuse and molestation were not recognized as social problems. In the 1950s and 1960s, there was a prevailing attitude that a man's wife and children were his property and his treatment of them was a private domestic matter (Ratcliff, 2002). As a result, older female prisoners who suffered childhood abuse traumas may have been unlikely or unable to attain succor from legal authorities and social service agencies. If abuse counseling is not available to these women in prison, they may spend their lives without having the ill-effects of abuse addressed or ameliorated. Additionally, contemporary older women grew up in an era that stressed modesty more than our modern times. Based on these assumptions, the physically and sexually invasive atmosphere of prison may be more detrimental.

Early Childhood Experiences

Although the focus of this chapter is primarily on adult abusive relationships, a small number of women felt compelled to discuss the sexual, physical, and emotional abuse they endured as children and adolescents. This sharing is consistent with the findings of earlier prison research emphasizing female victimization (Leonard, 2001; Logan et al., 2006). Additional research with incarcerated women has discovered childhood sexual assault rates ranging from 31 to 48 percent (Campbell et al., 2008). For the women in our sample, sexual abuse was the most frequently mentioned type of abuse, and the majority occurred within families of origin. The most graphically descriptive account of childhood sexual abuse came from a 58-year-old white woman:

> My dad would come into my bedroom every night and wake me up sucking on my breasts—every morning too. He would make me cook breakfast, then pull me down to him to suck on my breasts again and again. He used to make me follow him around like a puppy. He'd use a hand signal when he wanted to molest me. He's made me lie down naked on a blanket out in the end of a bean field so he could see and molest me.

However, several of the women also named other family members who took sexual liberties with them when they were youngsters. According to these accounts, some perpetrators frequently used physical violence or psychological abuse in the form of threats in order to keep the victim silent. The following serve to illustrate the magnitude of such abuses:

I was sexually abused by my brother from the age of eight to thirteen years old. He would beat me and use me the way he wanted to. He would tell me if I told, that he would tell Mama and Daddy that it was my fault. In my child mind, I believed him.

I was sexually abused when I was a child by my father. He told me that he would beat me until he killed me if I told anybody. I told my mother but she would not say a word. This abuse continued for several years and I felt terrible about the fact that I was alone and no one seemed to care.

I was a child with no one to turn to. I had to contend with being raped at my brothers' and my father's will—whenever they wanted to. I was beaten, have had a broken arm, broken both my feet from kicking, black eyes and bruising all over my body.

Inmates who provided these and similar testimonies also reported numerous negative consequences associated with their history of childhood abuse. Feelings of vulnerability, helplessness, and perceived inability to escape from abuse were frequently expressed. Other victims reported feelings of guilt and shame as a result of the trauma. As one woman stated, "This abuse made me feel dirty and alone and it made me not trust people." Another countered, "Until I came to prison, I thought I deserved punishment. I figured I wasn't a good person." These feelings of self-blame were linked with guilt feelings and reactions to abuse later in life. As one childhood sexual abuse survivor mentioned, "Later, when I was raped, I felt that it was my fault and therefore didn't even report it to the police or anyone else."

The deleteriousness of the types of abuse respondents reported cannot be overstated. Scientists have found that this abuse damages the chemistry and structure of the brain and adversely affects thinking, memory, and emotions (Conklin, 2004). Two respondents affirmed this actuality:

During my school years, I was mentally warped. I couldn't concentrate much less comprehend anything, so I didn't do very well. I quit two weeks before the end of my eighth grade year. I just didn't have the mental strength to continue.

So, from the beginning [of the abuse] up to recently, I completely shut myself down mentally and stopped emotionally growing. I still feel disconnected from where I should be in my life. My childhood—and as far as that goes—my entire life has been devastated and stolen from me. My life feels empty and worthless and I have not been able to overcome it. I let my family take advantage of me.

It is understandable that victims of childhood abuse would be anxious to leave home as soon as possible, and this could have created haste in finding a boyfriend or husband. However, several of the women mentioned going from an abusive situation in their family of orientation right into another with their chosen partner. As one inmate explained, "I married in 1968 to get away from my dad. That lasted 18 months. Then I married a second time to a very abusive man—mentally and physically." The link between childhood abuse and the likelihood of ending up in a violent adult relationship is complex, and attempted escape from childhood and adolescent abuse is but one factor. However, most women do not intentionally enter into adult relationships with batterers. The violent potential is often revealed later. As one victim acknowledged: "I married right after high school graduation. He would hold me and tell me that he loved me. He had never drank that I knew of until our honeymoon when, due to his age [19], he paid a man to buy him alcohol. He immediately became abusive and mean. Yes, I should have seen the writing on the wall, but I was blind!"

Adult Partner Abuse

Abuse is frequently categorized as verbal, physical, social, sexual, psychological, and controlling threats (Eliason, Taylor & Arndt, 2005). As Table 6.1 reveals, about 75 percent of participants reported their partner had made verbal insults toward them on a frequent basis. Additionally, about 80 percent of the women said their partner had frequently sworn at them, screamed and yelled at them, and insulted them in front of others. As one inmate stated, "He was always mentally abusing by insulting me by saying ugly things like I wasn't good for anything." Making statements like, "I'll beat or kill you if you tell anyone," or just "yelling obscenities" was frequently mentioned by those who were victims of repeated verbal abuse. Threats were also a common practice for perpetrators, who often used this tactic as a means of controlling their partners.

There is additional evidence that emotional abuse was a common pattern in the abusive relationships. Emotional abuse includes much more than an abusive husband calling his wife degrading names. This form of spousal abuse can have far-reaching repercussions for the victim and leaves scars that require long-term treatment. The overwhelming majority of abused women felt their partner had frequently made them feel stupid or unintelligent and that the abuser had little respect for the

Table 6.1 Partner Abuse Frequency by Abuse Type (percentage; n = 163)

Abuse Measure	Never	Rarely	Pretty Often	Very Often
Verbal abuse				
Verbal insults toward me	12.9	10.0	35.7	41.4
Told me I am ugly and unattractive	36.2	15.9	15.9	31.9
Insulted me in front of others	15.5	15.5	29.6	39.4
Screamed and yelled at me	10.0	10.0	30.0	50.0
Insulted or swore at me	8.6	11.4	28.5	51.4
Physical abuse				
Punched me with his fist	21.4	20.0	22.9	35.7
Beat me so badly I had to get medical help	29.0	20.3	18.8	31.9
Slapped me around my face and head	21.1	21.1	18.3	39.4
Tried to choke me	30.4	26.1	14.5	29.0
Pushed, grabbed, or shoved me	11.1	15.3	37.5	36.1
Social abuse				
Was jealous and suspicious of my friends	7.1	10.0	20.0	62.9
Acted like I was his personal servant	20.0	12.9	27.2	40.0
Didn't want me to socialize with friends	8.6	15.7	21.4	54.3
Sexual abuse				
Made me perform sexual acts	42.3	18.4	17.0	22.5
Forced me to have sex	37.1	11.4	22.8	28.6
Psychological abuse				
Made me feel stupid	20.3	10.1	24.6	44.9
Had no respect for my feelings	9.9	9.8	25.4	54.9
Treated me like I was unintelligent	22.1	14.7	20.6	42.6
Controlling threats				
Became angry when drinking too much	5.9	7.2	17.4	59.4
Became angry if I disagreed with him	9.9	12.6	39.4	38.0
Threatened me with a weapon	26.1	18.8	20.2	34.8
Ordered me around	9.9	14.1	19.8	56.3
Acted like a bully toward me	14.7	16.2	16.2	52.9
Acted as if he would like to kill me	11.8	14.8	30.9	42.6
Tended to be extremely jealous	7.4	5.9	29.4	57.4

victim or her feelings. For example, one older female described her controlling husband as someone who had little, if any, regard for her. As she stated, "He had sex with other women in front of me and other women stayed in my house with us. He would put me out and then beat me when I would leave." Two abused women illustrate how their abuser used "put downs" to make them feel worthless and reduce their self-esteem:

> He became violent without much warning and usually when he wanted to drink and couldn't. He'd pick fights over nothing so he could go off and drink. He'd put me down to make himself feel somehow superior since I was a college graduate and he'd only finished 9th grade.

> He always belittled me in public, but somehow made it look like my fault. He would get up and leave when we were in restaurants. The first few times the boys and I would leave and search for him. As they grew up, we started to finish our meal before searching.

Other emotional abuse included the severe humiliation of the victim—as the following woman's testimony demonstrates: "My husband slapped me in front of a room full of people. He made me dance in front of them, threatening with a pulled knife. I urinated on myself." Based on the responses presented in Table 6.1, it is evident that verbal, social, and psychological abuse as well as controlling threats played an important role in reinforcing the "sense of entitlement" common in traditional male abusers. It is obvious that many of the abused women lived in constant fear of their lives as they were frequently threatened with a weapon. When abusive husbands feel they have the right to "run the show," they tend to use any means necessary to control their victims. The use of controlling measures such as anger, verbal threats, weapons, or other bullying tactics make victims often feel they are at the mercy of these coercive acts, which are introduced to control, dominate, or punish them.

Other factors with emotional consequences include partners who exhibit jealousy and frequently attempt to isolate the victim. Perpetrators are often extremely jealous of their partners and invent or exaggerate the victim's attention to and from other men. Batterers may also be jealous of attention that victims receive from friends, family, and coworkers. As a result, abusers tend to isolate their partners. This is done in an attempt to control the victim as well as to hide the abuse. Victims are often compliant with isolation or seek it themselves in an attempt to guard the secret of abuse. The result is that battered women become cut off from sources of support and potential escape alliances (Gagne, 1998). As Table 6.1 displays, abusive partners were typically highly jealous and suspicious of their partners and seemed to constantly monitor their relationships with friends.

Perhaps one of the most obvious effects of domestic violence is the impact of physical injury that women frequently sustain. Not surprisingly, research indicates that battered women are more likely to visit emergency rooms and private physicians than nonbattered women (Greenfield, Rand & Craven, 1998). Both minor and severe injuries have been identified with women involved in intimate-partner violent relationships. Although the various forms of physical abuse presented in Table 6.1 were not quite as likely as other forms of abuse reported by this group of incarcerated older women, over 70 percent of the women stated that their partners had pushed, grabbed, or shoved them at least pretty often; whereas about 60 percent said they had been slapped around the face and head. Approximately one-third of the women reported their partners frequently punching them with their fist and beating them so badly they had to get medical help. For example, one battered inmate remarked, "[He] broke 17 bones in my body, gave me numerous cuts requiring stitches, black eyes, shot me in the face causing a broken jaw, [I] lost several teeth, [and] had many surgeries." A wide variety of other serious injuries were reported, including multiple broken bones and other head and eye injuries. The following are a sampling of the tragic physically abusive situations described by these older women in their 50s, who courageously reflect about their domestic abuse and violent histories:

He shot my dog in front of me. He was mad at the dog. He hit my horse in the nose with a metal pipe. He pushed me down and broke my wrist as well as kicking and throwing things at me. He was careful not to leave any marks.

In 13 years, we had about 30 violent encounters resulting in numerous broken bones, black eyes, stitches, etc. I finally left him in 1996. He found me and shot me in the face. He then called police and then waited for them. I had numerous surgeries, but obviously survived.

I have numerous scars on my neck, wrist, hand, and knee that came from his knife. He would choke me until I would fall down and pull my hair till I would think my eyes would come out. He told me I was no good and that he would knock my head off and use it for a trash can.

I mistakenly took lust for love and when I finally came out of this relationship the beatings started. I was pushed off the second story building which resulted in broken ribs, a broken arm, my eye socket and nose were torn and broken. The police did nothing because of my being unconscious. He told the police a story about me being a paranoid schizophrenic and that it was my idea to jump.

As for sexual abuse, over one-half of the women reported that they were forced to either have sex or their partner made them perform sexual acts against their wishes. Several women described violent and degrading encounters with their husbands that frequently led to multiple forms of abuse that occurred simultaneously:

> The worst part was he threw me on the bed, pulled my arms back, put his knees in my shoulders [to] hold me down. That night he rape[d] me and [urinated] inside of me. He kicked me between my legs, and hit me on the top of my head with his fists.

> The physical abuse was daily. I'd get things thrown in my face like coffee or water or other times I would be slapped. I've been in the shower only to have an AK-47 pointed at my face and told I was going to die and then later raped for hours.

Of course, other women also provided testimony regarding their sexual assault. Certainly the high rates of victimization across the life span of incarcerated women warrant further study in terms of perpetrators of abuse as well as the experiences of victims in order to develop more tailored treatment programs (Campbell et al., 2008).

Individual Risk Factors

Participants were asked to cite factors that contributed to crimes of violence against them. As the women gave examples of the violent episodes they had encountered over the years, several overriding themes emerged. The first of these discussed previously is the "power and control" batterer who utilizes violence to get his partner to comply with his wishes. We have already provided several examples of this risk factor. The second type of batterer frequently described is the mentally ill perpetrator who may suffer from depression, bipolar disorders, coexisting paranoid and schizophrenic disorders, and obsessive compulsive disorders. As one woman, who had all ten of her fingers broken, recalled, "He has a significant mental disorder. I would say he is bipolar, but he has never been diagnosed or treated." Other women complained of their partners having severe personality disorders, which they felt contributed to their abusive situations. Looking back, they can now see more clearly the complex domestic abuse situation they had encountered for years. As one inmate expressed, "I'm sorry all of this happened as I know now that he was sick. I tried to get him into a mental hospital, but he promised me on his release he would kill me and our sons." Another stated: "I feel that he was bipolar and he wouldn't take medication for it. I just felt that the more love and care I showed him would help, but I found out that I was not qualified to help my own husband. This situation was very frustrating, but you can't help people who won't help themselves."

An additional risk factor frequently mentioned for domestic partner violence among this group of inmates is regular drug and alcohol use. This is true whether one or both partners are using. As is well known, drugs and alcohol impair judgment. This impairment has been frequently linked to precipitating violence among batterers (Bogat, Levendosky & Von Eye, 2005; Walker, 2000). For female victims of domestic partner abuse, the relationship between substance use and domestic abuse is more complex. For instance, the use and abuse of drugs and alcohol has been related to partner assault as both a precursor and a consequence (Jarvis, Copeland & Walton, 1998). "Getting high" may be a means of escaping the stresses and pains of abuse for battered women, but it may also lessen a victim's ability and resolve to leave a violent relationship, and it may create a more volatile atmosphere and precipitate aggression.

Over half of the women stated that their abuser became angry when he drank too much. Once the violence did begin in the participants' intimate relationships, it often became severe. This became apparent as women gave examples of their most devastating episodes of abuse—including physical battering and rape:

He drank alcohol every day and stayed out with his friends all night, come home and want to have sex with alcohol smell on his breath. He'd hold me down until he finished.

He was on drugs real bad. We both were drinking a lot and we got to fighting and I had a knife and he was holding my hand with the knife so when he turned loose the knife, it went that way into him.

When we both were drinking, we'd both get high, and we both get to fighting. When he got mad, he did not care what he picked up and hit you with. I was injured numerous times when he lost complete control.

While not all alcoholic families appear to include physical, sexual, or emotional abuse, we know that substance abuse—alcohol abuse in particular—frequently emerges as the prominent risk factor contributing to family problems. In many cases, violent behavior results from a combination of the situation, consumption of the drug, and individual personalities involved (Flanzer, 2005). The excessive use of drugs or alcohol can act as a disinhibitor releasing pent-up anger, especially in those in a hyperirritable state and who possess a quick temper. Additionally, alcohol use has been found to cause women to downplay their own views of physical and sexual aggression (Logan et al., 2006; Norris & Kerr, 1993).

Should I Stay or Leave?

It is a common occurrence for abused women to express conflicted feelings about the intervention process. Many women expressed ambivalent emotions toward violent intimate partners, making the response a very complex decisionmaking process. While victims do not want the abuse to continue, they may want to maintain a relationship with the abuser in a safe, nonthreatening environment. Compared with younger women, older adults may have been together for many years and the victim may actually value the longevity of the relationship. Also, many older women may lack the opportunity for education or the possibility of acquiring job skills that would make them more financially independent (Zink et al., 2003). Cultural, spiritual, or intergenerational values may also make divorce or separation unthinkable. As one 63-year-old woman who has permanent injuries to her back and retina describes her abusive relationship:

> I was forced to stay with my husband because my family does not believe in divorce. He has beaten me frequently since our marriage began. After we had children he would threaten to kill them. I once left him and took the children and he called my family and threatened to kill himself. I had to return to that hell. He has knocked me down stairs more than once and one time it resulted in a premature birth. I had two miscarriages due to his abuse and once when I divorced him because he was sexually molesting one of our children, I was forced to remarry him because my family disowned me. This merely added an approval for him to continue the abuse.

Several other women also discussed the fact that family members tended to deny the abuse, blame the victim for their abusive situation, or be hostile to the idea of breaking up the family. Additional research has further argued that the notion that the family ought to be preserved at whatever cost has infiltrated the teachings of various religious institutions (Foss & Warnke, 2003; Nash & Hesterberg, 2009). This notion has led to inconsistent responses to domestic violence, if not substantial support for patriarchy and violence against women.

Other researchers have noted that women claim to remain in love with their abusers, and this prompts them to accept apologies and believe in promises to change (Anderson et al., 2003; Fugate et al., 2005). The cycle of violence, which includes shifts between violence and acts of loving contrition, may further cause dichotic emotions in women abused (Liang et al., 2005). Moreover, abusers often emotionally entrap victims by manipulating their self-esteem—telling them that they are loved, but they brought the abuse upon themselves (Wolf et al., 2003). As one inmate noted, "I loved him and I did not want to accept reality—that this was a deadly relationship. I still wanted to believe it was going to change, because he could be so nice." In particular, making a decision to leave can be difficult for women who have been in long-term relationships. Having weathered abusive situations for an extended period of time makes the decision even more difficult. One inmate in her 60s who was in an abusive relationship for 18 years illustrates this dilemma:

> A woman will continue believing that the man is going to change and keep going back like I did. He would come around and tell me he wouldn't hit me any more if I went back with him. He would end up hitting me and really beating me. So finally he grabbed the phone away from me when I was calling the police and tore it out of the wall hitting my oldest son. When I finally got away I never went back.

Actions to Stop the Abuse

For most victims of domestic abuse, the initial preference is to develop a strategy to end or reduce the significance of the abuse. Victims face difficult decisions as they decide how to proceed. Of course, they are concerned about engaging in behaviors that might escalate the abuse or they may fear for the safety of their children. The effectiveness of establishing appropriate interventions is often measured by the successes associated with a reduction in physical violence. Victims often turn to a variety of community agencies and other external supports. As Table 6.2 indicates, a common response to reduce abuse in a relationship was the attempt to get help from the police. Over half of participants (54.5 percent) said they called 911 (police) when abuse occurred, and in many instances, the abuse was reported multiple times with varying degrees of success. It should be noted that in 46 percent of the cases, the perpetrator was actually arrested.

As a rule, law enforcement's acknowledgment and response to

Table 6.2　Actions and Assistance to Stop the Violence (n = 163)

Intervention Measures	Percentage
Specific actions taken	
Tried to get a restraining order	40.0
Took out a restraining order	26.6
Filed for a divorce	53.2
Got a separation	30.5
Filed charges against him	40.0
Had him arrested	46.2
Called 911 when he abused you	54.5
Moved out of the home	71.2
Moved him out of the home	41.7
Tried to hide from him, leave, or run away	75.0
Sought outside help	
Courts/judge	30.0
Religious leader	16.9
Doctor/nurse	26.8
Counselor/therapist	18.3
Lawyer	23.9
Support group	8.5
Women's shelter	9.9
Family	63.4
Friends	60.9
Other	8.5

spousal assault has been slow in coming. Research has shown that police have historically neglected battered women's requests for protection (Moe & Ferraro, 2007). There remains a persistent tendency for police officers to view women reporting abuse as noncredible and unworthy of police time and effort. Officers who respond to domestic incidents often fail to report these as crimes or fail to file any report at all. Additionally, women who call the police risk their own arrest if they used physical force in defense (Leonard, 2002). Frequently, intervention through the criminal justice system, such as the filing of restraining orders or filing for separation, only increases the anger and aggression of the batterer. And, if a woman decides to pursue further legal action, she may find herself revictimized by prosecution members who demand descriptions of physical and sexual events (Ratcliff, 2002). Even today, with mandatory laws requiring officers to make an arrest when called to a domestic violence scene, some police officers would rather not get involved in a domestic matter. While some of the women reported that police intervention was effective in immediately stopping the violence, other respondents consistently reported mixed or negative experiences dealing with the police or the legal system as indicated by the following narratives:

> The police always responded, but no one was ever taken to jail. One time I just had the police take me from my husband and went with them to the police station. I called my mother to come and get me.

> The police I contacted said they couldn't do anything without blood-shed. The times he broke my bones or caused stitches he was briefly apprehended. He didn't do any significant time until he shot me.

> The police just looked at me and said you don't have a bloody nose or broke legs so I'm not going to report it. My attorney told me to go back home and let him file the papers to get my husband removed from the home. He attack[ed] me that night and I defended my life.

Consistent with earlier research, the reluctance of police to arrest a batterer at all or confine him for any substantial amount of time can prove detrimental for a vulnerable victim (Ferraro, 1997; Moe & Ferraro, 2007; Wolf et al., 2003). This lack of response has serious consequences because a woman risks retaliation from her abuser after procuring police involvement. Additionally, women who have ineffective or negative experiences with police response may become less likely to call for police help during future episodes of violence. Also, problems within the criminal justice system are the secondary reason women do not leave abusive relationships (Barnett, 2000). Several of the abused women quickly learned that the more frequently they called for police protection to no avail, the more likely their abusers learned that they could continue the abusive tactics without any major repercussions.

As Table 6.2 suggests, the battered women used a variety of other options in attempting to get their abuser to stop the violent behavior. Although there was no attempt to gather information that would have provided insights into the order of such strategies, this feedback does enable us to see the elaborate measures the victims used to escape their abusive situations. The most universal method (75 percent) was trying to hide, leave, or run away. Another 71 percent of the women said they tried to move out of the home. In other situations (41 percent), the women described moving the perpetrator out of the home. However, physically separating from the abuser was not always a successful strategy, as numerous women described overwhelming difficulty in leaving their violent relationships. Certainly, making the decision to leave an abusive relationship is difficult for many women; reaching a permanent separation can be even more difficult as the pulls and pushes of the emotional tie with the abuser may continue indefinitely.

The process of terminating the relationship usually involved leaving and returning several times. Of course, contributing factors that could inhibit leaving might include the presence of children, economic barriers, or simply the lack of determination to exit the abusive relationship. Likewise, research has also shown that ending relationships does not necessarily mean a cessation of violence (Zink et al., 2006). As one inmate voiced, "No matter what I did, where I moved, he always found me; even after the divorce. When he found me, he beat me even worse." Yet another battered victim, who had made an honest attempt for a clean break, describes how the abuse continued after the divorce: "He only agreed to give me a divorce if I allowed him to live in our basement. I did and it was as bad if not worse on me. He would come to my bedroom door and make sounds to let me know he was there and several times [he] broke in to force sex." Other women in the sample indicated that they never called the police or attempted to leave the relationship for fear of retaliation.

> The most devastating time was when my husband was under the influence of crack cocaine and I told him that I was divorcing him. He beat me severely and pulled his 9 millimeter on me and told me he'd kill me first. . . . He constantly called my friends' house and ordered me to come back home. They were afraid and told me I had to leave. Once when I return[ed] home, he flattened my car tires and assaulted me. I later had a miscarriage due to severe beating and being kicked.

In at least one situation, the victim was abused by none other than an officer of the police force. Many such victims do not report their victimization because they fear that the case will be handled by officers who know the abuser or simply will handle the case informally without taking an official complaint. This was the case for a battered woman of 22 years who eventually divorced her abusive husband with strong encouragement from her family. However, the emotional abuse continued when the ex-husband and his girlfriend continued to call and harass her. This battered woman provides the following summary, which describes an unhappy ending:

> All I can say about my abuse is my partner was a police officer and he would say to me all the time he was the law and he could do what he wanted to, and he did for 22 years. I finally got tired of his girlfriend calling for years and saying ugly things and telling me I was no good. I lost control and killed his girlfriend because I didn't know what to do. I was abused all over my body and mind.

Approximately one-half of the women who responded indicated they were charged with homicide, which ultimately ended the violence directed toward them. The overwhelming majority were either already separated or divorced, trying to leave or end the relationship, when the deadly event took place. It has been reported that battered women who strike back in a deadly fashion toward their abusers have been found to experience more severe trauma than other abused women (Bright & Bowland, 2008). Usually, those who respond with force have extensive abuse histories of incest and physical abuse as children as well as sexual and physical torture by their husband (Beattie & Shaughnessy, 2000). As one victim explained:

> I have been married three times and all were abusive. I grew up in abuse. My mother was mentally and physically abusive. I was molested for the first time as a small child [around 4 or 5 years of age]. I was later sexually abused by my uncle by marriage and then by my dad. I have been beaten with a baseball bat. I have had two black eyes and a broke nose numerous times. I have been arrested because I ran out of my house from him. My husband tried to have sex through my rectum and I wouldn't let him so he beat me with his fist and kicked me in my private area and stomach. All this was 21 years ago. That is how long I have been incarcerated.

In other cases, it was evident that some women killed their abusers because it was either the victim's life or their children's. Sometimes it may be a conscious choice, but other times it can be an immediate action taken for the purpose of self-defense.

> When he got off top of me and I was shaking so bad, the knife just hit him, but I did not know. It was never my intention to kill him, just to protect myself. He was chasing me and I shot him. Those last words I heard him say, "one of us ain't gonna live." I had heard those words over and over, but they never affected me, but they did this time when I seen the look in his eyes.

Searching for Community Support

Many times the choices available to victims of violence are limited or not realistic or reasonable. For example, in some cases, support groups or a safe shelter may not be available in every community. It has been acknowledged (Moe & Ferraro, 2007) that for some women who attempt to flee an abusive situation, homelessness and poverty are often inevitable consequences. One respondent who had reported her abusive relationship to the police around 20 times made this comment about the lack of community resources: "He came and cried and begged me to come back and I did. Boy I wish I'd never ever stayed after he started hitting me, but I had no place to go with my children. The welfare people told me they couldn't help me unless I had a home and to just go knock on people's doors and ask to stay." Some women have not always revealed the source or nature of their injuries due to fear of harm from their partner and due to shame and embarrassment. Research has revealed that, in the past, those in the medical community who treated the bruises and broken bones never inquired how the injuries occurred (Campbell et al., 2008; Coben, Forjuoh & Gondolf, 1999). Another problem associated with community response involves the political dilemmas associated with assigning abuse to a set of behaviors. It has been reported that significant dissimilarities continue to exist among state adult protective units in how programs are administered, and in how abuse is defined and reported (Goodrich, 1997).

Many of the women tried to go seek assistance from a variety of community resources (see Table 6.2). Some choices included women's shelters, support groups, religious leaders, and doctors along with several others. Seeking help from family (63.4 percent) and friends (60.9 percent) was the most common strategy participants used. Other studies have shown that abused women turn to family and friends for help more often than any other source (Fugate et al., 2005; Moe & Ferraro, 2007). Commensurate with our findings, it has been found that responses of friends and relatives vary greatly. Some researchers have found friends and family to be judgmental and lacking empathy (Moe & Ferraro, 2007). On the other hand, help from friends and family has been found to be an important form of external validation and a key element in a woman's decision and ability to leave a violent relationship (Jacobson & Gottman, 1998). Thus, the lack of support from loved ones can prove costly to the psyche of a battered victim. The following provides the mixed messages this victim was receiving from family and friends: "Police came once and threaten[ed] to lock him up so he begged off. His family and friends made excuses for why he was like he was. My friends and family kept begging me to leave and not take him back. Always said I wouldn't put up with it, but I did for four years." While some of the women stated that family and friends had provided adequate support, others reported getting little or no assistance. Another study of women who spent years in abusive relationships also reported that the responses of friends and family generally depended on several factors, such as the nature of the victim's relationship with her abuser, the number of times she had attempted to leave the abusive relationship, how many children were involved, and whether family and friends also had been threatened (Goodkind et al., 2003). As one woman in our study who had spent many years in an abusive relationship mentioned, "I know my family and friends got tired of my yo-yo rollercoaster relationships." Other inmates mentioned that their families were afraid of the abuser or that family and friends just did not want to get involved. In other cases, the women chose to remain silent about the abuse.

Surviving an Abusive Past

Domestic violence can have a far-reaching impact on its victims and society as a whole. Of course, physical injury is one of the most obvious consequences suffered by victims. Immediate injuries include bruises, contusions, cuts, and broken bones. These injuries generally heal rather quickly and are not perceived as highly serious by most people. However, some domestic violence victims face more serious consequences as a result of these types of injuries. For example, an older person who suffers a broken hip as a result of being pushed down may have significant complications during the healing process. Also, injuries that leave visible scars such as facial disfigurations; loss of teeth, fingers, or toes; or scars on the neck, arms, or legs can have a detrimental effect on the victim. Gunshot wounds, stabbing wounds, burns, and trauma to the head are also excessive injuries that may affect the long-term quality of life of certain victims. Some injuries may prove significant enough to result in loss of mobility due to an incomplete healing process.

In addition to various types of physical injuries suffered by victims of violent crime, victims of sexual assault endure extreme trauma leading to a variety of medical issues. For example, abused women report more symptoms of depression than do women in the general population (Arias, Lyons & Street, 1997; Campbell, Kub & Rose, 1996). Based on measures from the Hopkins Health Symptom Inventory, we found that older female inmates reporting being abused as a child or adult were significantly more likely to report higher levels of depression, somatization, anxiety, and chronic health problems when compared to those inmates who reported no abusive histories. Our finding is supported by a cross-sectional study of about 2,500 female inmates in state and federal correctional facilities, of which about one-half report suffering from an abusive relationship prior to incarceration (Lamb, 2010). This study further revealed that this random sample of imprisoned women were more likely to have been treated for PTSD, depressive and anxiety disorders, and a host of other mental health problems.

The long-term consequences of abuse can eventually take its toll on a battered victim. As we earlier documented, a frequent consequence of an abusive past is the participation in drugs or alcohol as a means of coping with the trauma encountered. Research indicates that higher levels of anxiety are reported for older women who are abused, and individuals experiencing multiple traumas are at particularly high risk for symptoms of distress (Hlavka, Kruttschnitt & Carbone-Lopez, 2007). The following account describes how one inmate is making some progress in recovering from an abusive past that started when the victim was in her early 20s and continued for 27 long years:

> I was emotionally distraught and turned to alcohol and drugs. I wanted to resolve the relationship but my feelings kept getting in the way. I just completed a residential substance abuse treatment program where I learned how to handle my feelings, situations, and to detach from relationships. I have learned to be my own person and to identify the difference between healthy and unhealthy relationships. I have to start with setting boundaries and exercising my rights as a person.

Similarly, other women talked about other successful strategies in overcoming the tendency to get involved in abusive relationships. One option mentioned by numerous women was to refrain completely from getting involved in any future relationship with men. "As I look back over my life and my relationships with men I now realize I never picked a man that didn't abuse me in some way. From all that I have read and heard from other women, it makes me think that a good man is hard to find. At the age I am now I believe that I will be better off by myself."

Despite the breadth of negative outcomes associated with violent and prolonged victimization, there is some evidence that many of the women are making an effort to cope with their abusive pasts. However, this can be a slow, tedious process as these women work through a vast range of emotions and trauma associated with their tumultuous pasts. It must be remembered that many of the women are not only dealing with victimization, but also social and emotional constraints and other indicators of social marginalization prior to incarceration.

Summary

This chapter documented that violence across the life span for older incarcerated women has been pervasive and severe. Moreover, patterns and experiences of abuse—as indicated by respondents—were found to be congruent with the abuse histories of women reported in other literature. First, women in this sample reported episodes of physical, sexual, and emotional abuse in childhood and adolescence. This has been found to be the primary commonality shared by adult women who end up in abusive partner relationships. Second, respondents reported that alcohol and drug use or abuse were factors involved with incidents of battering. The presence of narcotics has been associated with intimate-partner violence as both a symptom and a cause of the problem. Initially, some of the women tried to deny the deleteriousness of their abusive situations. However, most respondents eventually attempted to end the abuse. The most common response was to attempt to hide or run away. Additionally, most women tried to turn to others for help, including family, friends, and legal authorities. Some took legal actions including having their partners arrested, filing for separation, or filing for divorce. But, commensurate with findings from other research (Leonard, 2002; Ratcliff, 2002), participants reported that attempts to end abuse were futile or made matters worse.

Certain implications arise from the results of this chapter. First, the levels of physical and sexual assault reported in this study have potential for long-lasting psychological, physical, and behavioral outcomes. Thus, there are implications for interventions and programs in our prison systems. While on-site programs for survivors of domestic violence are slowly becoming available, there is a need for their increased frequency and availability (Browne, Miller & Maguin, 1999). It has been suggested that battered women would benefit from trauma and intimate-partner violence interventions while incarcerated (Eliason, Taylor & Arndt, 2005; Leonard, 2002). Not only would this improve the potential for prison adjustment, it would increase the chances of successful reintegration back into the community (Morash, Haarr & Rucker, 1995). Additionally, participants in this research stated a desire to talk about their histories of abuse and to help give support and voice to women currently in battering relationships. It is likely that this would be of benefit to both women incarcerated for violence against their abusers and women who may potentially share their fate.

7

Personal Transformation Behind Bars: An Intimate Look

NOT EVERYONE REACTS THE SAME WAY TO THE DEHUMANIZING influence of imprisonment. As Sharon McQuiade and John Ehrenreich (1998) have suggested, it is rather easy to construct an image of prison inmates as helpless with their lives totally controlled by the strict rules of a total institution. It should be noted, however, that people have the courage to overcome such an oppressed condition as they demonstrate the ability to carve out a successful niche behind bars despite what might seem like an overwhelming feeling of powerlessness and futility. Because of the unique nature of the interaction between inmates and their settings, one would expect a wide range of adaptive behaviors to emerge. As Thomas Schmid and Richard Jones have stated, "Most prisoners must negotiate the tensions between their preprison identity, the person who they appear to be in prison, and, finally, the one they actually become" (1993, p. 415). The following is a brief account of the personal transformation of one such older female as she provides a glimpse into her ever-changing prison experience.

Judy Holbird was first incarcerated from 1982 to 1985 in the Oklahoma prison system for committing a robbery in 1979. Several years later, she was sentenced to a total of 166 years for committing a series of similar robberies in Arkansas. For more than 20 years, the women's prison in Arkansas has been her home away from home. Judy has survived the harsh living conditions of three different prison compounds as she and her lifer friends have witnessed the rapid growth in the actual number of incarcerated women who share a common space. Her story provides a vivid account of the hidden world of women's prison. While this story is unique, Judy is no doubt representative of many other forgotten women who have spent the majority of their adult lives "aging in place" behind bars. Since age 21, Judy has lived with the painful loss of her father who, by all accounts, was murdered execution style in his driveway with a shotgun blast to the back of his head on January 23, 1968. This incident was especially difficult for Judy and her family because the murder was never solved. While the autopsy ruled out suicide or an accidental cause of death, the inexperienced sheriff failed to adequately preserve the homicide crime scene. Without a motive or any readily available evidence, the killer was never brought to justice. In addition to this tragedy, as a poverty-stricken victim of child and spousal abuse, her story mirrors the life experiences of so many incarcerated women today who, for a variety of reasons, now find themselves, 20 or 30 years after their crime, being warehoused alongside more-violent and less-adaptive younger offenders.

Judy mentioned that she discovered several years into her lengthy sentence that writing could be a valuable form of therapy in coping with her many stressful life experiences. As she notes: "My optimistic character developed when I realized my talent, my gift, was in writing down thoughts as an exercise like dear diary feelings. I feel the spirit burning with passion to let my words and thoughts, emotions, and facts be heard." In the course of presenting Judy's story, we will examine how she has survived the struggles of incarceration and created certain choices that have enriched her life while behind bars. Although it is impossible to touch upon all the facets of her life experiences, every attempt is made to exemplify Judy's strength, resiliency, and coping mechanisms as she transcends the loss of freedom and copes with the deprivations of imprisonment. Perhaps a good starting point is to explore a few of the more compelling aspects of her childhood as the very foundation of her existence is examined.

The Early Years

A Native American from the Choctaw Nation, Judy was born and raised in Red Oak, Oklahoma. Her childhood experiences were typical for any young female growing up in the 1950s in a small rural community such as Latimer County where traditional values prevailed. With two parents who loved each other and their children, Judy's upbringing was a rather disciplined one where whippings for misbehavior were generally the custom. Although frequently on the receiving end of her share of spankings, Judy never doubted that her parents cared for her deeply. She acknowledged that the "light of joy, happiness, love, and pride were in her parents' eyes for her." On the mere surface, Judy's early childhood was fundamentally sound as she experienced life with a family that exhibited the propensity to frequently help others whose lot in life was less fortunate. However, this innocent and sheltered childhood was rudely disrupted when this young girl was sexually molested by two uncles at two separate stages of her youth.

These abusive encounters set into motion a life-changing decision that would forever dramatically affect her life opportunities. For it was during that summer of 1962 that Judy, at age 15 and just having completed the ninth grade, first met the man that she would soon marry. Hoping to escape her abusive past, Judy entered into what would become a tumultuous relationship filled with numerous hardships and emotional pain. As Judy recollects, "I did not marry for love, but for the opportunity of getting to what I thought was a safer place." She acknowledges that the first thought of marriage was actually hers; when the time was right she did the actual proposing and to her delight marriage was imminent. Her personal career goal was to be a homemaker like her mother with three boys and three girls. She states "I wanted a working man and someone who wasn't too ugly looking for the children's sake . . . someone who valued home and family—someone like my daddy." As Judy recalls:

> I presented my skills of cooking, cleaning, laundering . . . I could even hunt, garden, tend to livestock, can/preserve foods, and I wasn't unpleasant to look at. I was also strong enough to do man's work. . . . When he first laid eyes on me, that's exactly what I was doing—bucking hay on the back of a flat bed truck in the middle of a hay field in the noon-time sun of Oklahoma in the July heat.

With a rather quick courtship, Judy married a man she hardly knew and who at the time of the marriage was, without her knowledge, AWOL from the army. Judy states that by the time she had become the mother of their first child, she knew that her husband was having sexual relations with other women. Married to an older and very controlling man who periodically was physically and sexually abusive, Judy found herself at his mercy. The family moved from place-to-place on a whim with ventures to Texas, Georgia, Arkansas, and California, and then finally back to Oklahoma. As Judy explains: "My husband never explained his decisions to me. It was just what he wanted done or what he did without explanation. A lot of decisions he made and put into place I know not even today how they came into being—his insensitive plan and how he came up with so many life changing decisions and moves during our marriage." Judy gave birth to five children, although her first child lived only a short time because of premature birth. By age 17, she had her first living child and at this young age led a life filled with hard work and heartbreak. While doing her very best to please her husband and finding ways to feed and clothe her children, the marriage that was so desired as a young teenager never reached its potential. After 17 years of marriage, Judy felt in many respects that she was married to a total stranger, someone she did not fully know or understand. With a life void of emotional closeness and togetherness, Judy acknowledges her awareness that the womanizing was becoming more obvious with each passing year. In fact, she describes an incident when her husband openly brought another woman into their life with the intention of proposing an "open marriage" arrangement. Realizing that she had only fallen in love with "the man he could be" and when it became obvious to her that he would never turn away from chasing other women, she made the decision to walk away. The negative consequence of Judy's marital journey is expressed with the following comment: "So you surely should know by now, as I do, that I've walked in some dark places—painful places—lonely places, and I have walked through things I would rather not of ever known or experienced."

Looking back many years later, Judy holds some regrets for not confronting her husband sooner, for she understands now that had she not left the relationship when she did, prison would probably not be a reality. However, she chose to hide her pain and anguish and to remain silent, suffering from emotional abuse and feelings of rejection.

Pathway to Prison

Scholars have suggested that women's incarceration can be attributed largely to a variety of unsolved social issues such as drug addiction, victimization, poverty, family fragmentation, and mental health problems (Acoca, 1998; Owen & Bloom, 1995; Salisbury & Van Voorhis, 2009). In Dana DeHart's (2008) study focusing on women's "pathways to prison," she reported that many of the women in her study talked about specific "turning points" in their lives that contributed to their participation in unlawful activities. For example, significant turning points over the life span could be times when women's lives changed rapidly as a result of situations such as divorce, violence, poverty, or illness. As a result, many women are forced to make hard choices with few viable options. At age 32, this view describes Judy's reaction to her "marginalized" state of existence:

In 1979, I reached my crisis point—breaking point. Starting out from nothing, dead broke, and where you have no education and no professional skills and yes even accepting a few handouts . . . I began waiting tables during the day and working as a bar waitress at night. I realized from my own financial concerns that I would benefit from a lump sum to put all my affairs in order to include the upcoming school year and needs for all four of my children. While drinking ice tea with several friends who were also facing their own financial crisis, the idea of conducting a robbery was conceived. I proposed the logical means as a robbery like in the old west days—Pretty Boy Floyd—Bonnie & Clyde—only not a bank, but a business that would have thousands of dollars in U.S. green cash on hand. We chose a business I'd once worked at some years before, both in the meat department and as a checkout cashier—a large supermarket that drew customers county wide and kept a large amount of cash on hand to cash government checks around the first of the month.

Using an elaborate disguise and 13 miles of two-lane state highway to reach her dirt road escape route, Judy pulled off the robbery working alone so her children and younger friends would not be implicated with armed robbery should there be any problems along the way. While the official record reported the robbery amount at over $13,000, Judy contends the take was in the neighborhood of $2,000. As Judy notes, "the money went too fast and accomplished almost nothing for my situation."

Although the robbery went off without a hitch, Judy was recognized and eventually arrested along with her teenage daughter, her lone codefendant, who was a passenger in the car. Judy describes in detail the testimony used to convict her for this crime. Since the evidence was only circumstantial in putting Judy at the crime scene, the first trial ended in a hung jury. However, a retrial resulted in her conviction and Judy, now at the age of 34, was sentenced to the least allowed time—a six-year sentence. Despite her classification as a violent crime offender, Judy was assigned to the Minimum Security Center in Oklahoma City. There she resided in a converted old motel serving much of her time as a trustee working at the Oklahoma Highway Patrol Training Center and in the pilot-project trash crew, where she picked up litter around highway medians, streets, and highway off ramps. Eventually, Judy became the first violent-crime female inmate to be placed on "house arrest" release with no monitoring attachments. At the work release center, Judy describes her many special privileges:

I was allowed to wear street clothes during all my incarceration. I had my own bath and bed linens as well as being allowed numerous personal items such as a TV, stereo, typewriter, tape recorder, alarm clock, camera and numerous electrical appliances such as coffeemaker, electric skillet, crock pot, a blow dryer and hot rollers and even a curling iron. True, your space was limited, but the living quarters were more in line with what is socially acceptable in a domestic setting.

A model prisoner who completed her GED in 1982, Judy was discharged in April of 1985, at which time she returned to her family and life on the outside. Her early release was made possible by the "extra" good time (three days for one served), which came off the back side of her six-year sentence. She left prison with a felony conviction against her name and $400 in cash saved while working at her prison job.

However, Judy's experience with the criminal justice system was far from finished, and a little under three years later in February of 1988, she became involved in another crime spree in Fort Smith, Arkansas. Now 41 years of age, Judy and her son Jared (age 21), daughter Lisa (age 24), and a family friend also in his 20s, and the only one with transportation, put together a scheme to rob a Pizza Hut, the Price-So-Low Grocery, followed quickly by the Mug and Jug. Again seeking money to support her family, Judy took the lead in planning and committing the crimes. Judy again went to great lengths to disguise her identity by wearing a wig, elaborate makeup, and multiple layers of clothing. While her children played a supportive role in the robberies, it was Judy who carried the gun and who personally confronted the cashiers. About three weeks after the first robbery, Judy was discovered in hiding at her daughter Lisa's newly rented house paid for by money from the robberies. It was at this residence that gunfire was allegedly exchanged between Judy and a rookie detective, resulting in both suffering gunshot wounds. Although Judy still adamantly contends that the officer actually shot himself trying to draw his weapon and that her gun never fired, the charges for this offense remained an important part of her sentencing. Due to the stacking of her numerous charges, Judy received 166 years for aggravated armed robbery, a felon in possession of a firearm, and the shooting of a police detective. For their assistance in one or more crimes, Jared received a 40-year sentence and Lisa, 5 years.

Early Years in ADC

The entrance into a prison setting is not always a smooth or easy transition for offenders to make. Long-term offenders who reflect back on their initial days of incarceration frequently describe the first few days, weeks, months of their sentences as causing them to experience feelings of shock or disbelief toward their surroundings (Leigey, 2007). Women, in particular, encounter numerous frustrations while learning how to cope effectively with the space restrictions that will be imposed on them. Living in close, confined quarters, for example, frequently requires these individuals to relinquish numerous sentimental items that would have otherwise provided them connections to persons who once held significant roles in their lives. In addition, the processes that are directly involved in downsizing one's personal possessions to the contents that can easily be stored in a small box may involve expressing their farewells to items necessary to engage in pastimes they have enjoyed for years (Genders & Player, 1990).

Judy was now about to begin a very different incarceration experience than the one she encountered in Oklahoma several years earlier. She entered prison this time wearing a temporary colostomy as a result of the "gut shot" received from the police detective. As Judy recalls her early prison days: "When I entered ADC [Arkansas Department of Correction] Women's Prison, I had a tight rein on my faith in God and a need to protect my family. I had my pride that would not crack to let others see me cry or in need. I had no grown children out in society to aid me in any manner. I had no husband or living parents either who might otherwise have provided me with assistance." Her sentence began in the punitive section of the prison at the Women's Unit in Pine Bluff before she was confined to the Mental Health Unit. Judy recognized this confinement as an extra precaution because the prison "campus" was actually minimum to medium security with no guard towers with guns and no double-fence razor wire normally associated with maximum security prisons. Although not perfect, the prison environment at this unit could be tolerated. The Mental Health Unit and other barracks had common social visiting areas, a kitchen area with appliances, not to mention bathrooms with private shower and toilet stalls. Her first job assignment in prison was as a laundry porter—washing, drying, and folding clothing. It was here that Judy developed a formal procedure for recording the outgoing and returned laundry and a system to track lost or stolen articles. According to Judy, her system eventually evolved into a standardized "form," which became a required procedure for keeping track of prison laundry and a more comprehensive version is still in use today.

When inmates initially arrived at this unit, they were allowed to wear free-world clothing. A new inmate could select five outfits of used free-world clothing for their very own and they could change out articles from time to time if they were unable to receive clothing from home. Inmates were allowed to receive boxes from home every six months until this privilege was halted in 1993. Inmates were also allowed to keep colored underclothing, housecoats, pajamas, and bedding. Those prisoners who were released from prison, but riding a bus home, were able to pick out clothes to wear home from the secondhand clothing room. This experience was nothing new for Judy who remarked, "I wore secondhand clothing all my life so I had no problem doing that in prison. . . . Clothes do not make a person, but one's selection of clothing can reflect that person's worth." The Pine Bluff Unit functioned with considerable donations from a variety of religious organizations. Hygiene products such as soap, toothpaste, deodorant, toothbrushes, hairbrushes, and combs were all donated and the indigent inmates received a monthly care package of these products. In looking back on her prison career, the early years at Pine Bluff were some of the best for Judy and the women serving time there.

It was at the Pine Bluff Unit where this inmate was also able to participate in the prison plasma program for inmates who were not on medications and currently held a clean health condition. Participants in the program gladly received $7.00 for each plasma donation and could donate up to two times a week. Although the amount eventually decreased to $5.00 per donation, this income provided Judy and other inmates with a financial independence most important to one's self-dignity. As Judy noted, "It meant a lot to me not to have to ask friends or family for money and to allow me simple pleasures such as coffee and tobacco, peanut butter and jelly, ramen noodles and crackers, baby powder, hard candy, and postage for mailing cards to loved ones." In addition, for extra money Judy indicated she often provided legal work for other inmates such as writing presentations for parole board reviews.

In 1993, a drastic change was in order for the female residents at the Pine Bluff Unit when they were relocated to Tucker Prison, a facility previously inhabited by male inmates. A former farm unit, Tucker had been earlier condemned by the state, but was now the new home for Arkansas's female offenders. The occupation of this facility is indicative of the plight of incarcerated women who frequently have been treated as second-class citizens in the criminal justice system for years. Judy summarizes the speech given to the assembly of women in the gym after being unloaded off the buses:

> Based on the current conditions, you'll find the housing areas need major work. The young boys who were housed here were rough and just tore up the place so please bear with us ladies. We will set things

right. . . . We're going to concentrate on one barracks at a time and as
one is renovated we'll fill it and then work on the next barracks just
emptied. Working in this manner we will renovate the entire housing
unit.

This was a challenging living arrangement for Judy, who spent her
first two years at the Tucker facility in a wheelchair because of significant back-leg pains from the bullet lodged in her lower lumbar region.
In fact, she was under full bed rest pending an examination from an outside medical specialist. Upon settling into their new home, it was discovered that the barracks' bathroom showers and sinks and individual
room sinks had only cold running water. In her assigned room, Judy also
discovered that her sink had a significant leak. The metal/chrome-plated
drain joint was decayed and rusted, leaving gaping holes where the
young boys who had occupied the facility prior to the women's arrival
had improvised with plastic wrap and electric tape to minimize leaking
onto the floor. To make matters even more challenging for the women,
for the first few days there was no running water going to the toilet stalls
whatsoever. Judy recalls that "I improvised with a gallon size bubble
gum bucket and by example showed and verbally instructed others on
how to bucket flush the toilets." Although the women had brought along
cleaning rags, Comet cleanser, and disinfectant packs, none of these
materials was helpful with the exposed naked electrical wiring, the bust-
ed holes in the walls big enough to walk through, or the large rats that
were running rampant.

However, in looking back at her five years at the Tucker Unit, the
experience was 110 percent better than the January 1998 transfer to the
newly constructed women's facility in Newport, Arkansas. The new unit
was owned and operated by a private company, Wackenhut, Inc., and
initially the majority of the first employees had little, if any, correctional
experience. According to Judy, the first 10 years spent at this facility
were the hardest of her incarceration because of the overcrowded confinement, abuse of discretion and power by correction officials, and the
majority population of druggies. Judy was confined to an overcrowded
open barracks, which was designed to house 32 inmates, but instead
housed a total of 48. The social area was downsized over the next two
years to make room for additional beds, but no extra toilets, face sinks,
or showers were added to accommodate the increased number of
inmates using these facilities. Such crowded conditions become especially difficult for older inmates such as Judy who frequently are more
likely to thrive in quieter living conditions away from the more aggressive and noisy inmates.

Adapting Across Time

Recent studies conducted on the psychological effects of incarceration have focused on prison adaptation, survival skills, and the methods or means of coping in the face of severely stressful conditions (Haney, 2006). It has been suggested that adaptation to imprisonment is largely imported and that various features of an individual's life prior to incarceration combine to affect the adaptation to imprisonment (Dhami, Ayton & Loewenstein, 2007). Different patterns of adaptation have emerged among prisoners who have been incarcerated for differing amounts of time. For example, those inmates serving long sentences have been shown to immerse themselves into the daily routine of prison life as a way of hiding their vulnerabilities associated with shrinking social contacts from family and friends on the outside (Cobden & Stewart, 1984). In essence, a process of transformation occurs as differing personalities find their own niche. Judy describes inmates in the following way:

> Prisoners are no different than the people of society and a prison community operates much like the places and people in all sectors of levels of society. You'll find the moochers, the whiners, and that class of movers and shakers who seem to flourish and prosper, but still use others to keep a superiority standing. They are the ones to watch out for. You'll easily recognize their flaunting as the devil's tools and they are quick to lie, control, and destroy.

Women who have served a long-term sentence also reported many more problems related to the environmental conditions of the prison compared to those who were relatively new to prison (MacKenzie, Robinson & Campbell, 1989).

In recent years, heightened attention has also been placed on the prison conduct engaged in by older, long-term offenders. As a collective, this group is composed of mature, well-behaved individuals who have no intent to cause disturbances for the larger institutional order. Instead, they may appear to preserve images of themselves as outstanding, model citizens of the prison community. Judy's story reveals, however, that the punitive nature of incarceration does provoke a segment of this population to occasionally provoke conflict for others who reside in their immediate presences. Typically, those who eventually become involved in disciplinary problems entered the system at young ages, have revolved through the system on repeat occasions, and have witnessed external (family) supports reduce the frequency of contact as

time progresses (McShane & Williams, 1990; Leigey, 2007). Any disturbances they provoke are likely to be minor disturbances. Occasionally,
for example, they may elect to ignore or overlook commands staff have
given them, use language that is considered to be unacceptable, collabo-
rate with others to have items they know are contraband delivered to the
institution, or even vandalize or destroy public property (Leigey, 2007).
In most states, elders who are serving long sentences do not cause these
problems with nearly the frequency as their younger counterparts. Some
have estimated that an inmate will reveal such signs of adjustment problems as infrequently as once per year (Florida Corrections Commission,
2002).

Erin George (2010) notes that lifers do not easily adjust to prison
life because it is easy; rather they develop successful coping strategies
to make the most of an extremely difficult situation. Just because prisoners are provided a roof over their heads, three meals a day, clothing, and
other amenities like showers, recreation periods, education programs,
and television, doesn't mean the rigors of a life in prison are not without
significant demeaning consequences. It is not the physical aspects of
confinement but the emotional pain that inmates find so debilitating.
These pains of imprisonment can eventually lead to feelings of being
totally overwhelmed, or in some cases, suicidal ideation. As Judy
reflects: "In the year of 2000, I did think deeply about if this is all there
is left for me? Why be content to just exist in prison bondage? My emotional breaking point was an overwhelming feeling of being tired and all
alone, feeling useless and forgotten. This low point became my multiple
character builders in both tolerance and patience."

It should be noted that Judy entered the ADC as a financially poor
and beaten down woman having lived a life filled with considerable pain
and sorrow. She had turned to crime as a way to provide financially for
her family and then was forced to live with the realization that such a
foolish choice also resulted in the incarceration of her two oldest children. Upon her arrival to prison, Judy experienced overstimulation and
resentment as she was immediately placed in the hole for security purposes. This negative cycle continued for Judy as she tried to manage her
feelings of anger, helplessness, self-hate, abandonment, and betrayal. If
an inmate does not possess adequate impulse control, these feelings are
often released in an ineffective manner such as through aggression
toward other inmates or for the correctional system as a whole. Thus, a
major turning point for long-term inmates is "to accept and hence give
their consent to those aspects of prison life that are out of their control"
(Johnson & Dobrzanska, 2005, p. 9). In other words, inmates eventually

consciously choose to submit to the prison culture rather than fight continuous battles they cannot win. Judy's turning point occurred in the year of 2000:

> After all, I can truthfully say today I am no longer of the same rebellious lawless character or the woman I was in 1979–1988 criminal season as an outlaw lifestyle or the same 1988–2000 prisoner slinging legal actions aimed at addressing the system's wrongs. My optimistic character developed when I realized my talent and gift was in writing down thoughts like one would if journalizing. I learned it can be important to share with others about past survivals be they yesterday or years ago.

Similar to the description provided by Robert Johnson and Ania Dobrzanska (2005) concerning the nature of mature coping among long-term inmates, Judy has accepted the limited situation of prison life and now more effectively copes with a life still filled with deprivation and daily challenges. Personal routines have been developed to afford a greater sense of autonomy as Judy has aptly carved out a niche that works for her. Despite her overall positive mental frame of mind, she still struggles with a painful past, as Judy bemoans, "Sometimes I look back at my crimes and connections and I feel I can't be helped. I feel an old-old anger still surfaces even after 40 years—the day my daddy was murdered!"

Avoiding the prison "jungle" Judy has so poignantly described is never an easy objective for long-term offenders to achieve. This ongoing process of finding an environmental sanctuary within a prison setting is a continuing struggle as inmates seek to find a place of refuge throughout their sentences. Some seek informal niches where prisoners engage in creative strategies as they organize elements of their surroundings into a plausible way of life (Hagel-Seymour, 1982). One such approach for adjustment to imprisonment is that of disengagement. Reminiscent of one prominent theory of aging, this view maintains that there is a mutual withdrawal between an aging person and other individuals leading to a valued position in society. Disengagement in prison involves a simplified life and a reduction of tension through the minimizing of interactions with others. Individuals such as Judy frequently attempt to avoid chaos and friction by seeking any opportunity they may secure to retreat to their personal cells for moments of much-needed privacy. When the communal social areas become too crowded or noisy, the inmate's cell, if such a structure is available, is considered a welcome safe haven. As Judy attests:

In a prison environment, I have found it necessary to detach myself often from the misery and misfortune of the people I am housed with or work with/around or even have interaction with from a class or program or church attendance. Maybe you don't understand, but then maybe you have never been in a physical bondage—connected to and with others! You need your own space, your private council.

Long-term offenders who have grown beyond a need for participation in structured activities desire quality time in more secluded locations where they can enjoy solitary pursuits. Reading or writing are two such forms of recreation that members of this population enjoy at the end of an otherwise stressful day (Zamble, 1992; Cowles & Sabath, 1996). Long-term inmates, more than most, live by the prison adage, "Do your own time." To this end, Judy maintains added control over life in prison by taking excellent care of herself and by engaging in numerous solitary pursuits. In an attempt to follow a passive path of least resistance, she laments:

Overall, I can honestly say that I have adopted a positive, healthy lifestyle. I have indeed chosen to grow old with dignity and grace. During the time I have served, I have become an avid reader and find enjoyment in studying intently the available reading materials. . . . I also like to walk in the warm sunshine, engage in deep reflection and meditation, and have contemplative, prayerful thoughts. . . . When I begin to have doubts about a particular issue I am struggling with, I can often change my anxious, worried mindset by opening the Bible.

However, as Judy reflects back on her imprisonment, it is obvious that she has encountered some painful experiences.

Thinking back on the changes I have observed while serving time is often a painful process. Many of my peers seem so well-adjusted to prison life . . . enjoying themselves as if nothing ever happened. . . . In here, these women are frequently allowed to "act out" . . . their language is simply intolerable: rude, crude, vulgar. . . . When they violate one of the policies, the employees tend to dismiss their behaviors without ever further investigating the situation. . . . I cannot tell you the number of times I have heard an officer say, "Oh, well that's just Misty, Joy, Jo Jo, or Trixie, being her usual self." . . . The aspect that bothers me the most, however, is that I know these individuals are setting themselves up to go through what I call a "revolving door." . . . By this, I mean that they will one day leave the institution, return to their former paths of crime, eventually be caught in the process, and come back to prison as if they had never left.

One example of sensitive information that is particularly painful for individuals who are serving life sentences to receive from external supports involves the death of mutual external supports. In prison environments, women may not always receive the option of speaking directly with close family members immediately after the events occur. Instead, news may be delivered to them through the chaplain or mental health professional's office. These conversations may even occasionally be overheard by other inmates or staff:

> I have been called to the Chaplain's office to receive notification of loved ones' deaths . . . once after my one and only husband died, and once following the death of an in-law. The procedures that staff members currently use to present to us traumatic news from home is almost as painful as the information itself. I cannot understand how administrators and trained professionals can be so cold, heartless, callous, and uncaring during a time of significant loss. . . . On both occasions, those who were in charge of telling me about the events used a gross lack of judgment in communicating the news to me. . . . I did not appreciate having to listen to my daughter's words of sorrow via a pre-recorded message . . . nor was I thrilled about being "interrogated" afterward.

However, as Judy reflects on her past, and the pains of imprisonment, she says:

> Sometimes, I just ponder how things have become a part of my past life and the emotions then and now. I find my emotions to be deeper and stronger in my mature years. Also, I find once I let a little piece of my heart's hurts out to others, especially witnessing to strangers, it's like a leaky faucet or a busted pipe. There's a steady flow of emotions and sometimes the release is downright humiliating. But if tears come to my eyes today, they are not necessarily tears of shame, guilt neither of pain nor of some depression. More often, they are linked to the anger of how I'm scrutinized by ignorant persons' lack of knowledge which creates unnecessary tragic events or conditions.

Preserving Family Relationships

Jean Miller's (1993) developmental theory on relationships claims that a woman's identity and well-being are found in her ability and motivation to maintain relationships with others, particularly family members. It has been found that both past and present relationship disconnections can have a cumulative effect on a woman's mental state throughout the life course, including increased anxiety, loneliness, and associated depressive symptoms (Miller & Silver, 1997; Poehlmann, 2005). Other research has found that regular visitations between incarcerated mothers and their children were associated with a more positive view of oneself and the parent-child relationship (Snyder, Carlo & Mullins, 2001). However, the opportunity for those confined to a prison environment to remain connected to family and friends can be influenced by a variety of factors, including length of sentence, prison location, and family attachment, to mention a few. The struggles that Judy has encountered to maintain a close connection to her family parallels several of these barriers.

Although hailing from a large family with three brothers and five sisters still living, four children, eight grandchildren, and nine great-grandchildren, there is much distance that now separates her family. Since her incarceration, the immediate family has scattered and now resides in two states (Oklahoma and Florida), so this is a considerable distance for family members to travel. As a result, social interactions have been severely limited and this barrier can make it extremely difficult to preserve family relationships. In her words:

> Fact is all my family (children, grandchildren, great grandchildren, brothers and sisters, in-laws and old friends from the past) seldom make contact with me. Some who do make contact don't feel it necessary to enlighten me of what's going on in the world at large or their day to day lifestyles. I do have a couple of friends who write on occasion and more often it's a note or a card. I have one sister who has been faithful and I can normally pick up a telephone and reach one of my children. I try to limit use of telephones because of the cost factor to family. Still it seems they need to "hear" my voice. They may e-mail or text-message one another but hearing my voice is an assurance to their peace of mind.

Although visits have been limited over the past 22 years of incarceration, Judy does remember conversations and emotions she experienced years ago. About one year after her initial entrance into the Arkansas prison system, Judy did receive one of her infrequent prison visits. This turned out to be an emotional occasion as Judy recalls:

> I got to see my other son when he came with his father to drive my oldest daughter home to Oklahoma. She was being released on parole after a year in ADC. She too like Jared was my family co-dependent. I had not seen my baby boy Jim for some eighteen months. In that time he had grown a bit taller and very much thinner. After I hugged him I commented on how skinny he had become. Jim's words in reply still

bring tears to my eyes for the words he uttered to me, "I miss your good biscuits and gravy mom!"

This visitation exchange was a vivid reminder for Judy that her availability to provide the day-to-day parenting functions she had become so accustomed to as a single parent was no longer possible. Judy's loss of the parenting role was an incidental consequence of her choice to choose a criminal lifestyle as a way to provide financially for her family. As a proud mother, this choice remains a constant reminder for Judy as she longs to return to the family she loves so much.

A few years later, Judy received yet another infrequent visit from two of her children. While it is apparent that separation between a mother and her children due to incarceration might affect their relationship, research has found that connections to family members are more likely to remain strong in the early stages of imprisonment (LaVigne et al., 2005). Again, based on the following account, the importance of family visits cannot be overestimated, especially at a time when both family members and the incarcerated are still coming to terms with a life where daily contact is no longer possible.

> I had one "surprise" visit from my two youngest children, Jim and Penny. They needed to see their mother in the flesh and drove the many miles to Pine Bluff to do that. This was truly a divine intervention touching my life. Two children barely old enough to travel the highways in an old battered auto with a simple heart's desire to see, touch, and talk to their mother. This visit is one of my heart's treasures, because even though we knew we were being watched and yes even our emotions were held close to our hearts, we could not have been more revealing if we had been naked and on display before a crowd of accusers like the Scribes and [Pharisees] who dragged before Jesus the woman taken in the act of adultery.

Judy maintains that visits in prison in Arkansas have never been more important to her than the financial, safety, security, and time factors of her children and grandchildren. Similar to other inmates, Judy personally never desired for her grandchildren, while small and minors in age, to even visit her in prison. The safety and security issues Judy refers to in the above narrative stem from a visitation experience that occurred in May of 1996 as two of her children were coming to see her. Judy provides a summary of the day that she still recalls so vividly:

> It was a very traumatizing experience on all family members even though only one made it to see me and she had to hitchhike the last

several miles. It is a story that I hope one day to share, but not until I can do so through the family who have more of a right to express how law enforcement used excessive force and uncalled for search and seizure upon my oldest daughter and youngest son. The EMS had to be called to stabilize my son when officers put guns to his head. My daughter relived the gunshots of a cop who shot me in 1988. It was that need to see her mom that brought her on to the Tucker Unit by a stranger. I held her and we cried. I was helpless to do anymore.

Since that day, Judy has been reluctant for her family to visit the state of Arkansas, and she has not had a family visit in the past 14 years. Judy is now more receptive of visits and speaks of the importance of "seeing" family members in the flesh and blood:

Now I've accepted it is time to let family make trips to see me. Visits in person can be more personal and confidential than letters or phone conversations. They can look me in the eye when I express what I am feeling or who is causing me to have problems. But mostly, the visits would be open for them to have access to me when they can afford to do so or at a time when they have time enough to make the trip.

Understandably, deciding to maintain connections with the world beyond the prison walls is not a task long-term offenders consider to be easily achieved. As Judy briefly discusses how her own family relationships have been dampened by incarceration, she speaks eloquently about the sacrifices she knows her children have made to preserve some semblance of a relationship with her throughout the duration of her sentence. This lifer, for example, occasionally references the financial burdens that spending on care packages, telephone calls, or (for those who desire on-site visitations) transportation and lodging impose on external supports in order to maintain frequent correspondences. Realizing that many family members may have limited resources available to assist them in funding this (added) necessity, Judy worries about the long-term implications that excessive reliance on credit cards could have on families as well as the time and emotional sacrifices that must also be made for those who wish to travel long distances to see their loved ones:

Families outside of prison seem to become accustomed to having to accept collect calls, send money, or schedule their lives around having to drop a card in the mail now and then. . . . I have no comprehension of how much it costs [in terms of money, time, and emotional labor] for family to actually care for a loved one who is in prison . . . but I do know the sacrifice that loved ones often make to keep the relationships alive are great.

In spite of the infrequent contact Judy has had with her family members, she still seems relatively satisfied with her family relationships and has maintained a positive attitude about her situation as it has unfolded over the many years of incarceration. As Judy remarks:

> Prayers are not measured by miles and neither is the love and joy of just being a part of one big family. As a family, we are not rich in the things of this world, but we are a family who knows the important things. To some people they would deem my family does not care about me, but what do they know? Love that is unseen is the deepest and matters of the heart are in God's promises.

Judy was determined to remain in the lives of her children even though she was serving time in another state. Due to the fact that for the first seven years in the ADC Women's Unit inmates had no telephone access, letters became the lifeline to the outside even when the communication flowed in only one direction. For Judy, writing letters soon became an important weekly pastime and an activity that not only serves to combat the countless hours of boredom, but also serves as an important way to "parent" from prison.

> I write in order to share and yes to seek answers through questions that might generate correspondence back. Letters are always important even where they are wrongly censored! But letters have always been an important method for sending messages. They were in the Bible and are still important for me today. While visits with family and even opportunities to do so in a prison can be controlled, limited or even denied, but as long as I have postage, pen, and paper, I can visit my loved ones.

Although Judy makes a concerted effort to stay connected with her family, she does acknowledge that with the passing of time she has become less relevant in their day-to-day lives. As she reveals:

> I'm human so what I see, feel, think, know and wonder about seems to have such little importance in the lives of my children or in the community. I must admit sometimes it does hurt my feelings to hear a daughter say over the phone, I've got the letter—it came a couple of weeks ago, but I just haven't had time to sit down and read it. I haven't even opened it. Is there something important in it I need to know or do now? Some who do make contact don't feel it necessary to enlighten me of what's going on in the world at large or their day-to-day life in the family circle—a family circle I was much the center of. This leaves me with a feeling of [being] less than important—something that has developed by not having day-to-day contact with family.

Although Judy shares her pain and disappointment resulting from the lack of quality interaction with her family with the passage of time, deep down inside she feels that if she were released, all of her children would rush to her as soon as they had the opportunity. She expresses, "They would need a mom hug. I'm sure they understand how I feel for Jared and Lisa both sat in prison waiting to go home too!"

It is natural for a mother to worry about her children, but parenting from prison can be a daunting task given the challenges of remaining involved in daily decisions. Similarly to life on the outside, sometimes disagreements may occur between an incarcerated parent and her children. This has been the case for Judy as she laments the strains of a life sentence and how "too many years of constant separation and distance" has led to a partially fractured family.

A tongue can cause problems where once as a parent or grandparent, I would have commented about something much differently. As a result, there are times when I no longer comment at all! For I have been outspoken to a point that I've lost contact from two of my children and grandchildren, and I know not if my comments set in a "guilt" phase or an "anger" one for no response was made to me. You can't fix what you don't know is damaged, especially where damage was already occurring. So though "words" can be fully powerful, the wrong words take away the zest of living. They bring on depression, sometimes counteracted with anger and feelings of rejection.

In spite of her differences with certain family members, Judy remains steadfast in her desire to continue to be available and do everything she can to assist her family. While her physical absence continues to take its toll on her ability to be a "central family figure" in her Choctaw tribe, this does not lessen Judy's strong emotional attachment or the constant worry about the present challenges facing her family members on the outside. Judy expresses the helplessness she feels from being tucked away in prison and a nonfactor in the lives of her children:

One of my grandsons has ADHD [attention deficit hyperactivity disorder] and it's mentally and physically hard on his parents. I also have a son-in-law with health problems (cancer) who will not live to see his children grown or young wife (my granddaughter) have anything in life except the burdens of a bunch of children to raise. I cannot help them in here and I try not to burden them needlessly, especially financially. I worry about my great grandchildren's safety at home, play and school because of all the dangers of kidnappers, child rapes and molesters who prey on young children. I realize I can't be there or contacted when some situation needs attention. I often hear after the fact.

With the passage of time, and now with great-grandchildren to worry about, Judy can simply long for the opportunity to reunite with her children and to be a presence in their everyday lives.

Judy's story provides evidence that prisoners who maintain family connections also adapt to new family roles. She is neither in a position to make a financial contribution to her family nor is she able to physically take care of or protect her grandchildren or great-grandchildren. Instead, Judy has done her very best to demonstrate caring and concern for her family by sending cards to acknowledge birthdays, calling home when possible, writing letters to encourage children's progress, and giving advice on how to handle different problems. Looking back on her role, Judy expresses the pride she feels for her family:

> I give praise to God for the good things I unknowingly taught my family. I am proud of them—their maturity, strength and survivor skills, and for their hope. And by their lives I am a blessed mother, granny, and great grandmother. It is helpful to know that I'm in family conversations even among the grandchildren and great grandchildren who have yet to meet me in person. They only know me from the ADC Inmate Information Website photo and the stories and songs my children, friends, siblings, and cousins who are older in years tell and share. This keeps the hope and heart's desire that one day someone will get a call saying we will release Judy Holbird on such day and such time.

It is evident that Judy continues to have a deep sense of respect for her family. As a child, Judy's family experience was a favorable one and she, no doubt, was greatly influenced by her own parents as they provided her with a model of responsibility. Although her responsibility as a parent has been curtailed by the choices she made, the commitment to her family remains especially strong.

Friends on the Outside

In addition to her family, Judy has maintained ties with her oldest and dearest living friend, Juanita. Now in her late 70s, this friend, mutual church member, and neighbor of the family has known Judy all of her life. Although they have not seen each other in many, many years (except by photograph), Juanita has faithfully written letters to Judy, which she terms as such "precious visits." This lifelong friend has provided information about the changes around her home of Red Oak, Oklahoma, of old friends from school days, or persons who are having health problems, or those who have passed to the next journey of life. This friendship bond has enriched Judy's life tremendously, as she states: "Juanita's letters, like old stories shared, are walks down memory lane. They have given me laughter, hope, tears, and encouragement. And she never fails to share the love of Jesus. Her Christian walk has been one I wish I could match."

Occasionally, this offender sentenced to 166 years has sought comfort and guidance from outside volunteers who come to the prison for the purpose of offering special programming. Religious retreats have been described as an occasion that permits women such as Judy to establish connections with persons who reside outside the prison walls. She notes several planned events that introduced her to a range of individuals who would continue to extend their companionship and support to her many years after the formal planned events concluded.

> When I was at the Tucker unit [between 1996 and 1997], I participated in a spiritually based retreat. . . . During that four day event, I met many outside volunteers . . . some of whom still attend events at the women's prison . . . or pass on their greetings through the occasional card or word from mutual acquaintances. . . . These volunteers have seen me struggle to overcome barriers, much pain and anger. . . . They have also, however, seen me at times with a joyful spirit. . . . Nearly any of these could tell you that I am just a normal old woman . . . that would be no danger to society.

Such social supports play an important role in determining successful prison adjustment, especially for those who desire contact with the outside world. Similar to life on the outside, having a set of friends who are supportive can play an important role in helping inmates cope with the stress associated with being prisoners. These new friends have the potential to provide support that they could not get from an otherwise deprived social network. Judy describes the following supportive outside relationship that has evolved over the years:

> I became acquainted with Vivian, a CRA [volunteer from an area religious group], at the women's unit in March 1998. Over a decade has passed since we first met, but seldom a week goes by that I don't chat with her . . . sharing much about my life, family, and faith. . . . She has consistently been there for me to pray about matters . . . whether over trivial issues such as getting a haircut, or more serious issues such as while I was struggling to quit smoking, deal with menopause, or refrain from suicide. Over the course of our relationship, I have also personally had the opportunity to meet her husband, who himself, has attended more than one center event. . . . Vivian and her

spouse could truly give anyone an accurate evaluation of the person I am today.

Friends on the Inside

Establishing a social support system, this long-term offender explains, is a challenging experience. She reflects back on the time she has served, conditions with which she has been presented, people met along the journey, and interactions with these people. In the process, she expresses amazement any lasting friendships could have been formed. At times, this lifer recalls, she has felt much like a stranger. While chronicling her account of life in prison, Judy explains that seeking and securing companionship are most difficult when one first arrives. Since she was not originally from the state where she is now serving time, Judy considered herself to be at a disadvantage to other women who may have had greater familiarity with the surrounding area. In addition, the number of inmates to whom she was suddenly exposed caused heightened, intense emotions. In large institutions, Judy notes, one may not know the names of each individual with whom you will be sharing time. Naturally, participation in available structured programming may provide some degree of assistance in acquainting offenders; yet, involvement is no guarantee.

However, Judy does consider a few of the thousands of inmates who have journeyed through her life as friends. These select ladies, whom she affectionately refers to as her "Christian sisters," include various inmate peers she has met, befriended, and grown fond of while she has been incarcerated. Although Judy explains only a limited few would be considered friends on the outside or someone she would be willing for her family to meet, there is a definite acknowledgment of the value these companions have added to her everyday life.

> I have had few lasting prison friendships, but consider the ones that I have made to be true blessings. . . . With these friends, I do not have to tally up columns of lies or regrets, but know that the positive memories we have shared can be preserved or savored over the years. With them, I feel confident in sharing together bad times, good news or just general pleasantries. We have weathered many storms together and will likely weather many more to come. Overall, I am very lucky to have found them.

"My prison friends," she recalls, "have faithfully stood next to me as I have withstood the various moments of pain, suffering, heartbreak, and yes, occasionally even despair." Each individual welcomed into her inner social circle has occupied sufficient time in the system to recognize the demands institutionalization can place on its offenders. Judy claims her closest acquaintances are a few of the "old timers" who started out with her at the Pine Bluff Unit. Because they understand the challenges one faces while attempting to cope in times of conflict, or refrain from breaking down psychologically and emotionally when tragic news is received from home, institutional supports fill a critical void.

Occasionally, however, those serving long sentences receive the rare privilege of preserving a connection formed within the prison walls after that acquaintance leaves the facility to establish a much-anticipated life as a law-abiding citizen. When this occurs, written correspondences from the free world may begin to take on a newly discovered, heightened importance. Word from these wonderful supports may serve as constant sources of inspiration, hope, and anticipation of brighter futures ahead. Stories of the barriers former peers have overcome to achieve and maintain respectable lives in the communities to which they have returned are always uplifting. Naturally, quick notes relaying little more information than "hello . . . and thinking of you" are appreciated as well.

Aging in Place

One of the most defining features of Judy's adaptation to prison is her emphasis on maintaining a healthy lifestyle. Although she entered prison with a bullet lodged in her spine as well as several minor conditions (such as arthritis in her bones and joints and blood clotting), these concerns do not cause her the degree of worry female lifers routinely have about physiological deterioration (Genders & Player, 1990). While the majority of inmates suffer from accelerated aging due to unhealthy lifestyles prior to incarceration (Reviere & Young, 2004), Judy has never been a consumer of drugs or alcohol. She notes that "in a prison setting, you will encounter inmates who have a range of disabilities." Some suffer physical or mental impairments caused by the natural aging process and others due to poor preincarceration lifestyle decisions (Reviere & Young, 2004). Personally, she is extraordinarily pleased to report that she very rarely needs treatment for any major illnesses.

> I take no medications and I function well for my age and far better than many inmates years younger. I figure that is because of the life and life style I live. I have never abused drugs or alcohol. I never

engaged in a wild sexual lifestyle prior to prison and for almost 23 years now I have been non-sexual. That too in a place like this is a very healthy way to be. The only medical care that I need is non-prescription drugs like Ben-Gay or Icy-Hot or just plain aspirins. . . . I have frequently refused routine checkups including procedures such as pap smears, rectal exams or mammograms. My medical records should confirm that I do not suffer from common colds and I normally refuse a flu shot when it is offered.

Judy reports that staying active has also been a beneficial trait for her good health. She is thankful that she has been able to endure the aches and pains that long-term incarceration imposes on offenders. Judy also realizes that many of her prison acquaintances have it much worse. Although Judy rarely takes any drugs whatsoever, she does recognize that many medications are dispensed freely to inmates. This is a troublesome issue for her as she can't help but question this policy, especially when witnessing the frequent sharing of medications among inmates. On other occasions she has even observed the wasteful practice of discarding medications as inmates frequently flush pills down the toilet.

The long-term effects of exposure to the stressors of imprisonment frequently take their toll on individuals who have few coping skills. Although Judy functions very well for her age, she readily admits watching other less-fortunate women's health deteriorate day-by-day. Judy attributes the marked decline in the women's health to the lack of any real emphasis by the prison staff to encourage a healthier prison environment coupled with inmates' lack of motivation. As she states:

> Women may not always receive the encouragement to eat healthily (and maintain a reasonable weight). . . . They may not be afforded the time or place to engage in the exercise needed to burn off excess calories. . . . Those who are not accustomed to routine physical exertion may even be inclined to sleep more than they would normally consider doing under free world conditions.

However, proper credit is given to the prison's medical staff for having taken ample precautions to ensure that the most vulnerable populations are routinely screened for potential problems before they have the opportunity to surface. This long-term offender discusses how the prison's health-care services make readily available to the women who are serving time in the facility annual physical examinations, mammograms, and pap smears, in addition to a range of ancillary services (routine dental and eye examinations). As she chronicles the journey through her most recent appointment, Judy vividly captures the thoroughness with which health-care staff tend to the patients who are seen in practice.

In March of 2009, Judy appeared before the Classification Committee for the purpose of determining her work eligibility. For several years she had been required to work strenuously and eventually suffered from fatigue poisoning of the body. Mental health services ruled that Judy was no longer able to receive proper medical care while residing in the mainstream prison population. As a result, she was relieved to learn that she would receive a transfer to the Special Program Unit for additional support. At the 12-bed unit she describes, eligible inmates are freed of the expectations to maintain rigorous physical activity. Although she documents throughout her journey the importance associated with keeping persons involved in structured pursuits to the maximum extent possible, Judy simultaneously recognizes that older adult populations often require modified work and responsibilities. Transfers to a less-demanding atmosphere, in her words, permits special needs offenders the relief that is due them. Specifically, she welcomes any opportunity that may be available to receive "fresh air, improved nutrition, and additional rest/peace," not to mention security staff that are much more accommodating in the Special Program Unit.

The Hope for Freedom

As this aging inmate continues her journey through the criminal justice system, she shares a similar concern that weighs heavily on the hearts of many elders who are now serving life sentences. Specifically, her thoughts turn to the experiences women would likely face if they received the opportunity to return home and spend their remaining years of life in mainstream society. Like so many other inmates serving long sentences, Judy continues to have hope—the hope that the day will come when she will have the opportunity to rejoin her beloved family. After so many years apart, there is the realization of the challenges ahead as the process of renewing her family ties unfolds. Yet, for now, this is the least of her worries, for with each and every passing day the lingering thought of going home always enters her mind.

> Someday I hope to rejoin my family and to go through the materials as I sit in the living room floor with my children, grandchildren, and great grandchildren. The stories I want to share of my time away are just as important as the stories I want to hear from them of the time I've missed. The memories are not all good nor are they all bad. The

gap just needs filling and that's my follow-up goal. This show and tell would take years of family time covering my Bible Study Certificate, Anger Management Certificate, Pal's Basic Life Principles and Pre-Release Certificate. From their world would be Birth Certificates and the stories all families share together.

Of course, it is realized that it will take a certain amount of time before she will be able to find her rightful position in the family system that was torn apart by her ill-advised quest to support her impoverished family via a life of crime. However, Judy has never been at a loss for words, and the following passage indicates she would welcome the opportunity to unite her family in her remaining golden years: "I want to answer honestly all questions my family might want to ask me from 'why?' to whatever my hidden motivation was. It needs to be talked out, expressed and exposed and an understanding reached. Because, I know I myself never even thought about some things at the time be it crime, sin or other." With Judy's recent request for a reduction in the number of years she must serve now under serious consideration by the parole board and a possible clemency by the governor, the hope for freedom heightens. Judy's heart has been warmed immensely as one of her grandsons whom she has not seen since 1988 has kindly requested that his grandmother come live with his family.

There are, however, feelings of insecurity that occasionally arise concerning what strategies elders would use to support themselves financially after leaving a system that has provided them with all basic essentials and few useful career skills. In fact, one of the primary themes resonating throughout her narrative focuses on the narrow range of job training programs currently available to older women who are serving long-term sentences. Understandably, an individual who entered into contact with the system during the peak of one's working years would desire the administration to assist them in developing useful skills. Although this inmate may not leave the institutional setting with time remaining to resume a lengthy career, she recognizes that self-sufficiency is a goal some would likely maintain well into their later years. In her own words, Judy explains:

When an inmate spends 20 plus years behind bars, she should be acquiring some form of work-related skills. . . . Meaningful prison jobs, for example, may include tasks in the areas of domestic labor . . . or other chores that involve making productive contributions to society. For those older, long-term offenders who will be leaving prison in good health, having this knowledge base may provide them the guidance, encouragement, and support needed to continue down the path toward rehabilitation. In essence, any employment that inmates engage in is essential in ensuring their returns to prison do not become parts of their natural lifestyles.

Of course, another challenge for those serving long sentences is adjusting to a different world from which they left. Over the past 20 or so years, there has been significant technological advancement that many lifers have never encountered. While exposed to many of the new technologies, most have had limited or no opportunity whatsoever to actually touch or use many of the recent discoveries.

I might have to be shown such things as how to operate a cell phone or a cordless one, for I've never experienced such. I figure my great-grandkids would be able to show granny many such things like turning on a TV or using a new CD-DVD or whatever the music and movies are on nowadays. I've never operated an answering machine for a telephone and some kitchen appliances would be strange to me, but I'm not worried about not being perfectly capable of caring for a home and kids.

Spending time in prison can serve as a life-changing experience, and Judy acknowledges that she has undergone a remarkable transformation during her many years of incarceration. This emotionally scarred, rebellious and confused woman at age 41, ten years later committed herself to changing for the better. With the assistance of several prison programs and personal reflections, Judy says, she transformed herself from the inside out, learned to be more selfless, and welcomed spirituality into her life. She finally faced the emotional turmoil caused by an abusive past, the premature death of her father, and her willingness to blame others for her situation.

There was a time in my life I was not a convicted felon, but you would have to go back over 30 years before I was arrested for a crime. We can all stop and think back to something when we made a choice we now, with maturity, age, and experience wish we had not made. Those questions like "what if I had stayed, did or did not" are those times in our life when finally enough is enough. We have to accept the road we're traveling on. I feel ashamed I did not recognize all these missed opportunities until I'd been in prison for seven years. I'd like to think if I would have made better choices in life—had I learned it sooner. Nothing would make a difference now and the only difference I can make is not available to me here today in prison. Nevertheless, I have an outlook that although a child can be taught wrong to start at some point during the growth stage of adolescence each individual will come to a knowing the right of it. I personally find it disgusting and a poor excuse and I have little tolerance when a grown woman blames her shortcomings—even her moral and/or criminal lifestyle on some time period of a childhood disadvantage. Any moment in time past it's not reversible. However, a difficult life can be fulfilling and even satisfying as well as educational. I still hope and pray. I forgive and I wait for another chance.

Over the years, Judy has learned the value of using humor as an important resource in helping her cope with the day-to-day life of imprisonment. She indicates that she has discarded her anger and left vengeance to God. As her relationship with God deepened, Judy expresses that she also found the love necessary to forgive, and that process includes herself. With these positive strides she has made over the past fifteen years, this reformed lifer now seeks to also educate others of all the wrongs and dangers that contributed to her life choices. More than ever, she feels confident about the person she has become and dreams of the opportunity to continue the life she left behind. Using her vivid memory of years past, Judy often reminisces:

I often think about taking a drive down one of those old country dirt roads or even the pleasure of a trip down a lesser traveled two-lane highway. There's a serene "freedom feeling" like leaving all my problems at the return-to-sender and just getting into that old solid built pickup truck or old car and rolling the windows down and driving without a plan, timetable, or schedule. Just moving like the wind as a spirit singing and smiling. In the drive, I would take whatever road that may look interesting being in no hurry, but to look at the beauty of the countryside and see the possibility of uncovering a treasure at some old abandoned home, barn or flea market.

For now, Judy will have to be content with her memories of those country dirt roads she longs to travel once again. Of course, she took some of those back roads years ago as she made her getaway from her initial grocery store robbery. However, things appear much different now for Judy. Although not always regularly attending church throughout her life prior to incarceration, she states, "Somewhere along the way in my life I lost sight of God—but God has revealed to me that wickedness has no season." Like other lifers, Judy's faith is a sustaining, vital aspect of her being, or as George stated in her book *A Woman Doing Life*, "a roadmap to forgiveness and calm that everyone deserves and needs" (2010, p. 159).

In the meantime, Judy waits anxiously for a decision about her future. One of just a handful of inmates technically serving life without ever having taken the life of another individual, will the parole board rule once more that her "sentence was NOT considered excessive?" Or will they reconsider the fact that the state originally offered 50 years as adequate punishment under a plea agreement, and will her time served under those circumstances be considered sufficient? Like many older women at the mercy of the state, Judy's biggest quandary is the unknown. What will be the fate of this Native American? Will ADC become her final destiny, or will Lady Luck provide a second chance? Having made her case with her steady march toward transformation, Judy emphatically pleads, "I long to return to my homeland of birth in Oklahoma where my heart, mind, and body seeks to live out my old age within the boundaries of the Choctaw Nation."

Postscript

Like the majority of lifers and other long-term inmates who seek redemption, Judy recently learned that her request to the governor of Arkansas to reconsider her initial 166-year sentence as excessive in nature was denied. Although selective states are now providing inmates with "second-chance" opportunities, especially those having served long sentences of 20 years or more, this was not to be the case for Judy. Nor has it been the case for many other aging women who, with vast histories of poverty, victimization, and abuse, find themselves serving the majority of their lives behind bars. These long-termers often find themselves feeling hopeless and helpless in a system that continues to feed on the very inmates who would otherwise be excellent candidates for reentry back to their communities. The pain and agony that a person must feel when such hopes are dashed under these circumstances is, no doubt, impossible to comprehend. However, in a recent letter, Judy does find the courage to share her recent disappointment with the realization of what it means to go back to "square one."

It has been a long, long, long time since the grief in my heart has hurt to the deepest corners of my very soul! The hardest part is still ahead—for I must write my family and let them know. But, the letting go of our hopes and dreams of time together is not easy to do. Yet, I do not see me living 4 to 6 years more in captivity. That's the range we have to recognize as how long it will be before I would qualify to reapply. I will inquire from the Governor to see what my standing is—even though I have no heart or inclination to try again. I don't know how my family will handle this. They have been holding on to the

Governor's words to Penny back in February, where from his mouth to her ears across the telephone line he said, "Yes, I believe your mother has done enough time." . . . There are thousands of females who have served time in the ADC out there who have known me in these many years. I pray they pray for us left behind.

Thus, it is easy to see why so many long-term inmates feel the public has forgotten them and why, after a time, no longer seek reentry back to society. The process described by Judy frequently becomes too painful to endure for the family and the inmate alike and over time inmates tend to give up hope, accept their fate, and withdraw deeper into the prison subculture.

As Judy revisits the mourning process, embracing the negative feelings accompanying her denial for freedom and the emotional struggle to reinvest in her extended life in prison, hopefully she will continue to engage in those activities which bring her strength, enjoyment, and hope: writing as therapy, her connections to family and friends on the outside, her spiritual life, and the inner peace she has found in transforming her life as a forgotten woman serving a lengthy determinant sentence. This proud Choctaw has proven time and time again her resiliency, and, if nothing more, her compelling story shared in these pages will serve as her legacy for her children, grandchildren, and great-grandchildren. They will know that despite her past mistakes, her love for them will never fade from behind these prison walls. And with her voice, we now understand more clearly the life experiences facing literally thousands of similar incarcerated women who only seek a "second chance."

8

Policy Issues and Future Concerns

U NTIL NOW, WE HAVE FOCUSED ON A WIDE RANGE OF ISSUES AND concerns older incarcerated women regularly encounter while navigating their ways through the complexities of the prison system. Specifically, we have thoroughly explored their voices in relation to their abusive pasts, adjustment and adaptation to evolving social relationships, the challenges of aging in a total institution with overriding medical and mental health issues, and the inmate's ultimate concerns with death and dying. Somewhat limited attention has been directed toward the growing concerns for older female inmates who may eventually qualify for reentry. The first portion of this chapter will address some of the initial concerns for this special population as they give consideration to transitioning from prison back to the community. The transition that individuals will encounter as they depart prison and return home to their families and communities is, no doubt, a dynamic social process. This is particularly true for so many older women who have, based on their lengthy sentences, spent a significant number of years in isolation.

Transition from Prison

Approximately 95 percent of individuals who are incarcerated in state prisons today can anticipate that they will eventually be leaving the institutions where they are currently serving time (Sabol & Couture, 2008). Interestingly, however, the literature clearly suggests that individuals most likely to be released back into the community lack the knowledge, skills, and resources that are necessary to begin new lives for themselves. Since the "tough on crime" approaches and policies that emerged during the 1990s, prison administrators have generally paid limited (if any) consideration to the need for ensuring that the time that is being occupied behind the prison walls is, in fact, constructive and preparing individuals for the lives they could be anticipated to lead after making the transition back into mainstream society. Several, for example, have spoken in considerable detail about the presence of a "waste management" model that has been implemented throughout institutions across the nation. In the process, these have highlighted that the populations who are most likely to be deeply and adversely impacted or affected by the challenges that reentry presents them are typically granted the least consideration when programs, services, and so on are being planned (Chiu, 2010). It is very uncommon, for example, for the criminal justice system to assume an active role in linking older offenders with area agencies on aging to begin coordinating the access to any age-related services that may be available to them upon their release (Higgins & Severson, 2009). In addition, programming that is designed for the purpose of reuniting older adult prisoners with external supports continues to lag behind those developed to assist young offenders (Stojkovic, 2007).

A number of studies have conceded that existing reintegration models for offenders center on male prototypes of change and fail to acknowledge that men and women have diverse transformation experiences (Blanchette & Brown, 2006; Herrschaft et al., 2009). Prior research on reentry suggests that the lack of close family connections, community separation, mental illness, chronic health conditions, and lack of education and the opportunity for stable employment are all critical factors in addressing the reintegration needs of women (Blanchette & Taylor, 2009). It is not uncommon, for example, for elders (specifically those of female gender) to regard the system as failing them in this critical dimension (Shantz & Frigon, 2009; Smyer & Gragert, 2006). Research (albeit scarce) is emerging to suggest the apparent failure of prison administrators to accommodate older individuals as they prepare to return home from prison. Such a reality can have far more severe consequences for them than would ordinarily be observed by their younger counterparts. The fact that sentencing policies are stricter (and providing individuals with longer periods of time behind bars) than was ever previously imagined, realized, or observed alone has had negative implications for this particular age group. In recent years, several have pointed to the fact that persons who will be departing during advanced age encounter numerous problems that would not likely be faced by other segments of the prison population at this critical moment in time solely because sentence lengths have left them bereft of various opportunities for longer periods of time (Aragon, 2007; Higgins & Severson, 2009; Stojkovic, 2007).

In order to understand how prison administrators prepare those older adults who will be leaving the system with health problems for their return home, consideration must first be directed toward discussing why this segment of the population is an ideal group to target for release. Overall, much of the research that has been conducted in this area has been inspired by a consideration of offender recidivism rates. Over the past several decades, for example, numerous scholars have pointed to an inverse relationship between the individuals' ages and their prospects of engagement in further criminal activities. Specifically, persons who are 45 years of age and older have been identified as posing a much smaller risk of being rearrested, reconvicted, or reincarcerated following their release from prison (Kerbs & Jolley, 2007; Chiu, 2010). With the onset of advanced age, persons who may have otherwise continued to be actively involved in various criminal activities have often witnessed age-related changes that have discouraged, distracted, or drawn them away from participation in criminal pursuits. When persons begin to exhibit personal characteristics or traits such as declines in physical strength, energy, or stamina and shifts from outward to inward expression of negative emotions, the desire or tendency to participate in crimes is generally considered to be greatly reduced (Kerbs, 2000).

Appropriate consideration should undoubtedly be extended to the needs, concerns, and feelings of elders who have begun the processes of applying for compassionate release. Those persons who have applied for release may frequently experience overwhelming feelings of anxiety associated with the extraordinary length of time required for the final decisions to be rendered. Although some older offenders will attempt to overcome these moments of angst by relying on their personal religious beliefs, rapid declines in health, or even interactions with fellow offenders they know have successfully negotiated the transition to construct views of positive outcomes (Leigey, 2007), for many, hope and optimism about their respective futures must eventually be shattered. Naturally, care must be taken when delivering the news to persons who are nearing the final moments of life with the anticipation of returning home to family and friends before they die (O'Connor, 2004).

Discharge Apprehension

Approximately 83 percent of older offenders who are serving sentences other than life without parole anticipate they will ultimately be released, with 27 percent of those who are serving life sentences holding similar expectations (Leigey, 2007). In general, elders who anticipate eventually being released began to focus on developing a transient niche as they anticipate the possibility of returning to the free world (Schmid & Jones, 1993). Surprisingly, even those who have a prior record of appearing before the parole board and receiving unsuccessful outcomes may continue to think they have a chance. Some, for example, may note that the processes involved in appearing in court have given them a stronger record, time to build a stronger case that will result in a successful outcome. Reasons given for anticipating their parole request will be approved include watching others who have applied and secured release, having a personal health status that is rapidly deteriorating, and having secured needed support from a prominent figure advocating on their behalf. As one inmate stated, "I've got 50 years to life, but I have yet to think of myself as a lifer. The sentence, in itself, does not stop me from trying to get back into court." While some women serve out their time in prison and will no longer be under the jurisdiction of the criminal justice system, other women talked with some ambivalence about the possibility of being released:

> Well, I am due for parole . . . and will meet the parole board next year. . . . Everybody—inmates and staff—tell me "You'll make it with no problem." . . . However, I have no illusions; they could find any reason in the world to put me off. . . . It might be a psych eval or severity of the crime. The older ones are the ones that the parole board never sends home. That's a shame because they'd never do anything wrong again. They'd never come back. Send them home; give them a chance.

> As I get closer to my release date, the little things such as the arts and crafts projects that I have held dear for so long no longer mean near as much to me. But, I am not willing to completely let go of them either. You just never know how things will actually turn out. I've watched others who thought they were leaving, but they are still here.

These statements are consistent with the view proposed by Thomas Schmid and Richard Jones that inmates' marginality and manifestations of ambivalence result from a conflict between an "outsider's and an insider's point of view" (1993, p. 458). In other words, as inmates enter into particular phases of their prison careers, new adaptation models must be invented. Although the women look to the outside for a fresh start, they also must emotionally deal with the possibility that parole may not be forthcoming.

Other studies conducted with inmates who are nearing release indicate that persons who are nearing this critical phase in their lives appear assured and confident that they have learned their lessons and will not be returning to prison, that they will do whatever it takes to ensure that "this time will be different" (Visher & Travis, 2003). Women who make up our sample were no exception. Several elders provided the following statements concerning the prospects of reentering mainstream society:

No, I'm not going to end up back in here. Oh no. No. I'm not on parole, so I don't have to worry. I've got a probated sentence that will be done.

No, I won't be back here. I can definitely say that. No way.

It's a lot different now because I am being honest. I wasn't honest last time. I was not honest, and it makes a difference. And I am not getting any younger. I have to change, or I could, you know, really end up here.

Craig Haney (2006) purports that, in many institutions, prison rehabilitation programming has inadequately prepared participants for their return to mainstream society. It is well documented that the days, weeks, and months that follow incarceration will impose considerable demands on female offenders. Such will, for example, be viewed as times when they must struggle to secure housing and employment, reestablish relations with family they once left behind, and enter into treatment for mental health concerns or problems with substance abuse. For those long-term inmates whose external support system may have abandoned them over the course of their sentences, those who are not or no longer employable, and those who have no knowledge of the steps they would need to take to secure assistance they need, the end result may be one of "institutional dependency." Coined as a concept to describe the psychosocial effects of long-term incarceration, offenders who have succumbed to this state and have withdrawn into a passive shell of their former existence rely on correctional officers and other staff members to perform all but the most basic activities for them and appear to be extraordinarily afraid of returning home to their former communities. For many, the psychological effects of long-term incarceration have robbed them of the coping skills that would ultimately be required to successfully reenter the free world—a world that may be much faster paced and more complex than the one they left. No amount of advance preparation, for example, can adequately prepare those individuals who have served long-term prison sentences for the myriad of technological advances to which their free-world counterparts have been introduced in their absences (Stojkovic, 2007). Several inmates spoke of their apprehensiveness about renewing their life on the outside, and the following provides a prime example: "Until now, everything I could possibly need (food, clothing, medical care, etc.) has been provided for me. Could I function without staff/peer support?" Similar to the research reported by Elaine Crawley and Richard Sparks (2006), other women voiced their fears of finding a suitable job once they were released. Here again, it is evident that age is a key factor in the subjective view of numerous women in our sample when coping with the challenges of making a successful transition. The following is representative of their concerns:

> I think older inmates have more concerns about what kind of jobs they are going to get. Because, you know, I can knock out 15 years, and will be almost 60 when I leave. I had a good job before I entered prison, with people working under me. And now, I have a criminal history. When I go back out, it will be completely different. I'll have to start over like a 16 year old, but I'll be about ready to retire. I'll eventually go on social security, but in the meantime, I'll need to work somewhere.

As inmates see their time of incarceration possibly coming to a close, it is obvious that the formulation of an outside plan becomes an important element of adaptation strategy. As these inmates reconstitute a mental orientation toward the outside, it is evident from the above narratives that their perspective reveals a sense of vulnerability. There is a certain apprehension about returning to a free world where, once again, they will be marginalized. As new images are to be constructed, questions arise from some about whether they will have sufficient resources or time remaining to fashion a new life. Others may be concerned about having committed a crime viewed as reprehensible by society and the lingering stigma associated with such behavior.

Haney (2006) has argued individuals who have served long-term prison sentences in particular may need assistance developing interpersonal communication skills as, by the very act of being institutionalized, they have learned to become and remain extraordinarily vigilant of their surroundings and distrustful of those with whom they must interact on a daily basis. In order to survive the conflicts, disputes, and frictions that occur in prison every day they are incarcerated without becoming the next target of victimization or exploitation, maintaining an exaggerated level of distance from one's neighbor becomes almost the norm. As the time progresses and one must reenter mainstream society, however, establishing a new identity, gaining community acceptance or support, is of utmost importance to women (Severance, 2005).

Family Reintegration

For many older offenders, maintaining quality, emotionally close rela-tionships with external supports can facilitate a successful transition back into mainstream society. The presence of family ties not only assists offenders navigating the hurdles that must be overcome to secure release, but also aids in identifying needed goods, services, information, and recreational or social opportunities following release (Singer et al., 1995). Without the love, support, and guidance of family, it would be nearly impossible for many to secure shelter, employment, Social Security or other governmental assistance, clothing, food, and other essentials that law-abiding citizens take for granted (Aday, 2003). It is often the family, for example, that provides older offenders who are nearing the times of their release the necessary confidence that they can maintain a healthy diet, exercise regimen, and visits to a health-care provider when they are ill. While the older offender has been incarcerat-ed, loved ones outside the institutional setting have had time to partici-pate in these practices, and they thus serve an invaluable purpose in passing on the healthy lifestyle characteristics they have developed to the elder who is now leaving prison for home (Loeb, Steffensmeier & Myco, 2007). Similarly, the presence of relatives may serve the invalu-able function of helping the women reestablish identities as productive, respectable members of the local community in addition to sharing strategies that would prove advantageous in reclaiming and building upon their roles as parents or grandparents to younger individuals who have entered the families in their absences.

Women who are in the processes of making the transition from liv-ing in institutional settings to establishing their own places of residence often report desiring help securing housing; counseling for mental health, drug, and alcohol problems; financial aid; vocational training; relationships with their children; religious affiliations; and new informal social supports (Singer et al., 1995). With the assistance of family who will willingly permit the former offender to live in their homes; resume the roles as spouse, parent, or other recognized kin; and assume the var-ied responsibilities associated with these positions, former inmates may thrive in achieving the goals they have established. Unsurprisingly, some evidence suggests that offenders whose relatives have also expressed interest in accompanying them as they participate in family therapy report greater success in making the transition into mainstream society following their parole (Visher & Travis, 2003). As most authors to explore the notion of release preparation have limited the scope of investigation to the lived experiences of younger or male prison populations, additional research is needed that focuses on the unique needs, desires, and realities associated with an older female population.

Although older offenders who have extensive family support are generally more likely than their unsupported peers to experience successful reentrance into mainstream society, several respondents acknowledged even those who have maintained the strongest connections to their relatives cannot be guaranteed the transition will occur with minimal friction. Family, for example, may be poorly equipped with the skills to respond to any physical, mental, cognitive, or emotional changes and transformations that the older offenders may have had while they were serving their given sentences. Persons who arrived at prison much earlier along the life course and have since aged in place, in particular, may find their relatives or other loved ones unable to or uncomfortable with providing them the care their conditions now warrant (Stojkovic, 2007). For a number, returning home will involve noticing members of their immediate family have changed in their absence. Individuals who had entered the setting while their children were young may encounter difficulties adjusting as they discover them to have since married, had children of their own, and established independent family units. Several women who recognized time had not indeed frozen in their absences explored the advantages associated with reentering the communities prior to reuniting with loved ones. One inmate examines the frictions she anticipates encountering upon reunification in noting:

> My daughter wanted me so bad to stay with her when I make parole. But I thought about it . . . and began to question about how it will affect us if I am staying in her home and we are living right underneath each other . . . this may not work. . . . I can't just come home after 20 years, act as if nothing happened. . . . She's grown, married, and with a kid. . . . And I'm not a fool enough to try to step in and play mom all of a sudden. We're going to have to work up to that, and it will be hard. . . . Some women are so starved for attention that they rush into it, and it's disastrous to begin with . . . so I'm trying to avoid this disaster.

Laura Shantz and Sylvie Frigon (2009) have mentioned that older women who are leaving the prison system are guarded in their interactions with others. Given their histories of low self-esteem and mental health problems, these individuals may be highly suspicious and more distrustful of family after serving long prison terms. A number of respondents, as the one who provided the following narrative, expressed strong reservations about attempting the transition, fearing any connections they may have formerly had with family, friends, and external supports could have been severed beyond repair.

> I really don't know that I will be able to re-establish a relationship with my family. . . . I want to feel there is some hope, but I can't say it. . . . Years ago, when I was in rehab, I said a lot of things about change, but my actions did not go along with my words. . . . So now, my family doesn't want to hear it. . . . I'm going to continue to try, but. . . .

Others, however, envision that under close supervision of professional guidance, relations can be mended:

> I have great family support right now from everybody, my daughter, my son, and I don't know how much they have told my daughter-in-law, but I'll find that all out when I go home. I really want to do some family counseling when I am released, and think it is imperative as they may have some questions they don't feel comfortable asking me without being in a safe place. And in my mind, the safest place is in a therapist's office.

Since the older adults will be arriving back home after having served time for their involvement in criminal activities, a sizable number will find themselves confronted with the challenge of relating to persons who may not always be receptive to conveying respect, empathy, or responsiveness to their given needs (Stojkovic, 2007). In the words of one woman who acknowledges her feelings of uneasiness or dread in making the transition:

> My feelings toward that lady, my stepmother, have not always been so good. . . . I have been working to change that . . . because I will see her again, if I don't drop dead in here or she out there. . . . I do not want to walk up to her after I am released with negativity. I didn't always feel this way, but I am now realizing I can't make her take my calls, send me money, or do other things for me while I am in prison. However, I can learn how to change my outlook on it even though it has taken a lot of work to get to this point.

Patricia O'Brien (2001) notes the new residence must be far enough away from external pressures that contributed to the inmate's offenses in the first place. Some are most likely to benefit from relocating some distance from their family, friends, and other close connections in order to receive the needed opportunity for a new beginning. Regardless, reentry can be a challenging adventure, especially for those who have been cut off from their family and friends for decades. The process may very well be a gradual one as the family system evolves to absorb mothers and grandmothers back into the fold. Certainly a gendered approach is important in underscoring the importance of developing more relevant reentry policies for women. This intervention strategy should include a relational pathway that includes the acknowledgment of dysfunctional intimate relationships stemming from long periods of victimization, drug abuse, and assorted mental and physical health problems (Blanchette & Taylor, 2009).

Prison Programs and Policies

Unfortunately, it is apparent that many older women, due to the nature of their crime and accompanying sentence, will more than likely never experience life on the outside again. Of special concern for these individuals is the need to establish new prison programs and policies for creating a prison setting more compatible for elders with special needs. Often factors such as the small number of older women that will be occupying later adulthood in this environment, budget considerations, inadequate staffing, and space restrictions have caused administration to overlook the unique needs of the aging female when planning for housing, programming, and services (Aday, 2003). Naturally, the dearth of attention granted to special circumstances experienced by aged and infirm women has resulted in many expressing their dissatisfaction with their living arrangements. Given the older female offender may encounter extreme levels of anxiety, depression, boredom, apathy, or despair when they are presented with various environmental and program constraints, it is imperative to identify and explore in further detail any recommendations for improving the state of their existing accommodations. Certainly, a gendered approach is necessary in responding more effectively to the needs of older women.

Living Accommodations

Mental and physical health problems afflicting older female prisoners are aggravated by the prison environment. Age-unfriendly settings have been found to penalize older women for functional and mental impairment. Placing the graying woman in settings where daily life is routinely characterized by the presence of inaudible staff orders, exhausting or demanding physical labor, or even so rigidly defined schedules that there is virtually no time to pause between activities can take its toll on nearly every aspect of the offender's well-being. Elders who are already experiencing problems with their hearing, for example, have frequently discussed the ramifications associated with being punished for failure to comply with policies they were unaware of. Furthermore, women who are situated in facilities where expectations do not become increasingly more lax with the onset of advanced age have occasionally reported suffering the unintended effects of serious (as well as, more frequently, minor) injuries due to being unable to navigate the demands imposed on them (Williams et al., 2006; Strupp & Willmott, 2005). It is not uncommon, for example, for women to report falling on the job, as they are climbing to and from their upper bunk accommodations, or even in passing between activities when they do not have someone in their immediate presence who is willing to assist them in overcoming some of the most commonly reported barriers or obstacles. Although we have talked in extensive detail about the invaluable role that social supports play in helping members of a graying prison population proceed through their daily activities, one cannot always depend on them to be readily available when assistance is most needed. As we have illustrated, staff may harbor strict reservations about assisting to fill a void where it may be needed.

Many of the problems that a graying female prison population faces on a routine basis are further complicated by the layout of contemporary women's prisons. Women's prisons, for example, are generally small in comparison to men's prisons—making security seem more rigorous and omnipotent. The small, often claustrophobic, environment denies privacy and curtails movement (Genders & Player, 1990). Moreover, the penal setting often forces two or more women to live within an arm's reach of one another and within the constant view of prison staff—both male and female. Thus, older women are denied the protection of modesty and the "respectability" normally deemed appropriate for older women (Wahidin, 2004). Privacy has been found to be a key factor in helping older adults mentally and emotionally adjust to institutionalized settings (Kane et al., 2003). A lack of privacy is especially detrimental for older women who grew up in an era that stressed modesty more stridently than our contemporary culture.

Since issues pertaining to space restrictions have been considered by many to be of paramount importance, one of the primary practices that was, at one time, regarded as taboo is the notion of double-celling, or the placement of more than one individual in a room designed, constructed, and intended to be a single-occupancy accommodation. In recent years, correctional budgets have failed to equip administrators with the resources necessary to safely house the desired number of inmates per institution. As some institutions filled to over 180 percent occupancy, many officials perceived themselves faced with no option but to assign more individuals to already cramped quarters. In essence, most jurisdictions eventually required two individuals to limit the necessary furniture and personal possessions to fit within a 60-square-foot area, or as Haney (2006) notes, the area of one king-sized bed. One institution in our study actually doubled-celled many inmates in a 48-square-foot area. While most who have examined issues concerning the presence of personal space as it is available within the context of prison settings focus exclusively on the experiences of male offenders, more attention should be given to the space restrictions now imposed in more and more women's facilities.

Literature concerning the long-term effects close confinement could indirectly have on inmates' psychological well-being has proliferated. Among studies to emerge, many documented positive correlations between space restrictions, perceived control over one's surroundings, and heightened levels of stress. John Gibbs's (1991) framework, which was based on the notion of environmental congruence, provided a compelling explanation of the processes by which the addition of inmates to already-crowded facilities creates unanticipated and unwarranted conflicts for the individuals who were residing in the locations at the time of their arrival. In general, inmates who report experiencing high environmental demands (as evidenced by the need for characteristics including safety, certainty, autonomy, and privacy) without the resources necessary to obtain the desired outcome appear to be at increased risk of suffering from symptoms indicative of poor institutional adjustment. Specific problems that inmates who lack a sense of choice in daily activities incur range from impaired interpersonal relations, adverse physiological reactions, symptoms indicative of mental illness, engagement in prison misconduct, restrictions to solitary confinement, and occasionally even mistreatment by exploitative staff (Bukstel & Kilmann, 1980; Gibbs, 1991; Haney, 2006).

Several of the most commonly identified issues to arise throughout the inmate narratives concerning their current living accommodations focused extensively on the absence of bedding appropriate for use by aged and infirm populations. Similar to prior research focusing on the needs of older offenders (Leigey, 2007; Loeb, Steffensmeier & Myco, 2007), our participants recognized the critical role that getting sufficient rest plays in maintaining optimum health but perceived themselves as limited in the degree to which they could personally control their sleep habits with the personal items they currently had available for their use. Without access to basic necessities such as lower bunks, comfortable mattresses, and sufficient pillows and blankets that their free-world counterparts take for granted, some elders described the rest they receive on a nightly basis in unfavorable terms. Several women, for example, indicated the mattresses they currently have are thin, flimsy, and when pressed against their aging bodies, cause significant pain to their already fragile bones and joints. Some women equated their current routine to sleeping on "metal and concrete" or "steel pancakes," whereas others reported that the level of discomfort was so intolerable they "never really get to sleep." Regardless of the pain endured from their provisions, those who openly shared their attitudes, thoughts, and feelings concerning this issue encouraged administrators to consider the implications that simple transformations such as the addition of more amenities could have on fostering a positive sleep experience.

One of the most commonly mentioned items these individuals requested throughout their stories was for the provision of lower-level bunking accommodations. As we have thoroughly discussed in earlier chapters, an estimated 85 percent of participants indicated they, indeed, needed lower bunks. While prison administrators do develop policies to ensure that inmates who would be physically unable to climb up ladders to top bunks receive special consideration whenever sufficient resources permit (Caldwell, Jarvis & Rosefield, 2001), the presence of written guidelines does not necessarily guarantee the aged and infirm receive these options. In many institutions, for example, the unique combination of financial constraints, space restrictions, and a growing number of persons who have physical health conditions that would warrant receipt of a lower bunk forces officials to accept the daunting task of determining which individuals have the greatest need. In some prisons, correctional personnel may even deliberately withhold assignment to lower bunks from those who truly could never independently reach the upper bunk as a form of discrimination, humiliation, or punishment (Leigey, 2007). Some scholars have reported cases involving officers who will reprimand individuals who are caught resting, napping, or sleeping on the bed of thoughtful peers, further inflicting punishment on the frailest offenders (Stoller, 2003). Although our participants provided no direct evidence of this occurring in their institutions, several expressed their desire for personnel to be more cognizant of their personal circumstances when selecting the most appropriate cells for them to reside in. Given the need identified in this study, it is evident prison administrators who will be preparing for the entrance of older women into the system will continue to be faced with the growing challenge of ensuring this population receives bunking assignments that are appropriate for their current levels of maneuverability.

Grouping Older Inmates

As the actual numbers of older female offenders increase, grouping this subpopulation into special housing units or designated areas specifically designed for or adapted to meet the unique needs of aging inmates should be considered. Older offenders with chronic illnesses are increasingly housed on a long-term basis in special needs facilities or medical units. For example, California has a licensed skilled nursing facility in the women's prison that provides constant, direct nursing care for its aging and infirm prisoners (Nadel, 1997), and, in particular, other special needs units have sprung up in countless men's facilities (see Harrison, 2006). Correctional policy should clearly define the goals and objectives of special units and perhaps specific criteria for admission should be developed. Combining similar populations, such as older female inmates with serious physical disabilities, can provide the protected environment old inmates may need to reduce environmental stressors.

Few of the older inmates representing the various facilities in this study reported being satisfied with their living conditions. One of the primary considerations that administrators who are presented with the inmate frustrations and criticisms must respond to as they prepare for the entrances of more older women into this environment involves recognizing, acknowledging, and basing decisions on the extent to which the existing facilities permit elders to age in place with dignity and grace. In general, individuals who are identified as aging in place are persons who are able to remain in their current residential locations even after they begin to witness marked declines in their physical functioning. For these elders, continued contact with familiar objects, recreational activities, and social supports who reside in close proximity to themselves are invaluable in helping them adjust to various unanticipated joys and sorrows encountered across the life course (Rosel, 2003). Satisfaction with one's housing arrangements may be particularly crucial for enhancing the overall quality of life for those elders who have, over the years, had to reduce their frequency of contact with the external world (Hooyman & Kiyak, 2008). It is no surprise to observe that the older women who composed our sample recognized their living environments as playing critical roles in either facilitating or hindering their levels of institutional adjustment.

Given the variety and complexity of concerns that older incarcerated persons frequently pose regarding institutional living, policymakers have recently begun to explore the most practical and economical approaches for responding to them. Among the potential solutions that have been proposed to resolve grievances elders have with their current living arrangements, the notion of segregated housing units has sparked considerable scholarly interest. Within the past several years, a substantial body of research has proliferated to recognize the needs unique to persons who are over 50 years of age and have health conditions that would preclude them from functioning effectively in the mainstream prison environment (Aday, 2003; Wahidin & Tate, 2005). Numerous scholars, for example, have argued that grouping offenders by their medical needs substantially increases the level of specialized care these individuals would receive while simultaneously permitting administrators to avert the expense of offering services in every facility where the aged and infirm would otherwise likely reside (Kerbs & Jolley, 2009; Thivierge-Rikard & Thompson, 2007).

Over time, it has also become increasingly more evident that many older women would view segregation as serving a critical social function. As we have extensively documented in previous chapters, females who are placed in direct contact with their younger counterparts often feel as if they have no viable option but to remain on guard for others who may use their physical frailties as signs of potential weakness and vulnerability. Several individuals, for example, have expressed that they regularly refrain from congregating in communal areas as these places within the larger institution appear to be prime locations for younger, assertive, and aggressive persons to prey upon them. For them, prolonged exposure to intolerable noise levels, insults, or threats of physical injury can substantially diminish the anticipation that would otherwise be associated with formerly enjoyable pastimes.

Decisions to segregate older women from their younger counterparts would undisputedly provide many individuals who are entering into later adulthood access to a number of privileges that would improve their feelings of safety and comfort. When comparing older inmates who were mainstreamed with those in a special facility, James Marquart,

Dorothy Merianos, and Geri Doucet (2000) discovered that most prisoners from both groups overwhelmingly supported the idea that older offenders required sheltering from the general prison population, especially from young inmates who might victimize them. Removing the more frail older offenders from the larger institutional climate, for example, is considered by many to serve the advantage of buffering or shielding them from minor or even major acts of exploitation. Specifically, many elders report valuing this practice as it substantially reduces their level of exposure to concerns such as verbal threats, taunts or teases, or financial exploitation (Kerbs & Jolley, 2009). In return, providing opportunities for age segregation would give many individuals who will be advancing in age in correctional facilities an added feeling of safety or security in knowing they would be reasonably safe and secure to participate in activities they would enjoy throughout their daily routines.

Nonetheless, any use of this alternative would need to be accompanied by efforts to ensure that the offenders' removal from mainstream environments would unlikely introduce them to additional extraneous burdens that could inhibit their opportunities for personal growth. In jurisdictions that have extended this option to male offenders, elders confined to geriatric facilities have occasionally reported suffering greatly from boredom or despair. For many, having limited options to engage in meaningful employment or structured activities results in them occupying countless hours in states of idleness. As previous research has appropriately illustrated, residence away from their more energetic, youthful peers causes some individuals to limit their daily affairs to sedentary pursuits such as reading, writing, watching television, taking naps, and snacking (Marquart, Merianos & Doucet, 2000).

Medical Policies Examined

Many women who made up our sample also recognized any comprehensive approach that would permit them easier access to needed medical services. Naturally, older women experience health complications that require greater use of screenings, diagnostic examinations, lab work, and follow-up services than other segments of the prison population (Aday, 2003; Morton, 1992; Nadel, 1997; Reviere & Young, 2004). Given the small number of elders who may reside in any one facility, however, institutions have historically failed in providing these offenders timely services on location. Instead, elders in greatest need of securing effective, efficient treatment for their conditions have often discovered themselves having to either wait extraordinary lengths of time before services are rendered or forced to leave the institution to receive care in area hospitals or other free-world facilities where specialized options would be available (Wahidin, 2004).

Because of the high prevalence of physical and mental health-care needs among older inmates, this group of offenders requires more frequent, complex, and costly medical services. As a result, most prisons today do require inmates to absorb some of that expense by using the managed-care strategy of inmate co-payments (Fisher & Hatton, 2010; Reviere & Young, 2004). Women who do manage to secure access to, contact with, and treatment from medical providers also often discover this policy creates excessive burdens and hardships on them. Participants frequently complained of being charged a co-pay by just going to medical regardless of whether any treatment was received. In recent years, administrators have received considerable scrutiny and pressure to initiate co-payment plans when responding to inmate populations. Advocates in favor of co-payments contend that such policies curtail or discourage inmate idle time, instill in individuals a sense of personal responsibility for managing their own health care, and reserve existing services for those who are most in need of treatment. Given offenders' high demand for medical care in comparison to their free-world counterparts, requests for specialized care or even second opinions when their conditions are not treated with the desired immediacy, as well as the frequent trips to sick call when they appear to be bored, lonely, or otherwise in need of attention and companionship, policymakers have often identified this option as one of the most effective deterrents to misuse and abuse of given privileges (Marquart, Merianos & Doucet, 2000; Aday, 2003; Stoller, 2003).

When inmates are presented with the news that they must assist in funding their own care, it is projected that they will routinely be involved in more stimulating health-promoting behaviors, avoid using health-related concerns as excuses to avoid work or other daily chores, and be prepared to listen to any health-related advice they may be provided when they do appear before the physician for care (Rold, 1996). However, countless women mentioned that they no longer participate in any preventive medical services, which can result in a more costly older inmate population down the road. Nonetheless, the prevalence of indigent populations who entered into the environment with preexisting conditions, and yet have neither the personal resources nor family with the resources necessary to assist them in securing medical care, have caused many to encourage the pursuit and exploration of more equitable alternatives.

Unsurprisingly, common themes resonating through some of the inmate narratives were deeply rooted in the primary arguments scholars have previously posed in favor of renegotiating existing practices involving inmate co-payments for sick-call visits. As William Rold (1996) explained over a decade ago, the very nature of incarceration severely restricts offenders' freedom to use any form of personal discretion in making decisions concerning health-related issues. Unlike the individual who experiences a common ailment while residing in mainstream society, those who notice themselves becoming ill while under the gaze of the penal system cannot easily secure amenities such as over-the-counter medications or privileges such as time off from work when they encounter the most common ailments. Moreover, those with mobility problems frequently find it extraordinarily challenging to ensure that ground-level accommodations are secured to minimize the risk of falls or other injuries. Given the infrequency with which these individuals are granted permission to promote optimum levels of health, safety, and well-being, some opponents of the use of co-payments have argued that it is the state's responsibility to provide care to every offender who goes through the system.

In keeping with findings from previous studies that focus on health care received by female offenders (Fisher & Hatton, 2010; Hatton, Kleffel & Fisher, 2006), members of our sample encouraged prison administrators to reconsider the processes by which co-payment amounts were determined, issued, or collected. Often, these individuals expressed their frustrations with having to pay a fee-per-service to purchase basic care, dental, and other ancillary services. Although the co-payment may be nominal (on average, $3 to $5 per service they must have performed), this penalizes those persons whose only form of financial support is the meager wages earned from prison employment. For a number of persons, the decision to seek treatment for any conditions may involve sacrificing any opportunities they may have to purchase from a range of additional commodities from the prison's commissary. Even more distressingly, those individuals who are incarcerated in institutions that require inmates to pay the small sum before the services are rendered have occasionally reported grievances associated with the fact that the care they have financed was never received. Supporting the notion that co-payments for prison health care can significantly reduce women's likelihood of requesting professional assistance when it is genuinely needed (Hyde & Brumfield, 2003), several participants urged policymakers to note the deleterious impact charges have on overall qualities of life.

Health Promotion Approaches

Chronic disease can often be managed through proper education, exercise, and healthy eating habits (Loeb & Steffensmeier, 2006; Stojkovic, 2007). As the cost of providing older female offenders access to needed medical care continues to rise, prison administrators will be presented with no option but to expand the range of services that emphasize disease prevention and health promotion. The limited body of research currently in existence concerning older offenders' receptivity to health promotion activities indicates members of this population are often very responsive to opportunities for change. Many elders, for example, earnestly desire to feel healthier, more mentally alert, and better about themselves in general (Loeb, Steffensmeier & Lawrence, 2008). Although few will have entered into the system having had opportunities to engage in healthy lifestyle practices, those who may have had the luxury of enjoying more diverse experiences share their expectations that such involvement will be continued throughout the duration of their given terms. Understandably, these individuals warmly welcome any options that would likely assist them in increasing their energy levels, expanding their social networks, and improving their senses of independence (Loeb, Steffensmeier & Myco, 2007).

One key component members of our sample associated with health promotion activities involved the development and maintenance of healthier diets. Similar to elders who reside in free-world settings (Arcury, Quandt & Bell, 2001), participants defined healthy eating in terms of the content of the food served as well as the structure of the overall meal experience. While many women recognized mealtimes as being a channel through which officials could regularly exert their power, force, and control over offenders—that is, by engaging in strategies such as planning mealtimes so inmates leave the dining areas full, sedated, and with limited energy to engage in rule-violating behaviors; selecting highly recommended foods from state-approved lists rather than those known to be rich in needed nutrients; and so on—they simultaneously recognized the long-term benefits that could be accrued from having greater variety available to them. In general, older incarcerated persons, for example, very frequently express an intense desire to eliminate those foods that are high in starch or caloric content that are presently on prison menus in favor of fresh fruits, vegetables, or meats (Janssen, 2007). The sentiment of many women is that more nutritional foods such as "more fruits and fresh vegetables" are sorely needed. As one inmates questioned, "How much starch can they put into our system?"

From a policy standpoint, any plans to ensure members of an aging prison population receive the full advantages associated with healthy eating must unarguably involve taking into consideration the amount of time necessary for inmates to travel from their previous activity to the dining hall, secure their food, and enjoy their meals. Given the prevalence of mobility problems and other health-related concerns that result in slower response time among older adults, it is unsurprising to note that those who must occupy later adulthood in prison regularly encounter problems arriving with sufficient time (Williams et al., 2007). As discussed in Chapter 2, numerous women did complain about the limited time that was made available to eat. Some mentioned the problems of digestion, dentures, or lack of teeth slowing down their eating process. However, there was little flexibility among prison security in providing any consideration for their special needs.

Although women may occasionally opt out of participating in traditional dining options in favor of snacking, preparing, or consuming meals in their personal cells, even these offenders will likely encounter a range of barriers they must overcome in order to receive balanced diets that would be considered high in nutritional value. Given the fact that many inmates rely on the food supply at the canteen, it was suggested that more nutritional foods and less sweets and sodium should be made available there as well. It was suggested that individuals who frequent the commissary report that healthier alternatives to meals in the mainstream dining hall are extremely expensive, often beyond the price the average working inmate could feasibly afford, and in some cases unavailable (George, 2010; Janssen, 2007; Leigey, 2007). Naturally, however, inmates will only benefit from the presence of alternative diets if they elect to comply with the procedures for securing them. As Marquart and colleagues (2000) have explained, elders must often undergo an intense application and screening process prior to their placement on lists for modified diets. Moreover, those individuals who have documented chronic conditions such as diabetes or hypertension must resist the temptations with which they may be presented to add salt or other seasoning to the otherwise bland foods the prisons serve.

Special Programming

As the number of older women who are occupying later adulthood in prison continues to rise, increased emphasis will also unquestionably be placed on accommodating their unique leisure and social needs. Until recently, members of this population had historically been overlooked, unacknowledged, or ignored when administrators planned vocational, educational, or recreational programming. Since these individuals made up the smallest segment of prisoners, frequently entered the system after years of passivity, lacked the strength or skills to participate in rigorous, structured activity, and had to be coaxed or prodded to become involved in existing opportunities, their voices were generally overshadowed by the concerns of their more assertive counterparts (Kratcoski & Babb, 1990; Aday, 2003).

Several states, however, are slowly beginning to recognize that older women do bring with them into the prison system a wide range of interests that can often be pursued through engagement in constructive activity. Administrators advocating on behalf of extending to this population more varied options for using their existing knowledge appear very receptive to the idea that every offender has some special talent that can be used for the betterment of self, the institution, and society at large. This point is well illustrated by one inmate in the Georgia system: "The prison staff here shows an interest in providing mentally and physically stimulating opportunities for an assortment of interest. They're generous with their time and given adequate information classify us in areas where we have an interest or sometimes experience that lends itself to fulfillment as well as mental stimulation." However, as a whole, the prisons housing inmates across this five-state region failed to offer activities especially designed for the older offender. Within other systems, for example, older women may receive encouragement to use their experiences with quilting, knitting, and other forms of needlework to sew clothing, blankets, toys, or other personal items for community organizations that are in need of these essentials (Janssen, 2007).

In recent years, the notion of establishing inmate support groups has emerged as one potential vehicle through which administrators could assist older women in coming to terms with mixed emotions they may have concerning their personal situations. Support groups are typically considered to be very safe environments within which participants can comfortably, freely, and openly discuss issues they may share with others. Within the prison setting, topics of exploration may include issues such as overcoming the deleterious effects of abusive relationships, addictive behaviors, or severance of external supports. For elderly women whose current problems stem from having previously encountered challenges asserting themselves while engaged in interpersonal interactions, active involvement in a group can permit them the invaluable opportunities to practice addressing their needs without the fear of potential abandonment. As they disclose intimate details concerning their lives with other offenders who, very frequently, will have greater understanding, awareness, and insight into the pains associated with their unique hardships than would family, friends, or acquaintances who reside outside the walls of the institutional setting; staff members; or trained professionals who also occupy time and space within the prison system, older inmates can find support groups to also be an invaluable resource for learning how to adjust to environmental demands that have been imposed on them. Additional themes that would likely seem important to persons who have yet to become accustomed to the fundamental nature of institutional living involve issues surrounding shared living and dining space; adherence to strict, inflexible rules or routines; interactions with apathetic, uncaring staff members; declines in physical functioning; and normal grief reactions that typically follow the unanticipated death of their newly identified friends and acquaintances. Although participation in support groups would unlikely have any major influence in changes to ways in which prisons currently operate (Schwartz, 2007), through their involvement in available support groups, older women can at least begin to resolve any feelings of anger, remorse, apprehensiveness, or despair (Aday, 2003).

The Ohio Department of Rehabilitation and Correction (1999) has implemented several programs, solely designed for older female offenders, that incorporate a strong support group modality. One end-of-life program teaches older offenders how to get their needs met in an assertive manner without major conflict or confrontation. Issues of loss due to chronic illness and death are also addressed in other programs. Providing appropriate care for dying prisoners is a growing problem and the program Heart to Heart provides a support system for offenders who are struggling with issues of their terminal illness. It provides information regarding such things as living wills. The program also improves the quality of life for dying offenders through interaction in an emotionally supportive environment. Another program, Life Beyond Loss, also teaches participants about the grieving process and how to apply techniques of grief resolution. Hospice care is now provided in many correctional facilities. Such programs provide counseling, crisis intervention, and closure in the form of funeral or memorial services.

Although participation in support, self-help, or mutual aid groups can undoubtedly prove to be an invaluable, enjoyable, and rewarding learning experience for older women who would otherwise likely have limited options for meeting their socioemotional needs, prior research conducted with elders who reside in free-world environments reminds us that involvement or engagement in this activity does not benefit every elder equally. Older individuals who have recently sustained the adverse effects of traumatic events and appear to still be in shock from these events may be better off attempting one-on-one counseling sessions prior to entering the group environment (Toseland & Rizzo, 2005). Specifically, persons who may be grappling with pressing personal issues or concerns that societal norms strongly discourage people from discussing in open settings may discover their attempt at seeking support within a public arena as placing them at increased risk of scrutiny among their peers (Kelly, 2004)

Staff Training

Among the myriad of recommendations our participants provided for enhancing older female offenders' current levels of life satisfaction, nearly all could be addressed through the use of increased staff training. As a growing body of literature has suggested, correctional personnel who must engage in prolonged communications with this population receive limited preparation for the enormous responsibilities they are expected to assume (Knapp & Elder, 1997–1998). At best, officers may be required to attend short seminars designed to only briefly familiarize them with the most fundamental knowledge concerning the various physical, cognitive, social, and emotional changes that accompany the aging process (Cianciolo & Zupan, 2004; Morton, 1992). In general, these sessions are typically structured to be one small component of a much larger in-service in which all employees within the institution must engage. As participants in these sessions, line staff, for example, may often be grouped and engaged in extensive dialogues with prison physicians or other professionals who receive more direct exposure to the aged and infirm in their daily practices. Although the use of group discussions, simulations, vignettes, and collaboration with their teammates may encourage employees to begin identifying and thinking about the ways in which their attitudes toward older adults in general, and older prisoners in particular, have been shaped by larger political, social, and environmental forces, a number of staff members may complete these activities with limited understanding about the relevance of training to their own positions of employment.

Specific groups of elders for whom correctional personnel will require additional training to assist them in responding in the coming years involve terminally ill offenders. As of this writing, an estimated 1,304 persons 55 years of age and older were identified as dying in state prisons annually, with the number of deaths due to illness or natural causes outpacing those from suicide, homicide, drugs, accidents, or unknown reasons (Mumola & Noonan, 2008). Although factors such as longer mandatory sentences have contributed to a rise in older persons spending their final years of life in the prison environment, correctional officers and other staff members have not received sufficient preparation for working with this segment of the population. Instead, personnel are frequently trained to harbor feelings of suspicion, distrust, and animosity toward the persons who are in their custody. Given the frequency with which personnel may encounter other inmates abusing sick-call lines or other medical services, they have historically failed to respond empathetically to the frailest among them. When presented with the occasional inmate who has a genuine need for comforting, they have often misconstrued any kind gestures or acts of generosity toward the dying as akin to "coddling" (Maull, 1991, 1998; Reviere & Young, 2004). Hopefully, the emerging presence of hospice in prison settings will play an important role in changing the prison culture from the current "penal harm" mentality to a more humanitarian one.

Information garnered from experiences older terminally ill persons confined in other total institutions have encountered in their interactions with employees can assist in filling a critical void in minimizing the friction that has regularly been observed in prison settings. As has been thoroughly documented in studies conducted with persons who are confined to nursing home environments (Kayser-Jones, 2002), the presence of effective communication skills may often play a crucial role in minimizing any feelings of abandonment or isolation that can accompany the dying process. Terminally ill persons whose family, friends, and other loved ones cannot be readily available to provide them much-needed around-the-clock support, and who do not have the strength that would be necessary to join peers in mentally stimulating activities occurring throughout the institution, may seek solace through staff interactions.

Summary

As the number of geriatric female offenders continues to swell, the voices of this distinct population will become increasingly more important in the development and implementation of prison policy. From the stories that the women in our sample generously shared, several recommendations can be made for enhancing the quality of life experienced by older women who are advancing in age behind bars. In general, their narratives have shared that a wide range of changes must be made in terms of how health-related, recreational, and social programming needs are addressed. Special consideration, the respondents observed, must be directed toward those women who arrived at prison at high risk for maladjustment, long-termers who are unlikely to return home to mainstream society in the foreseeable future, as well as terminally ill individuals who are currently striving to prepare themselves physically, mentally, emotionally, and spiritually for the end of life. In nearly every facility we visited, common themes identified and resonating throughout their stories focused on and provided invaluable insights into strategies that prison administration could adopt for improving the physical layout or structure of the facilities themselves, improving procedures for securing needed medical treatment, addressing ways interpersonal conflicts or disputes are resolved, and preparing or training staff to listen and accommodate their needs in a timely manner. Understandably, nearly all women had their own general and specific impressions about approaches that officials could adopt to establish more "age friendly" institutions. Nonetheless, the most salient and recurrent recommendations are outlined and discussed below.

Most importantly, care should be taken to ensure that any housing accommodations to which they are assigned are conducive to their age and gender-specific needs. Given the large number of older women who have entered the system with highly stressful, turbulent pasts, special emphasis should be placed on ensuring that their living quarters are as private as could be humanly achievable in a correctional setting of this nature. Ideally, for example, this practice would entail providing the geriatric female offender assignment to facilities where they have regular access to private or semiprivate sleeping quarters, bathrooms, dining halls, laundry facilities, dayrooms, and visitation areas (Caldwell, Jarvis & Rosefeld, 2001; Aday, 2003; Strupp & Wilmott, 2005).

In terms of the sleeping quarters, arrangements must be made to provide the older women with places they can call their own—spaces where they can retreat from the noise and chaos that routinely characterize institutional living to enjoy much anticipated rest and relaxation at the end of the day. Naturally, sufficient care should always be taken to afford those who require ground-level housing and lower bunks the needed provisions. In addition, attention should be directed toward making this climate one that would be relatively and reasonably comfortable for older populations. As we have illustrated throughout this chapter, this process would require prison administrators to provide the offenders themselves some degree of control over characteristics such as the temperature, lighting, and noise levels. Specifically, geriatric female offenders would benefit substantially from having access to thermostats they can personally adjust, comfortable bedding and mattresses, as well as additional blankets as circumstances warrant. Undisputedly, such amenities would be particularly necessary, welcomed, and greatly appreciated during the months when the weather is likely to be inclement and unbearable to even some members of mainstream society.

Given that none can realistically or objectively assess the level of pain that older women may routinely endure on a daily basis in relation to prolonged exposure to adverse environmental conditions, flexibility must be granted when their concerns are expressed. In order to ensure that incarceration is indeed treated as being "for punishment" instead of "to punish" in purpose, staff members must be actively encouraged to listen to the older adult when complaints are filed, questions posed, or concerns voiced. With the number of older women who will be occupying their later adulthood years behind prison walls projected to continue rising well into the twenty-first century, it is simply inexcusable to maintain the rigid policies that have come to shape, define, or characterize institutional routines. Older women, for example, must be granted some leniency or leeway in terms of soliciting, receiving, and enjoying the advantages associated with receiving support from their fellow offenders. As several elders in our sample generously shared, policies that restrict the level of instrumental help or assistance that one offender may provide to another can prove frustrating (if not dangerous) when the person on the receiving end of the exchange is currently advancing in age and, consequently, noticing declines in her levels of functioning. Moreover, the purposes of any institutional policies that require all inmates (regardless of age) to participate in various chores or routines must be reconsidered, reevaluated, and renegotiated if older adult populations are to thrive in this environment free from illness, injury, or exploitation. Rules or regulations that instruct inmates to take a specific path from one's cell to the dining hall or sick-call lines when shorter, alternative routes are clearly available, for example, serve no valuable purpose in working with this clientele.

Unarguably, each of the abovementioned recommendations would most effectively and efficiently be achieved through the establishment of special geriatric facilities. With all inmates above a certain age range residing together in one centralized location, administration receives the added advantage of being able to more easily identify the concerns held by this unique group and allocate resources accordingly. Although the exact age at which older women should be encouraged or determined eligible for entrance into these special units has yet to be established, several have recommended 55 as a starting point for designing age-appropriate facilities or cells (Strupp & Wilmott, 2005). Given that offenders, as a collective, tend to be on average 10 years older physiologically than their chronological age would suggest, this arrangement would prove indispensable in ensuring that older women receive access to needed programming and services well before the time that they would be needed. Such arrangements, for example, would assist administration in noting the special medical and other health-related needs that female offenders are likely to take on as they continue to travel together across the life course. In addition, they would prove essential in helping to train those staff members who will be working with them on an ongoing basis in the basic geriatrics needed to serve this population. As a significant number of the women who made up our small sample observed, however, this arrangement serves more than an indispensable medical or health-related function. For example, it proves to be invaluable in recognizing and responding to the need for program participation, interpersonal socialization, and friendship formation. Overall, our findings suggest, prison personnel must be willing and able to acknowledge that women who have grown old behind bars have varying interests from their younger counterparts, actively attempt to avoid communal social areas where much of the activity characterizing daily prison life is likely to occur, and generally refrain from making their needs known to others. Unless prison administrators, policymakers, correctional personnel, and others assume the initiative for identifying and tailoring provisions accordingly, most would appear relatively content with complacency or the adoption of a relatively sedentary lifestyle.

Final Comments

This book has addressed the fact that the number of women in US prisons has steadily increased over the past three decades. Unique to this growth has been the rapid increase in the number of older women behind bars. It is obvious that this is a diverse group of females who have found their way into the prison system, some for nonviolent crimes such as drug-related offenses, while others are serving long sentences for violent crimes. Regardless of circumstances that first brought them to prison or the harsher sentencing policies that have increased the length of prison sentences, federal and state policies and programs continue to neglect the health-care and programming needs of aging female inmates (Williams & Rikard, 2004). Understanding the lives of this forgotten population and the dynamic social world they encounter on a daily basis has been a worthy endeavor. While the number of older females imprisoned is still significantly smaller than their male counterparts, they are presenting challenging problems for institutions who with limited resources must respond to the special needs of this vulnerable population.

We have made every effort to provide a comprehensive view into the lives and characteristics of aging female inmates. It is an attempt to provide greater visibility for a group of older female inmates who entered prison with a variety of chronic health conditions, feelings of hopelessness and depression, as well as a variety of other gender-sensitive issues. When adjusting to a life in prison, the culture of violence endured by the incarcerated women at the hands of their abusers should not be ignored. Similar to other research, this project identifies the existing problem of imposing male standards for health care, housing, nutrition, and mental-health counseling on women prisoners (Zust, 2009). As we explored various facets of the women's lives, their personal narratives provided countless examples of the personal pains of imprisonment endured frequently at the cost of their dignity. There is also evidence of the hope for a second chance that is desperately clung to by the majority of these women, who despite being recipients of penal harm and undue punishment, seem to find a way to frame their lives in a most positive fashion given the circumstances of their sentence history.

As we conclude our body of work to share these women's experiences in the criminal justice system, it is imperative that the issues raised in this journey will somehow receive the appropriate attention from those responsible for influencing policy. Otherwise, older women in the criminal justice system will continue to be marginalized with inadequate care and without the necessary health-care standards to which they are entitled. It is apparent the current policies are often fraught with an ageist attitude leading to a disregard for the human spirit, particularly among so many women who are nearing the ends of their lives. It is important that the correctional system provide appropriate programming and therapy opportunities for those who have lived their entire lives under oppression and abuse. Creating a social environment within the confines of a harsh prison setting that fosters the development of interpersonal relationships is of equal importance.

The aging prison population will continue to pose a significant dilemma for decades to come as officials responsible for executing prison policy grapple with the problems associated with this special subgroup of prisoners. With an economic crisis that is challenging most state budgets to simply maintain the status quo, perhaps the time is ripe to consider alternatives to the traditional warehousing framework that has guided the unprecedented growth of the US prison system. This custodial approach has resulted in an increasing number of women being retained in prison for more than 20 or 30 years even though they have led model lives in prison. As Azrini Wahidin pointed out, "so many have faded into anonymity," and are now all but forgotten (2004, p. 196). In passing along the stories of these aging women and the conditions from which they came, this book will provide a significant step in recognizing the special needs of this prison subpopulation. With the women's courage to bare their souls and the authors' commitment to complete this project, the visibility of this group will no doubt be enhanced. Hopefully, the findings presented in this book will translate into forward-thinking prison policies that will be beneficial to both the older incarcerated women and the prison system alike.

References

Abramsky, S. (2004). "Lifers: Legal affairs." www.legalaffairs.org.

Acoca, L. (1998). "Defusing the time bomb: Understanding and meeting the growing health care needs of incarcerated women in America." *Crime and Delinquency* 44: 49–70.

Adams, K., & Ferrandino, J. (2008). "Managing mentally ill inmates in prisons." *Criminal Justice and Behavior* 35, no. 8: 913–927.

Adams, R. G. (1989). "Conceptual and methodological issues in studying friendships of older adults." In R. G. Adams & R. Blieszner (eds.), *Older adult friendships*. Newbury Park, CA: Sage, pp. 127–143.

Aday, R. H. (1994a). "Aging in prison: A case study of new elderly offenders." *International Journal of Offender Therapy and Comparative Criminology* 38, no. 1: 79–91.

———. (1994b). "Golden years behind bars: Special programs and facilities for elderly inmates." *Federal Probation* 58 (June): 47–54.

———. (2003). *Aging prisoners: Crisis in American corrections*. Westport, CT: Praeger.

———. (2005–2006). "Aging prisoners' concerns toward dying in prison." *Omega: Journal of Death and Dying* 52: 195–212.

American Correctional Association. 2010. *Adult and Juvenile Directory*. Alexandria, VA.

Ammar, N. H., & Erez, E. (2000). "Health care delivery systems in women's prisons: The case of Ohio." *Federal Probation* 64, no. 2: 19–27.

Anderson, M. A., Gillig, P. M., Sitaker, M., McCloskey, K., Malloy, K., & Grigsby, N. (2003). "'Why doesn't she just leave?' A descriptive study of victim reported impediments to her safety." *Journal of Family Violence* 18, no. 3: 151–155.

Anderson, T. L. (2006). "Issues facing women prisoners in the early twenty-first century." In C. M. Renzetti, L. Goodstein & S. L. Miller (eds.), *Rethinking gender, crime, and justice*. Los Angeles: Roxbury Publishing Company, pp. 200–212.

Anno, B. J. (2004). "Prison health services: An overview." *Journal of Correctional Health Care* 10: 287–301.

Anno, B. J., Gram, C., Lawrence, J. E., & Shansky, R. (2004). "Correctional health care: Addressing the needs of elderly, chronically ill, and terminally ill inmates." National Institute of Corrections. http://nicic.org.

Aranda, M. P., Lee, P., & Wilson, S. (2001). "Correlates of depression in older Latinos." *Home Health Care Services Quarterly* 20: 1–20.

Aragon, I. Z. (2007). "The need for reentry programs for released aging prisoners." Unpublished manuscript. California State University, Long Beach, CA.

Arcury, T., Quandt, S., & Bell, R. (2001). "Staying healthy: The salience and meaning of health maintenance behaviors among rural older adults in North Carolina." *Social Science and Medicine* 53: 1541–1556.

Arditti, J. A., & Few, A. L. (2006). "Mothers' re-entry into family life following incarceration." *Criminal Justice Policy Review* 17, no. 1: 103–123.

Arias, I., Lyons, C., & Street, A. (1997). "Individual and marital consequences of victimization: Moderating effects of relationship efficacy and spouse support." *Journal of Family Violence* 12, no. 2: 193–210.

Atchley, R. (1989). "A continuity theory of normal aging." *Gerontologist* 29, no. 2: 183–190.

Barak, Y., Perry, T., & Elizur, A. (1995). "Elderly criminals: A study of the first criminal offense in old age." *International Journal of Geriatric Psychiatry* 10: 511–516.

Barnett, O. (2000). "Why battered women do not leave: External inhibiting factors within society." *Trauma, Violence & Abuse* 1, no. 4, 343–372.

Beattie, L. E., & Shaughnessy, M. A. (2000). *Sisters in pain: Battered women fight back*. Lexington: University of Kentucky Press.

Beaulaurier, R. L., Seff, L. R., Newman, F. L., & Dunlop, B. (2005). "Internal barriers to help seeking for middle-aged and older women who experience intimate partner violence." *Journal of Elder Abuse & Neglect* 17, no. 3: 53–72.

Beck, A. J. (1999). *Prisoners in 1999*. Washington, DC: U.S. Department of Justice.

Beckett, J., Taylor, C. P., & Johnson, R. (2003). "Aging matters: Growing old in the correctional system." *Journal of Psychosocial Nursing and Mental Health Services* 41: 12–18.

Ben-David, S., & Siflin, P. (1994). "In quest of a lost father? Inmates' preferences of staff relation in a psychiatric prison ward." *International Journal of Offender Therapy and Comparative Criminology* 38, no. 2: 131–139.

Benton, J. P., Chistopher, A. N., & Walter, M. I. (2007). "Death anxiety as a function of aging anxiety." *Death Studies* 31: 337–350.

Bernstein, N. R. (1990). "Objective bodily image: Disfigurement and dignity." In T. F. Cash & T. Pruzinsky (eds.), *Body images: Development, deviance and change*. New York: Guilford Press, pp. 131–169.

Bill, L. (1998). "The victimization and revictimization of female offenders." *Corrections Today* 62 (December): 106–112.

Blanchette, K., & Brown, S. L. (2006). *The assessment and treatment of women offenders: An integrative perspective*. Chichester, NY: Wiley.

Blanchette, K., & Taylor, K. N. (2009). "Reintegration of female offenders: Perspectives on what works." *Corrections Today* 71, no. 6 (December): 60–63.

Bogat, G. A., Levendosky, A., & Von Eye, A. (2005). "The future of research on intimate partner violence: Person-oriented and variable-oriented perspectives." *American Journal of Community Psychology* 36, no. 1–2: 49–71.

Bolger, M. (2004). "Offenders." In D. Oliviere & B. Monroe (eds.), *Death, dying, and social differences.* New York: Oxford University Press, pp. 133–148.

Bond, G. D., Thompson, L. A., & Malloy, D. M. (2005). "Lifespan differences in the social networks of prison inmates." *International Journal of Aging and Human Development* 61: 161–178.

Bosworth, H., Kwang-Soo, P., McQuoid, D., Hays, J., & Steffens, D. (2003). "The impact of religious practice and religious coping on geriatric depression." *International Journal of Geriatric Psychiatry* 18: 905–914.

Bradley, R. G., & Davino, D. M. (2002). "Women's perceptions of the prison environment: When prison is the safest place I've ever been." *Psychology of Women Quarterly* 26: 351–359.

Braithwaite, R., Arriola, K. J., & Newkirk, C. (2006). *Health issues among incarcerated women.* Piscataway, NJ: Rutgers University Press.

Bright, C. L., & Bowland, S. E. (2008). "Assessing interpersonal trauma in older adult women." *Journal of Loss and Trauma* 13: 373–393.

Britton, D. (2000). "Feminism in criminology: Engendering the outlaw." *Annals, AAPSS* 571, no. 1: 57–76.

Browne, A., Miller, B., & Maguin, E. (1999). "Prevalence and severity of lifetime physical and sexual victimization among incarcerated women." *International Journal of Law and Psychiatry* 22: 301–322.

Bukstel, L. H., & Kilmann, P. R. (1980). "Psychological effects of imprisonment on confined individuals." *Psychological Bulletin* 88: 469–493.

Butler, R. N. (1969). "Ageism: Another form of bigotry." *Gerontologist* 9: 243–246.

Byock, I. R. (2002). "Dying well in corrections: Why should we care?" *Journal of Correctional Health Care* 9, no. 2: 102–117.

Caldwell, C., Jarvis, M., & Rosefield, H. (2001). "Issues impact today's geriatric female offenders." *Corrections Today* 65, no. 5: 110–113.

Campbell, J. C. (2002). "Health consequences of intimate partner violence." *The Lancet* 359: 1331–1336.

Campbell, J. C., Kub, J., & Rose, L. (1996). "Depression in battered women." *Journal of the American Medical Women's Association* 51, no. 3: 106–110.

Campbell, R., Greeson, M. R., Bybee, D., & Raja, S. (2008). "The co-occurrence of childhood sexual abuse, adult sexual assault, intimate partner violence, and sexual harassment: A mediation model of posttraumatic stress disorder and physical health outcomes." *Journal of Consulting and Clinical Psychology* 76: 194–207.

Carroll, L. (1982). "Race, ethnicity, and the social order of the prison." In R. Johnson & H. Toch (eds.), *The pains of imprisonment.* Beverly Hills, CA: Sage.

Casey-Acevedo, K., & Bakken, T. (2002). "Visiting women in prison: Who visits and who cares?" *Journal of Offender Rehabilitation* 34, no. 3: 67–83.

Chiu, T. (2010). *It's about time: Aging prisoners, increasing costs, and geriatric release.* Washington, DC: Vera Institute of Justice.

Christian, J. (2005). "Riding the bus: Barriers to prison visitation and family management strategies." *Journal of Contemporary Criminal Justice* 21, no. 1: 31–48.

Cianciolo, P. K., & Zupan, L. L. (2004). "Developing a training program on issues in aging for correctional workers." *Gerontology and Geriatrics Education* 24, no. 3: 23–38.

Cicirelli, V. G. (1997). "Relationship of psychosocial and background variables to elders' end-of life decisions." *Psychology and Aging* 12: 77–83.

Clemmer, D. (1940). *The prison community.* New York: Holt, Rinehart, and Winston.

Coben, J. H., Forjuoh, S., & Gondolf, E. (1999). "Injuries and health care use in women with partners in batterer intervention programs." *Journal of Family Violence* 14, no. 1: 83–94.

Cobden, J., & Stewart, G. (1984). "Breaking out: A perspective on long-term imprisonment and the process of release." *Canadian Journal of Criminology* 26: 500–510.

Cockerham, W. C. (1991). *This aging society.* Englewood Cliffs, NJ: Prentice Hall.

Cohen, S., Gottlieb, B. H., & Underwood, L. G. (2001). "Social relationships and health: Challenges for measurement and intervention." *Advanced Mind Body Medicine* 17: 129–141.

Cohn, F. (1999). "The ethics of end-of-life care for prison inmates." *Journal of Law, Medicine, & Ethics* 27: 252–259.

Coker, A. L., Smith, P. H., Bethea, L., King, M. R., & McKeown, R. (2000). "Physical health consequences of physical and psychological intimate partner violence." *Archives of Family Medicine* 9: 451–457.

Coker, A. L., Smith, P. H., McKeown, R. E., & King, M. J. (2000). "Frequency and correlates of intimate partner violence by type: Physical, sexual, and psychological battering." *American Journal of Public Health* 90: 553–559.

Comfort, M. L. (2003). "In the tube at San Quentin: The secondary prisonization of women visiting inmates." *Journal of Contemporary Ethnography* 32, no. 1: 77–107.

Conklin, J. E. (2004). *Criminology.* Boston: Pearson.

Cowles, E. L., & Sabath, M. J. (1996). "Changes in the nature and the perception of the long-term inmate population." *Criminal Justice Review* 21, no. 1: 44–61.

Cranford, S., & Williams, R. (1998). "Critical issues in managing female offenders: Women offenders have unique needs which impact the ways in which staff manage them." *Corrections Today* 60, no. 7: 130–134.

Crawley, E. (2005). "Institutional thoughtlessness in prison and its impact on the day-to-day prison lives of elderly men." *Journal of Contemporary Criminal Justice* 21, no. 4: 350–363.

Crawley E., & Sparks, R. (2006). "Is there life after imprisonment?" *Criminology and Criminal Justice* 6: 63–82.

Curry, L. (2001). "Tougher sentencing, economic hardships, and rising violence." *Corrections Today* 65: 74–76.

Deaton, D., Aday, R. H., & Wahidin, A. (2009–2010). "The effect of health and penal harm on aging female prisoners' views of dying in prison." *Omega* 60: 33–50.

DeBell, J. (2001). "The female offender: Different, not difficult." *Corrections Today* 63, no. 1: 56–61.

DeHart, D. D. (2008). "Pathways to prison: Impact of victimization in the lives of incarcerated women." *Violence Against Women* 14: 1362–1381.

Deichman, E. S., & Kociecki, R. (1989). *Working with the elderly.* New York: Prometheus Books.

Derogatis, L. R., Lipman, R. , Rickels, K., Uhlenhuth, E. H., & Covi, L. (1974). "The Hopkins symptom checklist (HSCL): Self report symptom inventory." *Behavioral Science* 19: 1–15.

Dhami, M., Ayton, P., & Loewenstein, G. (2007). "Adaptation to imprisonment: Indigenous or imported?" *Criminal Justice and Behavior* 34, no. 8: 1085–1100.

Ditton, P. M. (1999). *Mental health and treatment of inmates and probationers.* Washington, DC: Bureau of Justice Statistics.

Dobbs, D., Eckert, J., Rubenstein, B., & Keimig, L. (2008). "An ethnographic study of stigma and ageism in residential care or assisted living." *Gerontologist* 48: 517–526.

Dressel, P. L., & Barnhill, S. K. (1994). "Reframing gerontological thought and practice: The case of grandmothers with daughters in prison." *The Gerontologist* 34, no. 5: 685–691.

Dutton, D. G. (2007). *Rethinking domestic violence.* Vancouver: University of British Columbia Press.

Dutton, D. G., & Golant, S. K. (1995). *The batterer: A psychological profile.* New York: Basic Books.

Ebersole, P., & Hess, P. (1998). *Toward healthy aging.* St. Louis: Mosby.

Edwards, T. A. (2000). *Female offenders: Special needs and Southern state challenges.* Atlanta, GA: Council of State Governments, Southern Office.

Eliason, M. J., Taylor, J. Y., & Arndt, S. (2005). "Assessing intimate partner violence in incarcerated women." *Journal of Forensic Nursing* 1, no. 3: 106–111.

Enos, S. (2001). *Mothering from the inside: Parenting in a women's prison.* New York: State University of New York Press.

Everard, K. M., Lach, H., Fisher, E. B., & Baum, M. C. (2000). "Relationship of activity and social support to the functional health of older adults." *Journals of Gerontology Series B: Psychological Sciences and Social Sciences* 55: 208–212.

Fagan, T. J., & Lira, F. T. (1978). "Profile of mood states: Racial differences in a delinquent population." *Psychological Reports* 43: 348–350.

Falter, R. G. (1999). "Selected predictors of health services needs of inmates over age 50." *Journal of Correctional Health Care* 6: 149–175.

Fazel, S., Hope, T., O'Donnel, I., & Jacoby, R. (2001). "Hidden psychiatric morbidity in elderly prisoners." *British Journal of Psychiatry* 179: 535–539.

Fearn, N. E., & Parker, K. (2005). "Health care for women inmates: Issues, perceptions and policy considerations." *California Journal of Health Promotion* 3, no. 2: 1–22.

Ferraro, K. J. (1997). "Battered women: Strategies for survival." In A. P. Cardarelli (ed.), *Violence between intimate partners.* Boston: Allyn and Bacon, pp. 124–140.

Fingerman, K. (2004). "The role of offspring and in-laws in grandparents' ties to their grandchildren." *Journal of Family Issues* 25, no. 8: 1026–1049.

Fisher, A. A., & Hatton, D. C. (2010). "A study of women prisoners' use of co-payments for health care: Issues of access." *Women's Health Issues* 20, no. 3: 185–192.

Flanagan, T. J. (1980). "The pains of long-term imprisonment: A comparison of British and American perspectives." *British Journal of Criminology* 20, no. 2: 148–156.

———. (1981). "Dealing with long-term confinement: Adaptive strategies and perspectives among long-term inmates." *Criminal Justice and Behavior* 8, no. 2: 201–222.

———. (1982). "Correctional policy and the long-term prisoner." *Crime and Delinquency* 28: 82–95.

———. (1995). *Long-term imprisonment: Policy, science, and correctional practice.* Thousand Oaks, CA: Sage.

Flanzer, J. (2005). "Alcohol and other drugs are key causal agents of violence." In D. R. Loseke, R. J. Gelles & M. M. Cavanaugh (eds.), *Current controversies on family violence.* Thousands Oaks, CA: Sage, pp. 163–174.

Florida Department of Corrections Annual Report (2002). Tallahassee, FL: Florida Corrections Commission.

Fortner, B. V., & Neimeyer, R. A. (1999). "Death anxiety in older adults: A quantitative review." *Death Studies* 23: 387–411.

Fortner, B. V., Neimeyer, R. A., & Rybarczyk, B. (2000). "Correlates of death anxiety in older adults: A comprehensive review." In A. Tomer (ed.), *Death attitudes, and the older adult: Theories, concepts, and applications.* Philadelphia: Taylor and Francis, pp. 95–198.

Foss, L. L., & Warnke, M. A. (2003). "Fundamentalist Protestant Christian women: Recognizing cultural and gender influences on domestic violence." *Counseling and Values* 48, no. 1: 14–23.

Foucault, M. (1995). *Discipline and punish: The birth of the prison.* New York: Vintage Books.

Freeman, R. M. (2003). "Social distance and discretionary rule enforcement in a women's prison." *The Prison Journal* 83: 191–205.

Fugate, M., Landis, L., Riordan, K., Naureckas, S., & Engel, B. (2005). "Barriers to domestic violence help seeking." *Violence Against Women* 11, no. 3: 290–310.

Furer, P., Walker, J. R., & Stein, M. B. (2007). *Treating health anxiety and fear of death.* New York: Springer.

Gagne, P. (1998). *Battered women's justice.* New York: Twayne.

Gallagher, E. M. (1990). "Emotional, social and physical health characteristics of older men in prison." *International Journal of Aging and Human Development* 31, no. 4: 251–265.

———. (2001). "Elders in prison: Health and well-being of older inmates." *International Journal of Law and Psychiatry* 24: 325–333.

Gamliel, T., & Hazan, H. (2006). "The meaning of stigma: Identity construction in two old-age institutions." *Aging & Society* 26: 355–371.

Garrard, J., Rolnick. S. J., Nitz, M. M., Luepke, L., Jackson, J., Fischer, L. R.,

& Leibson, C. (1998). "Clinical detection of depression among community-based elderly people with self-reported symptoms of depression." *Journals of Gerontology Series A: Biological Sciences and Medical Sciences* 53: M92–M101.

Genders, E., & Player, E. (1990). "Women lifers: Assessing the experience." *The Prison Journal* 70: 46–57.

George, E. (2010). *A woman doing life.* New York: Oxford University Press.

Gesser, G., Wong, T. P., & Reker, G. T. (1987). "Death attitudes across the life span: The development and validation of the death attitude profile." *Omega: Journal of Death and Dying* 18: 113–128.

Gibbons, J. J., & Katzenbach, N. B. (2006). "Confronting confinement." www.prisoncommission.org.

Gibbs, J. J. (1991). "Environmental congruence and symptoms of psychopathology: A further exploration of the effects of exposure to the jail environment." *Criminal Justice and Behavior* 18: 351–374.

Girshick, L. B. (1999). *No safe haven.* Boston: Northeastern University Press.

Glamser, F., & Cabana, D. (2003). "Dying in a total institution: The case of death in prison." In C. Bryant (ed.), *Handbook on Death and Dying.* Thousand Oaks, CA: Sage, pp. 495–501.

Goffman, E. (1961). *Asylums: Essays on the social situation of mental patients and other inmates.* Garden City, NY: Doubleday.

Goodkind, J. R., Gillum, T. L., Bybee, D. I., & Sullivan, C. M. (2003). "The impact of family and friends' reactions on the well-being of women with abusive partners." *Violence Against Women* 9, no. 3: 347–373.

Goodrich, C. S. (1997). "Results of a national survey of state protective services programs: Assessing risk and defining victim outcomes." *Journal of Elder Abuse & Neglect* 9, no. 1: 69–86.

Gosselin, D. K. (2005). *Heavy hands: An introduction to the crimes of family violence.* Upper Saddle River, NJ: Pearson.

Granse, B. L. (2003). "Why should we even care? Hospice social work practice in a prison setting." *Smith College of Social Work* 74, no. 3: 359–375.

Greenfield, L. A., & Snell, T. L. (1999). "Women offenders." Bureau of Justice Statistics Special Report. US Department of Justice Office of Justice Programs.

Greenfield, L., Rand, M., & Craven, D. (1998). *Violence by intimates: Analysis of data on crimes by current or former spouses, boyfriends and girlfriends.* Washington, DC: US Department of Justice.

Greer, K. R. (2000). "The changing nature of interpersonal relationships in a women's prison." *The Prison Journal* 80: 442–468.

———. (2002). "Walking an emotional tightrope: Managing emotions in a women's prison." *Symbolic Interaction* 25, no. 1: 117–139.

Gutheil, Irene A. (1991). "Intimacy in nursing home friendships." *Journal of Gerontological Social Work* 17, no. 1–2: 59–73.

Hagel-Seymour, J. (1982). "Environmental sanctuaries for susceptible prisoners." In H. Toch (ed.), *Pains of imprisonment.* Thousand Oaks, CA: Sage, pp. 267–284.

Hairston, C. F. (1991). "Family ties during imprisonment: Important to whom and for what?" *Journal of Sociology and Social Welfare* 28: 87–104.

Ham, J. N. (1980). "Aged and infirm male prison inmates." *Aging* (July–August): 24–31.

Haney, C. (2006). *Reforming punishment: Psychological limits to the pains of imprisonment*. Washington, DC: American Psychological Association.

Harlow, C. W. (2003). *Education and correctional populations*. Washington, DC: Department of Justice.

Harrison, M. T. (2006). "True grit: An innovative program for elder inmates." *Corrections Today* 68 (December): 46–49.

Harrison-Ross, P., & Lawrence, J. E. (1998). "Health care for women offenders." *Corrections Today* 60: 122–129.

Hatton, D. C., Kleffel, D., & Fisher, A. (2006). "Prisoners' perspectives of health problems and health care in a US women's jail." *Women & Health* 44: 119–136.

Hayslip Jr., B., & Kaminski, P. L. (2005). "Grandparents raising their grandchildren: A review of the literature and suggestions for practice." *The Gerontologist* 45: 262–269.

Heflick, N. A. (2005). "Sentenced to die: Last statements and dying on death row." *Omega: Journal of Death & Dying* 51: 323–336.

Henderson, D., Schaeffer, J., & Brown, L. (1998). "Gender-appropriate mental health services for incarcerated women: Issues and solutions." *Family & Community Health* 2, no. 3: 42–53.

Heney, J., & Kristiansen, C. (1998). "An analysis of the impact of prison on women survivors of childhood sexual abuse." In J. Harden & M. Hill (eds.), *Breaking the rules: Women in prison and feminist therapy*. New York: Haworth, pp. 29–44.

Hensley, C., Koscheski, M., & Tewksbury, R. (2002). "Does participation in conjugal visitations reduce prison violence in Mississippi? An exploratory study." *Criminal Justice Review* 27, no. 1: 52–65.

Herrschaft, B. A., Veysey, B. M., Tubman-Carbone, H. R., & Christian, J. (2009). "Gender differences in the transformation narrative: Implications for revised reentry for female offenders." *Journal of Offender Rehabilitation* 48, no. 6: 463–482.

Higgins, D., & Severson, S. E. (2009). "Community re-entry and older adult offenders: Redefining social work roles." *Journal of Gerontological Social Work* 52, no. 3: 784–802.

Hirschell, J. D., & Buzawa, E. (2002). "Understanding the context of dual arrest with direction for future arrest." *Violence Against Women* 8: 1449–1473.

Hlavka, H. R., Kruttschnitt, C., & Carbone-Lopez, K. C. (2007). "Revictimizing the victim: Interviewing women about interpersonal violence." *Journal of Interpersonal Violence* 22, no. 7: 894–920.

Hoffmann, H. C., Dickinson, G. E., & Dunn, C. L. (2007). "Communication policy changes in state adult correctional facilities from 1971–2005." *Criminal Justice Review* 32, no. 1: 47–64.

Hooyman, N. R., & Kiyak, H. (2008). *Social gerontology: A multidisciplinary perspective*. Boston: Addison-Wesley.

House, J. S., Landis, K. R., & Umberson, D. (1988). "Social relationships and health." *Science* 241: 540–545.

Hunsberger, M. (2000). "A prison with compassion." *Corrections Today* 62, no. 7: 90–92.

Hyde, R., & Brumfield, B. (2003). "Effects of co-payments on the use of medical services by male and female prisoners." *Journal of Correctional Health Care* 9, no. 4: 371–380.

Jacobi, J. V. (2005). "Public health: Obligations and opportunities." *American Journal of Law and Medicine* 31: 447–478.

Jacobson, N. S., & Gottman, J. M. (1998). *When men batter women: New insights into ending abusive relationships.* New York: Simon & Schaster.

James, D., & Glaze, L. (2006). *Mental health problems of prisons and jail inmates.* Washington, DC: Bureau of Justice Statistics.

Janssen, L. M. (2007). "Aging behind bars: Adaptation of older women." Unpublished thesis. Oxford, OH: Miami University.

Jarvis, T. J., Copeland, J., & Walton, L. (1998). "Exploring the nature of the relationship between child sexual abuse and substance use among women." *Addiction* 93, no. 6: 865–875.

Jeffery, J. E., & Lubkin, I. M. (2002). "Chronic pain." In I. M. Lubkin & P. D. Larson (eds.), *Chronic Illness.* Boston: Jones & Bartlett.

Jiang, S., & Winfree, L. T. (2006). "Social support, gender, and inmate adjustment to prison life: Insights from a national sample." *The Prison Journal* 86: 32–55.

Johnson, C. L., & Troll, L. E. (1994). "Constraints and facilitators to friendships in late late life." *The Gerontologist* 34: 70–87.

Johnson, R., & Chernoff, N. (2002). "Opening a vein: Inmate poetry and the prison experience." *The Prison Journal* 82, no. 2: 141–167.

Johnson, R., & Dobrzanska, A. (2005). "Mature coping among life sentence inmates: An exploratory study of adjustment dynamics." *Corrections Compendium* 30, no. 6: 8–9, 36–38.

Johnson, R., & McGunigall-Smith, S. (2008). "Life without parole, America's other death penalty." *The Prison Journal* 33: 328–346.

Johnson, R., & Toch, H., eds. (1982). *The Pains of Imprisonment.* Beverly Hills, CA: Sage.

Jose-Kempfer, C. (1990). "Coming to terms with existential death: An analysis of women's adaptation to life in prison." *Social Justice* 17, no. 2: 110–125.

Kalish, R. A. (1985). "The social context of death and dying." In R. H. Binstock & E. Shanas (eds.), *Handbook of Aging and the Social Sciences.* New York: Van Nostrand Reinhold, pp. 149–170.

Kalish, R. A., & Reynolds, D. K. (1974). "Widows view death: A brief research note." *Omega: Journal of Death and Dying* 5: 187–192.

Kamerman, J. B. (1988). *Death in the midst of life: Social and cultural influences on death, grief, and mourning.* Englewood Cliffs, NJ: Prentice Hall.

Kane, R. A., Kling, K. C., Bershadsky, B., Kane, R. L., Giles, K., Degenholtz, H. B., Liu, J., & Cutler, L. J. (2003). "Quality of life measures for nursing home residents." *Journals of Gerontology* 58A, no. 3: 240–248.

Kayser-Jones, J. (2002). "The experience of dying: An ethnographic nursing home study." *Gerontologist* 42, supplement 3: 11–19.

Kelly, T. B. (2004). "Mutual aid groups for older persons with mental illness." *Journal of Gerontological Social Work* 44, no. 1–2: 111–126.

Kerbs, J. J. (2000). "Arguments and strategies for selective-decarceration of older prisoners." In B. D. Dunlop & M. B. Rothman (eds.), *Elders, crime, and the criminal justice system.* New York: Springer, pp. 229–250.

Kerbs, J. J., & Jolley, J. M. (2009). "A commentary on age segregation for older prisoners." *Criminal Justice Review* 34: 119–139.

Kiser, G. C. (1991). "Female inmates and their families." *Federal Probation* 55, no. 1: 56–63.

Klug, L., & Sinha, A. (1987). "Death acceptance: A two-component formulation and scale." *Omega: Journal of Death and Dying* 18: 229–235.

Knapp, J. L., & Elder, K. B. (1997–1998). "Assessing prison personnel's knowledge of the aging process." *Journal of the Oklahoma Criminal Justice Research Consortium* 4: 50–54.

Knight, K. H., & Elfenbein, M. H. 1996. "Relationship of death anxiety/fear to health-seeking beliefs and behaviors." *Death Studies* 20: 23–31.

Koons, B. A., Burrow, J. D., Morash, M., & Bynam, T. (1995). "Expert and offender perceptions of program elements linked to successful outcomes for incarcerated women." *Crime & Delinquency* 43: 512–533.

Krabill, J. J., & Aday, R. H. (2005). "Exploring the social world of aging female prisoners." *Women & Criminal Justice* 17, no. 1: 27–54.

Kratcoski, P. C., & Babb, S. (1990). "Adjustment of older inmates: An analysis of structure and gender." *Journal of Contemporary Criminal Justice* 6: 264–281.

Kruttschnitt, C., Gartner, R., & Miller, A. (2000). "Doing her own time? Women's responses to prison in the context of the old and new penology." *Criminology* 38: 681–717.

Kubiak, S. P. (2005). "'I came to prison to do my time—not to get raped': Coping within the institutional setting." *Stress, Trauma, and Crisis: An International Journal* 8, no. 2–3: 157–177.

LaBelle, D. (2002). "Women, the law, and the justice system: Neglect, violence, and resistance." In J. F. McDonough & R. C. Sarri (eds.), *Women at the margins: Neglect, punishment, and resistance.* New York: Haworth Press, pp. 347–374.

Lamb, G. (2010). "Examining the mental and physical health conditions found in a national sample of females abused prior to incarceration." Unpublished thesis. Middle Tennessee State University.

Laughlin, J. S., Arrigo, B. A., Blevins, K. R., & Costin, C. (2008). "Incarcerated mothers and childhood visitation: A law, social science, policy perspective." *Criminal Justice Policy Review* 19, no. 2: 215–238.

LaVigne, G., Naser, R. L., Brooks, L. E., & Castro, J. L. (2005). "Examining the effects of incarceration and in-prison family contact on prisoners' family relationships." *Journal of Contemporary Criminal Justice* 21: 314–335.

Leigey, M. (2007). "Life while serving life: Examining the correctional experiences of older inmates serving a life sentence." Unpublished dissertation. University of Delaware.

———. (2010). "For the longest time: The adjustment of inmates to a sentence of life without parole." *The Prison Journal* 90, no. 3: 247–268.

Leonard, E. D. (2001). "Convicted survivors: Comparing and describing California's battered women inmates." *The Prison Journal* 81, no. 1: 73–86.

————. (2002). *Convicted survivors: The imprisonment of battered women who kill*. New York: State University of New York Press.

Liang, B., Goodman, L., Tummala-Narra, P., & Weintraub, S. (2005). "A theoretical framework for understanding help-seeking processes among survivors of intimate partner violence." *American Journal of Community Psychology* 36, no. 1–2: 71–84.

Liang, J., Krause, N., & Bennett, J. (2001). "Is giving better than receiving?" *Psychology & Aging* 16: 511–523.

Liebling, A. (1999). "Doing research in prison: Breaking the silence?" *Theoretical Criminology* 3, no. 2: 147–173.

Lindquist, C. H. (2000). "Social integration and mental well being among jail inmates." *Sociological Forum* 15: 431–455.

Lockhart, L. K., Bookwala, J., Fagerlin, A., Coppola, K. M., Ditto, P. H., Danks, J. H., & Smuker, W. D. (2001). "Older adults' attitudes toward death: Links to perceptions of health and concerns about end-of-life issues." *Omega: The Journal of Death and Dying* 43: 331–348.

Loeb, S. J., & Steffensmeier, D. (2006). "Older male prisoners: Health statuses, self-efficacy beliefs, and health promotion behaviors." *Journal of Correctional Health Care* 12, no. 4: 269–278.

Loeb, S. J., Steffensmeier, D., & Lawrence, F. (2008). "Comparing incarcerated and community-dwelling older men's health." *Western Journal of Nursing Research* 30, no. 2: 234–249.

Loeb, S. J., Steffensmeier, D., & Myco, P. M. (2007). "In their own words: Older male prisoners' health beliefs and concerns for the future." *Geriatric Nursing* 28, no. 5: 319–329.

Logan, T. K., Walker, R., Jordan, C. E., & Leukefeld, C. G. (2006). *Women and victimization: Contributing factors, interventions, and implications*. Washington, DC: American Psychological Association.

Loper, A. B., Carlson, L. W., Levitt, L., & Scheffel, K. (2009). "Parenting stress, alliance, child contact, and adjustment of imprisoned mothers and fathers." *Journal of Offender Rehabilitation* 48: 383–503.

Lowenthal, M. F., Thurnher, M., & Chiriboga, D. (1975). *Four stages of life: A comparative study of women and men facing transition*. San Francisco: Jossey-Bass.

Luke, K. P. (2002). "Mitigating the ill effects of maternal incarceration on women in prison and their children." *Child Welfare* 81: 929–949.

Lundstrom, S. (1994). "Dying to get out: A study on the necessity, importance, and effectiveness of prison early release programs for elderly inmates suffering from HIV disease and other terminal-centered illnesses." *BYU Journal of Public Law* 9: 155–188.

Lynch, M. (2001). "Pain as the fifth vital sign." *Journal of Intravenous Nursing* 24: 85–94.

Lyness, J. M. (2004). "Treatment of depressive conditions in later life, real world light for dark tunnels." *JAMA* 291: 1569–1575.

MacKenzie, D. L. (1987). "Age and adjustment to prison." *Criminal Justice and Behavior* 14: 427–447.

MacKenzie, D., Robinson, J. W., & Campbell, C. S. (1989). "Long-term incarceration of female offenders: Prison adjustment and coping." *Criminal Justice and Behavior* 16, no. 2: 223–238.

Maeve, M. K. (1999). "Adjudicated health: Incarcerated women and the social construction of health." *Crime, Law & Social Change* 31: 49–71.

——. (2000). "Speaking unavoidable truths: Understanding early childhood sexual and physical violence among women in prison." *Issues in Mental Health Nursing* 21: 473–498.

Maeve, M. K., & Vaughn, M. S. (2001). "Nursing with prisoners: The practice of caring, forensic nursing or penal harm nursing?" *Advances in Nursing Science* 24, no. 2: 47–64.

Maggio, R. (1996). *The new beacon book of quotations by women*. Boston: Beacon Press.

Mahan, S. (1984). "Imposition of despair: An ethnography of women in prison." *Crime & Justice* 7: 101–129.

Mara, C. M. (2002). "Expansion of long-term care in the prison system: An aging inmate population poses policy and programmatic questions." *Journal of Aging and Social Policy* 14, no. 2: 43–61.

Marquart, J., Merianos, D., & Doucet, G. (2000). "The health-related concerns of older prisoners: Implications for policy." *Ageing and Society* 20: 79–96.

Marquart, J. W., Merianos, D. E., Hebert, J. L., & Carroll, L. (1997). "Health conditions and prisoners: A review of research and emerging areas of inquiry." *The Prison Journal* 77, no. 2: 184–208.

Martin, C. D., & Salovey, P. (1996). "Death attitudes and self-reported health-relevant behaviors." *Journal of Heath Psychology* 1: 441–453.

Maull, F. M. (1991). "Dying in prison: Sociocultural and psychosocial dynamics." *The Hospice Journal* 7, no. 1–2: 127–142.

——. (1998). "Issues in prison hospice: Toward a model of hospice care in a correctional setting." *The Hospice Journal* 13, no. 4: 57–82.

McHugh, K. E. (2003). "Three faces of ageism: Society, image, and place." *Ageing and Society* 23: 165–185.

McPherson, M., Smith-Lovin, L., & Cook, J. M. (2001). "Birds of a feather: Homophily in social networks." *Annual Review of Sociology* 27: 415–444.

McQuiade, S., & Ehrenreich, J. (1998). "Women in prison: Approaches to understanding the lives of a forgotten population." *Affilia: Journal of Women and Social Work* 13: 233–246.

McShane, M. D., & Williams, F. P. (1990). "Old and ornery: The disciplinary experiences of elderly prisoners." *International Journal of Offender Therapy and Comparative Criminology* 34: 197–212.

Menec, V. H. (2003). "The relation between everyday activities and successful aging: A six-year longitudinal study." *Journal of Gerontology: Social Sciences* 58B: 74–82.

Mezey, M., Dubler, N., Mitty, E., & Brody, A. (2002). "What impact do settings and transitions have on the quality of life at the end of life and the quality of the dying process?" *The Gerontologist* 42: 54–67.

Miller, J. B. (1993). "Growth through relationships." *Advanced Development* 5: 13–25.

Miller, J. B., & Silver, I. P. (1997). *The healing connection: How women form relationships in therapy and in life*. Boston: Beacon Press.

Miller, S. L. (2006). *Victims as offenders*. New Brunswick, NJ: Rutgers University Press.

Miller, S. L., & Meloy, M. L. (2006). "Women's use of force: Voices of women arrested for domestic violence." *Violence Against Women* 12: 89–115.

Miller, S. L., & Wellford, C. (1997). "Patterns and correlates of interpersonal violence." In A. P. Cardarelli (ed.), *Violence between intimate partners*. Upper Saddle River, NJ: Pearson, pp. 20–47.

Minichiello, V., Browne, J., & Kendig, H. (2000). "Perceptions and consequences of ageism: Views of older people." *Ageing and Society* 20: 253–278.

Moe, A. M., & Ferraro, K. J. (2007). "Criminalized mothers: The value and devaluation of parenthood from behind bars." *Women & Therapy* 29, no. 3–4: 135–164.

Morash, M., & Schram, P. J. (2002). *The prison experience: Special issues of women in prison*. Prospect Heights, IL: Waveland Press.

Morash, M., Bynum, T., & Koons, B. A. (1998). *Women offenders: Programming needs and promising approaches*. Washington, DC: US Department of Justice.

Morash, M., Haarr, R. N., & Rucker, L. (1995). "A comparison of programming for women and men in U.S. prisons in the 1980s." *Crime and Delinquency* 40: 197–221.

Morton, J. B. (1992). "An administrative overview of the older inmate." National Institute of Justice Research in Brief. Washington, DC: US Department of Justice.

Mullins, L. C., & Lopez, M. A. (1982). "Death anxiety among nursing home residents: A comparison of young-old and the old-old." *Death Education* 6: 75–86.

Mumola, C. J. (2000). "Incarcerated parents and their children." Bureau of Justice Statistics Special Report. Washington, DC: US Department of Justice.

Mumola, C. J., & Noonan, M. E. (2008). "Deaths in custody: Local jail deaths 2006–2008." Bureau of Justice Statistics Special Report. Washington, DC: US Department of Justice.

Nadel, B. (1997). "BOP accommodates special needs offenders." *Corrections Today* (October): 76–80.

Nash, S. T., & Hesterberg, L. (2009). "Biblical framings of and responses to spousal violence in the narratives of abused women." *Violence Against Women* 15, no. 3: 340–361.

National Institute of Corrections. (1997). *Prison medical care: Special needs populations and cost control*. Washington, DC: US Department of Justice.

Neeley, C., Addison, L., & Craig-Moreland, D. E. (1997). "Addressing the needs of elderly offenders." *Corrections Today* 59, no. 5: 120–123.

Negy, C., Woods, D. J., & Carlson, R. (1997). "The relationship between females, coping and adjustment in a minimum security prison." *Criminal Justice and Behavior* 24, no. 2: 224–233.

Norris, J., & Kerr, K. (1993). "Alcohol and violent pornography: Responses to permissive and non-permissive cues." *Journal of Studies on Alcohol* 11: 118–127.

North, C. S. (2002). "Somatization in survivors of catastrophic trauma: A methodological review." *Environmental Health Perspectives* 10, no. 4: 637–640.

O'Brien, J. (1980). "Mirror, mirror: Why me?" *Nursing Mirror* 150: 36–37.

O'Brien, P. (2001). *Making it in the "free world": Women in transition from prison.* New York: SUNY Press.

O'Connor, M. (2004). "Finding boundaries inside the prison walls: Case study of a terminally ill inmate." *Death Studies* 28: 63–76.

Ohio Department of Rehabilitation and Correction. (1999). *A comprehensive approach to addressing the needs of aging prisoners.* Columbus, OH.

Owen, B. (1998). *In the mix: Struggle and survival in a women's prison.* Albany, NY: Springer.

Owen, B., & Bloom, B. (1995). "Profiling women prisoners: Findings from national surveys and a California sample." *Prison Journal* 75, no. 2: 165–185.

Patenaude, A. L. (2004). "No promise, but I'm willing to listen and tell what I hear: Conducting qualitative research among prison inmates and staff." *The Prison Journal* 84, no. 4: 69S–91S.

Pehlmann, J. (2005). "Incarcerated mother's contact with children, perceived family relationship, and depressive symptoms." *Journal of Family Psychology* 19: 350–377.

Petersilia, J. (2003). *When prisoners come home: Parole and prisoners reentry.* New York: Oxford University Press.

Phillips, S. D., & Harm, J. J. (1998). "Women prisoners: A conceptual framework." *Women & Therapy* 20, no. 4: 1–9.

Plichta, S. (2004). "Intimate partner violence and physical health consequences: Policy, practice and implications." *Journal of Interpersonal Violence* 19: 1296–1323.

Poehlmann, J. (2005). "Representations of attachment relationships in children of incarcerated mothers." *Child Development* 76, no. 3: 679–696.

Pollock, J. M. (2002). *Women, prison and crime.* Belmont, CA: Wadsworth.

———. (2004). *Prisons and prison life: Costs and consequences.* Los Angeles: Roxbury.

Pruzinski, T., & Cash, T. (1990). "Integrative themes in body development, deviance, and change." In T. Cash & T. Pruzinski (eds.), *Body images: Development, deviance, and change.* New York: Guilford Press, pp. 337–349.

Rasch, W. (1981). "The effects of indeterminate detention—Study of men sentenced to life imprisonment." *International Journal of Law and Psychiatry* 4: 417–431.

Ratcliff, K. S. (2002). *Women and health: Power, technology, inequality, and conflict in a gendered world.* Boston: Allyn and Bacon.

Rawlings, W. K. (1992). *Friendship matters: Communication, dialectics, and the life course.* New York: Aldine de Gruyter.

Reed, M. B., & Glamser, F. D. (1979). "Aging in a total institution: The case of older prisoners." *Gerontologist* 19, no. 4: 354–360.

Reitzel, L. R., & Harju, B. L. (2000). "Influence of locus of control and custody on intake and prison adjustment depression." *Criminal Justice and Behavior* 27, no. 5: 625–644.

Renzetti, C. M., Goodstein, L., & Miller, S. L. (2006). *Rethinking gender, crime, and justice.* New York: Oxford University Press.

Reviere, R., & Young, V. D. (2004). "Aging behind bars: Health care for older female inmates." *Journal of Women and Aging* 16, no. 1–2: 55–69.

Richards, B. (1978). "The experience of long-term imprisonment: An exploratory investigation." *The British Journal of Criminology* 18, no. 2: 162–169.

Riley Jr., J. W. (1970). "What people think of death." In O. G. Brim, H. E. Freeman, S. Levine & N. A. Scotch (eds.), *The dying patient.* New York: Russell Sage, pp. 30–41.

Roberto, K. A., & Reynolds, S. G. (2002). "Older women's experiences with chronic pain: Daily challenges and self-care practices." *Journal of Women and Aging* 14, no. 3–4: 5–23.

Roberto, K. A., Perkins, S. N., & Holland, A. K. (2007). "Research on persistent pain in late life: Current topics and challenges." *Journal of Women and Aging* 19, no. 3–4: 5–19.

Rocke, C., & Cherry, K. E. (2002). "Death at the end of the 20th century: Individual processes and developmental tasks in old age." *International Aging and Human Development* 54: 315–333.

Rold, W. J. (1996). "Charging inmates for medical care: A legal, practical, and ethical critique." *Journal of Correctional Health Care* 3, no. 2: 129–135.

Rose, B. M., & O'Sullivan, J. M. (2002). "Afterlife beliefs and death anxiety: An exploration of the relationship between afterlife expectations and fear of death in an undergraduate population." *Omega; Journal of Death and Dying* 54: 229–243.

Rosel, N. (2003). "Aging in place: Knowing where you are." *International Journal of Aging and Human Development* 57, no. 1: 77–90.

Rosen, D. M. (2001). "Mass imprisonment and the family: A legal perspective." *Marriage and Family Review* 33, no. 3–4: 63–82.

Ross, P. H., & Lawrence, J. E. (1998). "Health care for women offenders." *Corrections Today* 60, no. 7: 122–129.

Rowe, J. W., & Kahn, R. L. (1998). *Successful aging: The MacArthur Foundation study.* New York: Pantheon Books.

Ruiz, D. S. (2002). "The increase in incarcerations among women and its impact on the grandmother caregiver: Some racial considerations." *Journal of Sociology and Social Welfare* 29: 179–297.

Sabath, M. J., & Cowles, E. L. (1988). "Factors affecting the adjustment of elderly inmates to prison." In B. McCarthy & R. Langworthy (eds.), *Older offenders: Perspectives in criminology and criminal justice.* New York: Praeger, pp. 178–195.

Sabol, W. J., & Couture, H. (2008). "Prison and jail inmates at midyear 2007." Bureau of Justice Statistics Special Report. Washington, DC: US Department of Justice.

Salisbury, E., & Van Voorhis, P. (2009). "Gendered pathways: An empirical investigation of women probationers' paths to recidivism." *Criminal Justice Behavior* 36: 541–566.

Santos, M. G. (1995). "Facing long-term imprisonment." In T. J. Flanagan (ed.), *Long-term imprisonment: Policy, science, and correctional practice.* Thousand Oaks, CA: Sage, pp. 36–40.

Sappington, A. A. (1996). "Relationships among prison adjustment, beliefs, and cognitive coping style." *International Journal of Offender Therapy and Comparative Criminology* 40: 54–62.

Schafer, N. E. (1994). "Exploring the link between visits and parole success. A survey of prison visitors." *International Journal of Offender Therapy and Comparative Criminology* 38, no. 1: 17–32.

Schmid, T. J., & Jones, R. S. (1993). "Ambivalent actions. Prison adaptation strategies of first-time and short-term inmates." *Journal of Contemporary Ethnography,* 21, no. 4: 439–463.

Schwartz, K. (2007). "Remembering the forgotten: Psychotherapy groups for nursing home residents." *International Journal of Group Psychotherapy* 57, no. 4: 497–514.

Seijeoung, K. (2003). "Incarcerated women in life context." *Women's Studies International Forum* 26, no. 1: 95–100.

Sellen, J. L., McMurran, M., Cox, W. M., Theodosi, E., & Klinger, E. (2006). "The personal concerns inventory (offender adaptations) measuring and enhancing motivation to change." *International Journal of Offender Therapy and Comparative Criminology* 50: 294–305.

Severance, T. A. (2005). "You know who you can go to: Cooperation and exchange between incarcerated women." *The Prison Journal* 85: 343–367.

Shadmi, E., Boyd, C. M., Hsiao, C., Sylvia, M., Shuster, A., & Boult, C. (2006). "Morbidity and older persons' perceptions of the quality of their primary care." *Journal of the American Geriatric Society* 54: 330–334.

Shantz, L. R., & Frigon, S. (2009). "Aging, women and health: From the pains of imprisonment to the paints of reintegration." *International Journal of Prisoner Health* 5, no. 1: 3–15.

Shearer, R. A. (2003). "Identifying the special needs of female offenders." *Federal Probation* 67, no. 1: 46–51.

Sherman, L. W., & Beck, R. A. (1984). "The specific deterrent effect of arrest for domestic violence." *American Sociological Review* 49: 261–271.

Silver, C. B. (2003). "Gendered identities in old age: Toward (de) gendering?" *Journal of Aging Studies* 17, no. 4: 379–397.

Silverman, I. J., & Vega, M. (1996). *Corrections: A comprehensive view.* Minneapolis/St. Paul, MN: West Group.

Singer, M. I., Bussey, J., Song, L.Y., & Lunghofer, L. (1995). "The psychosocial issues of women serving time in jail." *Social Work* 40, no. 1: 103–113.

Smyer, T., & Gragert, M. (2006). "Health issues of aging prisoners." In P. M. Burbank (ed.), *Vulnerable older adults: Health care needs and interventions.* New York: Springer, pp. 57–74.

Smyer, T., Gragert, M., & LaMere, S. (1997). "Stay safe! Stay healthy! Surviving old age in prison." *Journal of Psychosocial Nursing and Mental Health Services* 35, no. 9: 10–17.

Snell, T. L., & Morton, D. C. (1994). "Women in prison: Survey of state prison inmates, 1991." Report NCJ 145321. Washington, DC: US Department of Justice.

Snyder, Z. K., Carlo, T. A., & Mullins, M. M. (2001). "Parenting from prison: An examination of a children's visitation program at a woman's correctional facility." *Marriage & Family Review* 32: 33–61.

Speroff, L., Rowan, J., Symons, J., Genant, H., & Winborn, W. (1996). "The comparative effect on bone density, endometrium, and lipids of continuous hormones as replacement therapy: A randomized controlled trial." *Journal of the American Medical Association* 276: 1397–1403.

Stein, M. B., & Barrett-Connor, E. (2000). "Sexual assault and physical health: Findings from a population-based study of older adults." *Psychosomatic Medicine* 62: 838–843.

Stevens, N., & Van Tilburg, T. (2000). "Stimulating friendship in later life: A strategy for reducing loneliness among older women." *Educational Gerontology* 26: 15–35.

Stojkovic, S. (2007). "Elderly prisoners: A growing and forgotten group within corrections vulnerable to elder abuse." *Journal of Elder Abuse & Neglect* 19, no. 3–4: 97–117.

Stoller, N. (2003). "Space, place, and movement as aspects of health care in three women's prisons." *Social Science and Medicine* 5: 2263–2275.

Strupp, H., & Willmott, D. (2005). *Dignity denied: The price of imprisoning women in California*. San Francisco: Legal Services for Prisoners with Children.

Sudnow, D. (1967). *Passing on: The social organization of dying*. Englewood Cliffs, NJ: Prentice Hall.

Suitor, J. J., Pillemer, K., & Keeton, S. (1995). "When experience counts: The effects of experiential and structural similarity on patterns of support and interpersonal stress." *Social Forces* 73: 1573–1588.

Sykes, G. M. 1958. *The society of captives: A study of a maximum security prison*. Princeton, NJ: Princeton University Press.

Taylor, P. J., & Parrott, J. M. (1988). "Elder offenders: A study of age-related factors among custodially remanded prisoners." *British Journal of Psychiatry* 152: 340–346.

Taylor, W. D., McQuoid, D. R., & Ranga Rama Krishnan, K. (2004). "Medical comorbidity in late-life depression." *International Journal of Geriatric Psychiatry* 19: 935–943.

Tewksbury, R., & DeMichele, M. (2005). "Going to prison: A prison visitation program." *The Prison Journal* 85, no. 3: 292–310.

Tewksbury, R., & West, A. (2000). "Research on sex in prison during the late 1980s and early 1990s." *The Prison Journal* 30: 368–378.

Thivierge-Rikard, R. V., & Thompson, M. S. (2007). "The association between aging inmate housing management models and non-geriatric health services in state correctional institutions." *Journal of Aging and Social Policy* 19, no. 4: 39–56.

Thoits, P. (1986). "Social support as coping assistance." *Journal of Consulting and Clinical Psychology* 54: 416–423.

Toch, H. (2006). *Living in prison: The ecology of survival*. Washington, DC: American Psychological Association.

Tonry, M. (1995). *Malign neglect: Race, crime and punishment in America*. New York: Oxford University Press.

Toseland, R. W., & Rizzo, V. M. (2005). "What's different about working with older people in groups?" *Journal of Gerontological Social Work* 44, no. 1–2: 5–23.

Touhy, T. A., & Jett, K. (2008). "Pain and comfort." In P. Ebersole, P. Hess, T. Touhy, K. Jeff & A. S. Luggen (eds.), *Toward healthy aging*. St. Louis, MO: Mosby, pp. 269–293.

Travis, J., McBride, E. C., & Solomon, A. L. (2005). "Families left behind: The hidden costs of incarceration and reentry." Urban Institute Justice Policy Center. www.urban.org/publications/310882.html.

Unger, J. B., Anderson Johnson, C., & Marks, G. (1997). "Functional decline in the elderly: Evidence for direct and stress-buffering protective effects of social interactions and physical activity." *Annals of Behavioral Medicine* 19, no. 2: 152–160.

US Department of Justice, Bureau of Justice Statistics. (1998). *Sourcebook of Criminal Justice Statistics*. Washington, DC: US Government Printing Office.

———. (2004). *Sourcebook of Criminal Justice Statistics*. Washington, DC: US Government Printing Office.

———. (2009). *Sourcebook of Criminal Justice Statistics*. Washington, DC: US Government Printing Office.

Valera, E. M., & Bernbaum, H. (2003). "Brain injury in battered women." *Journal of Consulting and Clinical Psychology* 71: 797–804.

Vaughn, M. S. (1999). "Penal harm medicine: State tort remedies for delaying and denying health care to prisoners." *Crime, Law, and Social Change* 31: 273–302.

Vaughn, M. S., & Collins, S. C. (2004). "Medical malpractice in correctional facilities: State tort remedies for inappropriate and inadequate health care administered to prisoners." *The Prison Journal* 84, no. 4: 505–534.

Vaughn, M. S., & Smith, L. G. (1999). "Practicing penal harm medicine in the United States: Prisoners' voices from jail." *Justice Quarterly* 16, no. 1: 175–231.

Vega, W. M., & Silverman, M. (1988). "Stress and the elderly convict." *International Journal of Offender Therapy and Comparative Criminology* 32, no. 2: 153–162.

Viney, L. (1984). "Concerns about death among severely ill people." In F. R. Epting & R. A. Neimeyer (eds.), *Personal meaning of death*. Washington, DC: Hemisphere, pp. 143–158.

Visher, C. A., & Travis, T. (2003). "Transitions from prison to community: Understanding individual pathways." *Annual Review of Sociology* 29: 89–113.

Vogt, A. S. (2007). "Perceived age discrimination and mental health." *Social Forces* 86, no. 1: 291–311.

Vuolo, M., & Kruttschnitt, C. (2008). "Prisoners' adjustment, correctional officers, and context: The foreground and background of punishment in later modernity." *Law and Society Review* 42, no. 2: 307–336.

Wahidin, A. (2004). *Older women in the criminal justice system: Running out of time*. London: Jessica Kingsley.

Wahidin, A., & Tate, S. (2005). "Prison (e)scapes and body tropes: Older women in the prison time machine." *Journal of Body and Society* 11: 59–79.

Walker, L. E. A. (2000). *The battered women syndrome*. New York: Springer.

Walsh, C. E. (1990). "Needs of older inmates in varying security settings." Unpublished doctoral dissertation. Rutgers University.

Warren, J. (2002). "Inmates' families pay heavy price for staying in touch." *Los Angeles Times*, February 16, p. 6.

Warren, J. I., Hurt, S., Loper, A. B., & Chauhan, P. (2004). "Exploring prison adjustment among female inmates: Issues of measurement and prediction." *Criminal Justice and Behavior* 31, 624–645.

Watson, R., Stimpson, A., & Hostick, T. (2004). "Prison health care: A review of the literature." *International Journal of Nursing Studies* 41, no. 2: 119–128.

Watterson, K. (1996). *Women in prison: Inside the concrete womb*. Boston: Northeastern University Press.

West, H. & Sabol, W. (2010). *Prisoners in 2009*. Washington, DC: Bureau of Justice, US Department of Justice.

Westerhof, G. J., Katzko, M. W., Diffinann-Kohl, R., & Hayslip, B. (2001). "Life contexts and health-related selves in old age: Perspectives from the United States, India & Congo/Zaire." *Journal of Aging Studies* 15: 105–126.

Williams, G. J. (1989). "Elderly offenders: A comparison of chronic and new elderly offenders." Unpublished master's thesis. Middle Tennessee State University.

Williams, M. E., & Rikard, R. V. (2004). "Marginality or neglect: An exploratory study of policies and programs for aging female inmates." *Women and Criminal Justice* 15, no. 3: 121–141.

Williams, J. W. (2006). *The aging inmate population: Southern states outlook*. Lexington, KY: Southern Legislative Conference.

Williams, B., Lindquist, K., Sudore, R., Strupp, H., Wilmontt, D., & Walter, L. (2006). "Being old and doing time: Functional impairment and adverse experiences of geriatric female prisoners." *Journal of the American Geriatrics Society* 54, no. 4: 702–707.

Wilson, D. G., & Vito, G. F. (1986). "Imprisoned elders: The experience of one institution." *Criminal Justice Policy Review* 1, no. 4: 399–421.

Wilson, K. S., & Spink, K. S. (2006). "Exploring older adults' social influences for physical activity." *Activities, Adaptation & Aging* 30, no. 3: 47–60.

Wink, P., & Scott, J. (2005). "Does religiousness buffer against the fear of death and dying in later adulthood? Findings from a longitudinal study." *The Journals of Gerontology, Series B: Psychological Sciences and Social Sciences* 60: 207–214.

Wolf, M. E., Ly, U., Hobart, M. A., & Kernic, M. A. (2003). "Barriers to seeking police help for intimate partner violence." *Journal of Family Violence* 18, no. 2: 121–129.

Woods, S. J. (2005). "Intimate partner violence and post-traumatic stress disorder symptoms in women." *Journal of Interpersonal Violence* 20: 394–402.

Wright, K. N. (1989). "Race and economic marginality in explaining prison adjustment." *Journal of Research in Crime and Delinquency* 25: 67–89.

———. (1991). "A study of individual, environmental, and interactive effects in explaining adjustment to prison." *Justice Quarterly* 8, no. 2: 213–233.

Young, D. S. (2000). "Women's perceptions of health care in prison." *Health Care for Women International* 21, no. 3: 219–234.

Young, D. S., & Smith, C. J. (2000). "When moms are incarcerated: The needs of children, mothers, and caregivers." *Families in Society* 81: 130–142.

Young, V. D., & Reviere, R. (2001). "Meeting the health care needs of the new woman inmate: A national survey of prison practices." *Journal of Offender Rehabilitation* 34, no. 2: 31–48.

———. (2006). *Women behind bars; Gender and race in US prisons.* Boulder, CO: Lynne Rienner.

Zaitzow, B. H. (2003). "Doing gender in a women's prison." In B. H. Zaitzow & J. Thomas (eds.), *Women in prison: Gender and social control.* Boulder, CO: Lynne Rienner, pp. 21–38.

Zamble, E. (1992). "Behavior and adaptation in long-term prison inmates: Descriptive longitudinal results." *Criminal Justice and Behavior* 19, no. 4: 409–425.

Zamble, E., & Porporino, F. J. (1988). *Coping, Behavior, and Adaptation in Prison Inmates.* New York: Springer.

Zink, T., Jacobson, C. J., Regan, S., Fisher, S., Fisher, B., & Pabst, S. (2006). "Older women's descriptions and understandings of their abusers." *Violence Against Women* 12: 851–865.

Zink, T., Regan, S., Jacobson, J., & Pabst, S. (2003). "Cohort, period, and aging effects: A qualitative study of older women's reasons for remaining in abusive relationships." *Violence Against Women* 9: 1429–1441.

Zweig, J. M., Schlichter, K. A., & Burt, M. R. (2005). "Assisting women victims of violence who experience multiple barriers to services." *Violence Against Women* 8, no. 2: 162–180.

Zosky, D. L. (1999). "The application of object relations theory to domestic violence." *Clinical Social Work Journal* 27: 55–69.

Zupan, L. (1992). "Men guarding women: An analysis of the employment of male correctional officers in prisons for women." *Journal of Criminal Justice* 20: 297–309.

Zust, B. L. (2009). "Partner violence, depression, and recidivism: The case of incarcerated women and why we need programs designed for them." *Issues in Mental Health Nursing* 30: 246–251.

Index

About the Book

RONALD ADAY AND JENNIFER KRABILL OFFER A COMPLETE PICTURE of the experience of older women prisoners and the distinct challenges these women present for correctional institutions.

The authors integrate their quantitative findings with the voices of individual inmates to explore essential concerns such as health, inmate and family relationships, prison adjustment, and end of life issues. They also consider the enduring impact of intimate partner violence. While painting a vivid portrait of struggles to build lives behind bars, the authors share critical insights into the social forces that shape women's contact with all stages of the criminal justice system.

RONALD H. ADAY is professor of sociology at Middle Tennessee State University. JENNIFER J. KRABILL is a research associate at the Tennessee Center for Gerontology and Geriatric Research.